The Indian Uprising of 1857–8

Anthem South Asian Studies
Series Editor: Crispin Bates

Ranganathan, Muali (ed.) *Govind Naraya's Mumbai* (2007)

Banerjee-Dube, Ishita *Religion, Law and Power* (2007)

Fraser, Bashabi (ed.) *Bengal Partition Stories* (2006)

Chattopadhyaya, Brajadulal *Studying Early India* (2006)

Brosius, Christiane *Empowering Visions* (2005)

Mills, James (ed.) *Subaltern Sports: Politics and Sport in South Asia* (2005)

Joshi, Chitra *Lost Worlds: Indian Labour and its Forgotten Histories* (2005)

Dasgupta, Biplab *European Trade and Colonial Conquest* (2005)

Kaur, Raminder *Performative Politics and the Cultures of Hinduism* (2005)

Rosenstein, Lucy *New Poetry in Hindi* (2004)

Shah, Ghanshyam *Caste and Democratic Politics in India* (2004)

van Schendel, Willem *The Bengal Borderland* (2004)

The Indian Uprising of 1857–8

Prisons, Prisoners and Rebellion

Clare Anderson

ANTHEM PRESS
LONDON · NEW YORK · DELHI

Anthem Press
An imprint of Wimbledon Publishing Company
www.anthempress.com

This edition first published in UK and USA 2007
by ANTHEM PRESS
75-76 Blackfriars Road, London SE1 8HA, UK
or PO Box 9779, London SW19 7ZG, UK
and
244 Madison Ave. #116, New York, NY 10016, USA

British Library Cataloguing in Publication Data
A catalogue record for this book is available from the British Library.

Library of Congress Cataloging in Publication Data
A catalog record for this book has been requested.

1 3 5 7 9 10 8 6 4 2

ISBN 978 1 84331 249 9 (Hbk)
ISBN 978 1 84331 295 6 (Pbk)

Cover illustration: 'Criminals From Calcutta', by Egron Lundgren,
courtesy of the National Museum, Stockholm

Printed in India

CONTENTS

ACKNOWLEDGEMENTS

Many people and institutions have facilitated this research and it is a pleasure to express my gratitude formally. I carried out archival research in the Oriental and India Office Collections of the British Library (London) and in the National Archives of India (New Delhi). I thank profoundly the archivists and the staff of both institutions, as also those based at the National Archives of Mauritius (Coromandel) and Tamil Nadu State Archives (Chennai), where inadvertently I picked up further references. I conducted research on convict transportation with the assistance of a personal research fellowship from the Economic and Social Research Council (award no. R000271268, 2002–6) and I completed the manuscript as Caird Senior Fellow at the National Maritime Museum (Greenwich). The University of Leicester granted me study leave during this period. I would like to thank the council, museum, and university.

I would like to thank colleagues who helped me in various ways. Dave Anderson, David Arnold, Lionel Caplan, Marina Carter, Clive Dewey, Ian Duffield, Tony Farrington, Durba Ghosh, Will Gould, Sumit Guha, Andrea Major, Barbara Metcalf, Anshu Mondal, Doug Peers, Frances Pritchett, Gavin Rand, Satadru Sen, Taylor Sherman, Peter Stanley, Jon Wilson, and Francis Xavier offered advice, discussed ideas, read drafts, and assisted with references. I owe a special word of thanks to Deborah Sutton for help in New Delhi. The talented Simon Barnard drew the map. Most of all I thank Christopher Shackle for his enormous scholarly generosity in translating the poetry of Munir Shikohabadi, and allowing me to use that translation here. In addition, he supplied all poetic annotations and references, and dated the chronograms. I hope my historical analysis does justice to his literary expertise.

I have presented the themes that I explore in this book at a number of research seminars, workshops, and conferences, and I am grateful to those who engaged with and critiqued work-in-progress papers. They include the Centre of South Asian Studies Research Seminar, University of Cambridge (2005); *Captivity: from Babylon to Guantanamo Bay* conference, UCL (2005);

Convicts Discussion Network workshop, University of Leicester (2005); South Asia Seminar, University of Leeds (2006); Institute of English Studies Inter-University Post-Colonial Studies Research Seminar, University of London (2006); British Association of South Asian Studies annual conference (2006); and *Cultures of Confinement* workshops, SOAS (2004–6). I much regret that the convenor of the Cambridge seminar, Raj Chandavarkar, did not live to see the fruits of our discussions in print.

At Leicester, I am grateful to colleagues in the School of Historical Studies, and the interdisciplinary post-colonial research group, especially Huw Bowen, Sally Horrocks, Prashant Kidambi, Claire Mercer, and Peter Musgrave.

Finally, I would like to thank Crispin Bates, series editor for Anthem South Asian Studies, for his support of my research over many years. Thanks also to my editor Paolo Cabrelli and the anonymous reader of the manuscript. All errors and omissions are, of course, my own.

I dedicate this book to my dearest Sam and our children Hugh and James, with much love and affection.

A NOTE ON THE TEXT

Given the incarceration of undertrial and convicted prisoners (civil and criminal) in the same penal institutions during this period, the descriptive categories 'jail' and 'prison' are used interchangeably. In order to distinguish residents of jails from those transported overseas, the terms 'prisoner' and 'convict' are used to denote inmates of mainland Indian jails and penal settlements respectively.

Place names have been transliterated according to modern conventions (hence Kanpur not Cawnpore), though where places have changed their name since the mid-nineteenth century, the nineteenth-century appellation has been retained (hence Madras not Chennai).

Finally, the terms 'mutiny-rebellion', 'revolt', and 'uprising' refer to widespread army and civilian unrest across north India during 1857–8.

MAP

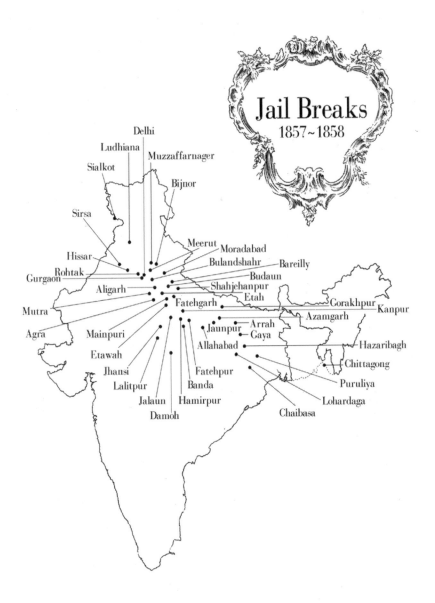

Jail Breaks
1857~1858

CHAPTER 1
INTRODUCTION

O come and look!
In the bazaar of Meerut.
The Feringi is waylaid and beaten!
The whiteman is waylaid and beaten!
In the open bazaar of Meerut.
Look! O Look![1]

Few events in the history of the British Empire have attracted as much interest or controversy as the Indian mutiny-rebellion of 1857–8. Since its immediate aftermath historical readings of the tumultuous events that swept across north India during these years have focussed largely on the causes of the revolt, and explanations for it are many and various. This reflects the multi-faceted character of the military and popular uprisings that fuelled and sustained events. Widespread mutiny in the Bengal army was accompanied rapidly by massive civil unrest, and few communities in rebellious areas in the North-West Provinces, Awadh, and western Bihar were unaffected. Though British and Indian historians have claimed variously that the unrest was 'mutiny', 'rebellion', or 'war of independence', it is impossible to capture the essence or meaning of the revolt in such simplistic, singular ways.[2]

Mutiny first erupted in the cantonment of Meerut on 9 May 1857, provoked by the fettering and imprisonment of a group of *sowars* (cavalrymen) and sepoys (from the Persian *sipahi*, meaning native infantry) who had refused to use a new issue of cartridges allegedly greased with animal fat. Military mutiny fanned civil unrest and that night sepoys and rebels broke open the town's two prisons. This triggered a pattern of revolt that was repeated over and again during the military and civil disturbances that gripped north India during 1857–8. In a stark challenge to the notion that the nineteenth century witnessed an uncontested imperial expansion of the carceral continuum, altogether mutineers and rebels attacked 41 prisons, mainly in the North-West Provinces and western Bihar, and released just over 23,000 prisoners, many of whom subsequently slipped out of the purview of the colonial state. This left the British with an unprecedented penal crisis, for notwithstanding the many thousands of escaped prisoners hiding out in the districts, making for home or joining the rebel cause, rebels damaged and destroyed a large number of jails. Gradually, Company troops quelled the revolt, but in many towns and cities there were no secure buildings to hold either recaptured prisoners or mutineers and rebels under arrest. British fears about the further spread of rebellion in territories associated with India led to the temporary abandonment of the transportation of convicts to existing penal settlements in the Straits Settlements (Pinang, Melaka, Singapore) and Burma (Arakan, Tenasserim Provinces). In this context, extant yet still vague proposals to settle the as yet unsuccessfully colonized Andaman Islands in the Bay of Bengal rapidly took shape, and in 1858 the British established a penal colony for the reception of mutineer-rebel convicts at the new site of Port Blair.

This book's point of departure is mutiny-rebellion jail-breaking and its consequences. It is not an exhaustive rewriting of the events of 1857–8; rather its aim is to use the revolt and its aftermath to probe the nature and meaning of incarceration in colonial north India. The pages that follow will examine the reflexive processes that characterized the relationship between colonial cultures of confinement and north Indian communities during the period to the 1860s. The book's central premise is that the mutiny-rebellion was a decisive moment in the history of Indian imprisonment, for it consolidated the colonial jail as a crucial site of provocation and coalescence concerning British interventions into cultural affairs. As we will see, mutineer-rebels targeted jails during the revolt not only for practical purposes such as the acquisition of labour and supplies, but also because they saw them as one of the principal instruments of colonial rule and the multiple cultural and religious transgressions that implied. In turn, in seeking solutions to the crushing penal crisis facing north India post-1858, though in many ways the mutiny-rebellion assured continuity in long-term penal trends it also secured innovative changes in the agenda of overseas transportation. The revolt of 1857–8 thus marked an important moment in the colonial history of incarceration both as a mode of control and as a social institution.

The Indian Uprising

During 1857–8 over one hundred thousand troops - over two-thirds of the entire Bengal army – mutinied. Almost all the cavalry and artillery and 70 infantry regiments rose against their commanders. The enlisted men were mainly small landholders. The majority of the infantry (who made up the bulk of the army) were *Brahmins* (of the priestly caste) or other high-caste Hindus, and most of the cavalry (numbering about 19,000) were Muslims or Pathans. Forty thousand came from the newly annexed Kingdom of Awadh.[3] Widespread social unrest both accompanied mutiny and spread across Awadh and the North-West Provinces to western Bihar, constituting the largest and most threatening rebellion in the history of the nineteenth-century British Empire. We know little about the impact of the revolt in other areas. Bombay in the west and Madras in the south were seemingly unaffected, though this seems rather anomalous for sepoy disaffection itself can be traced back to southern India.

In what historians view commonly as a precedent for the more general uprising of 1857–8, in 1806 several regiments mutinied at Vellore after soldiers were ordered to appear bare cheeked and wear new headgear with a leather cockade (rosette). *Quranic* mores meant that Muslims did not shave or in some cases even trim their beards, while Hindu religious tradition proscribed the wearing of leather. Further factors in the run-up to 1857–8 were army disquiet over the professional threat posed by the opening up of service to recruits from non-traditional regions or castes, ineffective army leadership, limited prospects for promotion, grumblings over discriminatory pay (British soldiers received better wages), and the General Service Enlistment Act (1856) which made service outside the Bengal Presidency (including in Awadh) compulsory. Not only did the act remove the financial benefits of foreign service, it threatened potentially customs relating to caste. Christian missionaries, and even military commanders like the evangelical General Hugh Wheeler who was commanding the troops at Kanpur at the outbreak of mutiny, were by this time preaching openly to sepoy regiments, and fears about loss of caste if not forced conversion to Christianity were widespread.

By the beginning of 1857 rumours about a new rifle cartridge issue were circulating among regiments. Allegedly, the cartridges were encased in gelatine-stiffened paper and greased with pig or cow fat. Because the ends needed to be bitten off before use they transgressed the cultural mores of Muslims, for whom pigs were unclean, and of Hindus, to whom cows were sacred. The first sign of discontent itself was in February, when the regiment at Berhampur refused to use new cartridges and so its officers disarmed and dismissed it. There was a further mutiny at the Barrackpur cantonment in March. A few weeks later, the third Bengal cavalry in Meerut also refused to accept newly issued cartridges. Officers arrested, court-martialled, and sentenced eighty-five *sowars* to ten years' imprisonment. Their fellow cavalrymen broke out in open defiance, shooting dead the lieutenant of the eleventh Bengal native infantry, John Finnis, and any other Europeans they could lay their hands on, looting and setting fire to cantonment bungalows, breaking open the city's two jails (and so releasing their fellow *sowars*), and in what marked the start of widespread military, social, and economic revolt made for Delhi where they framed a constitution and proclaimed the somewhat elderly and frail Bahadur Shah II Emperor of Hindustan. Some accounts claim that he was an unwilling leader, but whether or not this was the case his involvement gave the revolt a sort of legitimate sanction and over the course of the weeks that followed troops across the region followed the Meerut *sowars*, rising in protest and defiance. Their violent mood and interventions in the precipitation of disorder more generally shocked the British, who had not anticipated the extent and significance of widespread army discontent or the speed with which it instantaneously and dramatically spilled over into massive civil disturbance. The British were driven out of large areas of the North-West Provinces and Awadh. However, despite the anticipation of European communities elsewhere in northern India, there was no general rising in the Panjab or Bengal. The Company was able to use loyal soldiers reinforced by British troops diverted to India to begin the military campaign to defeat the rebels. Tactically, the rebels had failed to spread outwards and so the British were able to attack each of their north Indian city strongholds in turn. By January 1859, British forces had quashed the mutiny-rebellion, though of course sporadic local unrest continued unabated over the months and years that followed.

Certainly, the most famous single explanation for the cause of the mutiny-rebellion is the disaffection of sepoys around the rumoured issue of greased cartridges, in the broader context of increasing unease around racially or culturally discriminating pay and working conditions. And yet the close relationship between the mutiny and social revolt suggests that the rebellion meant something more to Indian communities. Some historians have contextualized the sepoys' growing sense of disaffection within general public fears of forced conversion to Christianity. By the middle of the nineteenth century, British and American missionaries were a familiar presence in Indian towns, cities, and villages. Some Company officials too were evangelical in their open proselytization, leading to the supposition among Indians that the government supported missionaries. Military commander General Wheeler, for instance, preached openly to the sepoys under his command in Kanpur. 'I have told them plainly that they are all lost and ruined sinners both by nature and by practice,' he wrote in April 1857.

'As to the question whether I have endeavoured to convert sepoys and others to Christianity, I would humbly reply that this has been my object.'[4] Educated communities viewed such attitudes as 'dangerously intrusive'.[5] It is little wonder that many Indians regarded missionaries as the religious arm of the Company.[6]

In this reading, the mutiny-rebellion was a local response to the general assault on 'native tradition' that invariably, some would say inevitably, accompanied East India Company expansion across South Asia, beginning with the utilitarian philosophy that characterized William Bentinck's 'Age of Reform' (1828–35). Like missionary activity generally, historians cite often the promotion of western education, the extension of the right of inheritance to religious converts (1850), and the Hindu Widow Remarriage Act (1856) as evidence of inappropriate and unpopular cultural interference in this respect. Though it did not mention Christian conversion directly, the first intervention in practice benefited Christian converts alone, as previously they had been unable to inherit property. The measure sparked protests from caste Hindus because Christians were unable to perform the religious duties associated with the appeasement of their ancestral spirits. The second act extended legislative interference on the social norms of widowhood. Large numbers of young girls were promised in marriage, and the not at all uncommon circumstance of their intended husband's untimely demise left many, often still pre-pubescent, as outcastes. The act's intention was to facilitate their remarriage and therefore mitigate the effect of the supposedly degrading practices to which widows were subject: the shaving of the head, living outside the family or even community compound, and taking water from separate wells. The act was unpopular among Hindus, not simply on religious grounds but undoubtedly also because it was bound up with the desire on the part of the colonial state to strengthen its hold over land, which the claims of remarried widows threatened potentially to disrupt through subdivision.

A number of contemporary Indian commentators explained the mutiny-rebellion in part through reference to the religious threat posed by Company administration.[7] Rumours about the Company's adulteration of flour in the bazaars accompanied fears about the alleged introduction of greased cartridges, triggering and directing rebellion. As Ranajit Guha shows, such rumours were an important element of rebellion in a pre-industrial, pre-literate society.[8] Indian perspectives were echoed in Britain where, although the causes of the mutiny-rebellion were debated fiercely, many contemporaries gave much import to religious interference in explaining the motive for revolt. To be sure, rebel cries of *'deen'* and *'deen ka jai'* (religion, victory to religion) as also *'dharam'* (duty) sounded in the countryside, towns, and cities throughout these turbulent months. Revolutionary Messianism was a further feature of unrest, with rumours about an imminent end to British rule circulating regularly during the first half of the nineteenth century.[9] Marking one hundred years since British victory at the Battle of Plassey, 1857 assumed symbolism as the year in which Indians would drive Europeans, sometimes called *firingi* (Christian westerners) and sometimes Nazarenes (followers of Jesus of Nazareth), from India. Tapti Roy has argued persuasively that rebels perceived the revolt as 'an imperative course of action' for upholding religion.[10] And religion, of course, was not a fixed and unchanging set of beliefs, but a vehicle through which new political concerns could be expressed and status claims made.[11] In an important intervention on the political theory of the revolt, Rajat Kanta Ray shows how codes of personal conduct were linked to matters of public duty. Religion and realm became closely tied by communities uniting against a common enemy. 'In the people's own consciousness,' he wrote, 'these were wars of religion.'[12] Or, as Rudrangshu Mukherjee puts it in an invocation of the social basis of religious protest noted by Karl Marx, religion was 'the sigh of the oppressed.'[13]

British contemporaries could not understand the suddenness and extent of the revolt and so concluded that it must have been pre-planned. This led to a further explanation: that the revolt was not simply a religious response to threats posed by Christianity but a religious conspiracy. Some nineteenth-century British writers argued that the rebellion was a plot masterminded by high-caste *Brahmin* Hindus angry at the Company's evangelical zeal and fearful of the continuing loss of privilege that interventions like the remarriage of widows implied. Others claimed that it was a Muslim *jihad* (holy war), declared in the context of the decline in political authority experienced by Mughal elites. And yet while religious feelings and concerns were a central element of how rebels themselves viewed the revolt, evidence for religious conspiracies is at best limited. Hindu kingship was fragmented, localized, and in some cases allied to the Mughal regime. Despite famous Hindu leaders like Lakshmibai (the Rhani of Jhansi), Tantia Tope (in Central India) or Kuer Singh (in Bihar),[14] Hindus generally did not share the common interests necessary to inspire the religious plot claimed by some contemporary observers. In the years running up to the mutiny-rebellion there was, on the other hand, a series of Islamic movements that combined religion with socio-economic protest. For instance, followers of Sayyid Ahmad (who had declared *jihad* against the Sikhs in 1826) in Rai Bareilly, later a rebel stronghold in southern Awadh, formed a *fara'izi* (dutiful observance) movement that melded revolt with religious duty in northern and eastern Bengal throughout the 1850s.[15] Islamic revivalist groups had a strong presence during the mutiny-rebellion, and several *maulvis* (clerics, intellectuals) declared *jihad* against a foreign power that they believed was on the verge of defeat. Militant *ghazis* (warriors of the faith) promoted the rebel cause in Delhi; they were joined by Muslims in other cities like Allahabad and by peasants in the district of Awadh. Even Hyderabad, a native state largely unaffected by rebellion, faced a declaration of holy war and an attack on the British Residency. Yet these *jihadis* never presented a serious threat because theological and broader social divisions hampered leadership, organization, and unity.[16] Moreover, during this period there is much evidence of the syncretism of Muslim-Hindu cultural practice.[17] Often Hindus and Muslims were more united than divided in the intertwining of notions of religion and realm into the broad category of 'Hindustan', which hardly smacks of communal conspiracy.[18] More generally, it is not clear why religious concerns fanned revolt in the north only.

The causes of the mutiny-rebellion were more widespread than religious interpretations alone suggest. Contemporary, nineteenth-century, and post-colonial interpretations also locate the genesis for unrest, if not rebel aspirations, additionally if not rather in the social and economic dislocation of Company policy. However, as for religious explanations it is still unclear why rebellion erupted in the north of the subcontinent and not elsewhere. Many changes related to land and the collection of revenue. The Company assumed responsibility for revenue collection (*diwani*) in Bengal and Bihar in 1765, taking over direct administrative control in 1772. At first it adopted various strategies, including farming out the *diwani* (*ijaradari*) or giving land to local magnates or tax collectors (*zemindars*). Permanent revenue settlement came in 1793, when the Company created the principle of landed property and clarified the relationship between the state and the cultivator. *Zemindars* became hereditary landlords with all the implied legal rights and restrictions. Not all were grateful for their new status because they acquired considerable responsibility for raising revenue from their tenant cultivators and some faced a considerable reduction in income. The creation of landlord interest was a strategy designed to promote social stability by encouraging investment by what was in effect a new landed gentry. Within twenty years, however, critics were arguing that far from assuring loyalty and dynamism the permanent settlement encouraged stagnation.

Later *mahalwari* land settlements in the North-West Provinces aimed to cut out the middleman and were based on collective village settlements or the 'restoration' of village *zemindary*. The British often over-assessed land, however, and unlike the permanent settlement of Bengal and Bihar, revenue demands increased constantly. There was a perhaps surprising degree of bankruptcy and repossession for arrears, and *zemindars* even fell into the clutches of creditor *banias* (moneylenders). Though not a traditionally landowning class themselves, *banias* made considerable inroads into the acquisition of property and upset the 'traditional' social order in the region, especially as most ex-*zemindars* stayed on the land as tenants. It is certainly indicative that during 1857–8 most of the countryside in the North-West Provinces went over to the rebel cause. The rebels first destroyed publicly *bania* records of debt and then reinstated traditional hereditary proprietors. Others as elsewhere across north India used the general chaos to settle old political, social, and economic scores. In an attempt to play down what were clearly widespread Indian grievances with Company policy, often British chroniclers of the day dismissed the nature and extent of such civil rebellion. In contrast, now historians view the especially pernicious impact of new land settlements in the North-West Provinces as one cause of rebellion there.

The Company developed a system of subsidiary alliances with the independent princely states, guaranteeing their defence and external security but following a policy of non-intervention in their internal affairs. It was not long, however, before they set their sights on annexation. In 1830 Mysore in the south was the first state to face the Company's axe. A device called the Doctrine of Lapse was used to gain control of other independent territories. If a prince had no heir, precedent demanded the adoption of a son to succeed him. After 1848 the Company refused to recognize these adoptive heirs, and over the course of the next seven years took control of seven states, causing considerable resentment by Indian elites. Rebel leader Lakshmibai, for instance, was from newly annexed Jhansi. Other types of interference in aristocratic affairs caused bad feeling also. For example, the Company had refused a pension and the dignity title *peshwa* to the most prominent leader in the revolt, Nana Sahib (Maharaja of Bithur), after his adoptive father died in 1851.

The Company annexed Awadh and its capital at Lakhnao in 1856, not as a lapsed territory but on the grounds that the *nawab* (ruler), Wajid Ali Shah, had mismanaged his government to such a degree that the whole state was corrupt. It deposed the *nawab* and disinherited his son. Company annexation had especially profound social consequences for Awadh because the political settlement that accompanied it gave land to a *zemindar* class to the exclusion of the great landholder kings *(taluqdārs)* already under pressure from subdivision. Local resentment was such that after Delhi Awadh became the main centre of the 1857–8 uprising. Generally historians accept now that the annexation of Awadh was one of the principal causes of the mutiny-rebellion more broadly. In the aftermath of annexation, discontent and resentment brewed in the popular local Urdu press. One Muslim leader, *Maulvi* Ahmadullah, preached *jihad* in Lakhnao until the Company posted troops at his residence. He later moved to Faizabad where the British arrested him and placed him in jail.[19] Some tens of thousands of ex-soldiers from the *nawab*'s disbanded army were unemployed and the revolt in Awadh assumed all the proportions of a populist movement, with rebels seeking to reverse the annexation and restore their king. To this end the ex-Queen Mother (Hazrat Mahal) co-operated with military and Muslim religious leaders and the British faced particularly fierce opposition in the high-caste villages from where most of the mutinous Bengal native infantry was recruited. News of their grievances had spread quickly, reinforcing the more general sense of socio-economic disquiet across north India. Interestingly, often the newly created landlord class came out in favour of dispossessed *taluqdārs*. Their actions expressed both genuine fears about the economic implications of the new land settlement and widespread resistance to the passing of an old order in which local magnates were viewed as representations of the Hindu deity Lord Shiva, around which systems of patronage and honour circulated.

Trade was another area of economic transition under the Company, and by the time of the mutiny-rebellion India's trading position had been reversed. It exported raw materials such as cotton or opium rather than finished products, and imported piece goods like textiles in lieu of raw materials. Protective British domestic trade policies affected profoundly the market for Indian cotton textiles, impacting on urban based weavers in negative ways. Indeed, grain and tax riots were features of social protests in towns and cities throughout the first half of the nineteenth century. Though Indian merchant houses profited, and local intermediaries retained importance in some areas, notably the expanding opium trade, by drawing the subcontinent into the global economy and its instability, and by changing local patterns of production and consumption, Company policy altered fundamentally patterns of Indian trade. While some magnates rode the potential storm to carve out new sources of profit for themselves, the shift in the structure of trade was an important stimulus to unrest, especially in urban areas, with weavers and artisans making rebellious expressions of their lost livelihoods during 1857–8.

The effects of land settlement, annexation, and changing trade patterns squeezed communities already teetering on the margins of society. Joining the dispossessed rural aristocracy and the new landlord classes in revolt were an impoverished or culturally fearful peasantry, geographically and economically displaced *adivasi* (tribal) communities, and a marginalized urban workforce, all of whom had quite different and often competing claims on the Company state. With the Company's creation of a rural landowning aristocracy and its associated peasant class, increasingly non-sedentary tribal pastoralists were forced out of traditional grazing areas and into the hardships of wage labour. Vast swathes of the north Indian peasantry rebelled in 1857–8, with revolt sparked off by an explosive combination of local fears and concerns about impending economic hardship in the face of revenue demands, and loss of status or prestige in relation to other communities more favoured by East India Company rule. There were *adivasi* rebellions throughout the first half of the nineteenth century, most famously the Kol rebellion of 1831–2 and the Santal *hul* of 1855–6, in Chota Nagpur and Santal Parganas. *Adivasi* communities used the revolt as a means to protest against moneylenders and other exploitative agents of the Company, though groups like the Kols and Santals had little sympathy with the army that had crushed them previously and so did not necessarily support the mutinous sepoys. Indeed, in one notorious incident a group of *adivasis* actually blocked the progress of the sepoy rebels in Ranchi.[20] In cities across Awadh, the North-West Provinces and western Bihar, marginalized weavers and artisans, almost half of whom were Muslims,[21] came out in support of local rebel *maulvis*. Though we know relatively little about the urban dimensions of the revolt, no doubt their social and economic dislocation in part explains the broad appeal of city *jihadis*.[22]

An important historiographical layer in the repertoire of causative explanations is the suggestion that the mutiny-rebellion was India's first war of independence, in which disaffected communities of all kinds united against a common British enemy. In this reading, the revolt was not an expression of diverse social, political, economic, and cultural complaints, but a coherent nationalist movement. Such interpretations came to prominence with the writings of imprisoned revolutionary leaders in the twentieth century. Hindu nationalist V.D. Savarkar, for instance, penned *The Indian War of Independence* in 1909, shortly before the government transported him to the penal colony in the Andaman Islands on a charge of sedition.[23] Given the extent of the political, social, and economic discontent that underlay the revolt, the notion that it was an anti-colonial movement is an attractive proposition, for it provides a framework through which the grievances of various rebels can be expressed, in the countryside and in the towns, and for the inclusion of social groups such as low-caste Hindus or *adivasis* who are often represented historically as common bazaar ruffians (*badmash*) without the consciousness of their social betters. Critics of this view, however, point to the lack of evidence of nationalist feeling and the absence of a united or effective leadership with broad appeal. According to their reading of events the mutiny in the army simply sparked off a chain of revolt among those with other, disparate grievances which although perhaps traceable to the restructuring of colonial economy and society did not at the time constitute anti-colonial war.[24] Indeed, it has been argued that in its widespread desire to see a return to the old order, the uprising was more of a counter-revolution than a forward-looking nationalist one.[25]

The mutineer-rebels did not force the British out of India. In general historians agree that the failure of the revolt in military terms was due to a combination of the fragmented nature of discontent, ineffective leadership, inappropriate tactics in failing to move out of northern centres (or perhaps a lack of tactics altogether), the successful mobilization of British troops, and a perhaps surprising degree of Indian loyalty to the Company, for many large *zemindars*, native princes, traders, and bankers supported the British. One historian has argued that the low caste too remained excluded from most rebel notions of solidarity, something which the Company took advantage of in recruiting them in large numbers in support of their assault on anti-British strongholds.[26] As C.A. Bayly has pointed out following Eric Stokes' refusal to generalize experiences into causal links, who collaborated with the British and who revolted against them is not simply explained by the sort of causative factors discussed above, for there were many exceptions to apparent social, economic, cultural or religious connections.[27]

Mirroring contemporary writing on the mutiny-rebellion which almost always sought to understand and therefore to prevent future discontent, frequently historians discuss the revolt in relation to the issue of causation.[28] This makes the question of loyalty and rebellion perplexing.[29] However, research on the causes of revolt has told us much more about local (or even individual) responses to East India Company policies of various kinds than the trajectory or meaning of the mutiny-rebellion itself. Equally, there are still large gaps in our knowledge both about the local and precise impact of British policy in the years leading up to 1857 and local patterns of mutiny-rebellion, especially in the cities.[30] Additionally, while contemporaries and historians have discussed Indians' religious grievances and fears of conversion, they have not in general linked them to the threat that the Company posed to social and moral values and principles and ideas more generally (*dharma*).[31] The nature and extent of forms of religious repression that threatened a profound impact in these respects, notably with regard to colonial violations of religion and caste in jails, have barely surfaced in historiographical debates at all.

Historians accept that the mutiny-rebellion was not the unique and unprecedented event contemporaries often spoke of, but part of what Bayly has described as endemic armed revolt across early colonial India.[32] Landholders and landlords, tenants and peasants, itinerant communities, religious and caste-based groups, villagers, city dwellers, and townspeople were all involved in the instigation of periodic disputes, riots, and rebellions during the first half of the nineteenth century. Each episode can be traced, however indirectly, to a Company policy which sought to increase revenue and monopolize political authority. Tax rates were higher and collection was more vigorous. Interference in succession disputes or the affairs of regions that had never before come under the direct rule of the centralized Mughal Empire was common. Cash cropping encouraged the settlement of peasants and others on traditionally pastoral land. Often, the British catalogued local resistance against such measures as expressions of unique forms of 'native criminality'. In an array of marvellously detailed and nuanced studies historians have carefully deconstructed the criminal archive to reveal fascinating yet untold stories in the run-up to the uprising, not simply of law and (dis)order but of colonial oppression and Indian responses to perceived wrongs.[33]

Many historians have grappled with the issue of how to extract subaltern experiences and perspectives from colonial archives and studies of 1857 are no exception. Scholars have shifted the focus away from the actions of officials or military and rebel leaders towards subaltern groups, viewing them as important historical actors in their own right. This has reversed the usual relationship between the historical centre and margins in order to move away from the regular concentration on the bravado of British and Indian heroes. In their accounts of the revolt, both K.S. Singh and Pankaj Rag focus on ordinary Indian rebels, for instance, while Roy was concerned largely with subaltern experiences and views.[34] Gautam Bhadra examines four 'ordinary and yet complex' insurgent personalities, and Guha the sovereignty, consistency, and logic of *adivasi* and peasant rebels.[35] In a marvellous unravelling of 'the prose of counter insurgency' Guha resuscitates peasant consciousness through a close 'reading against the grain' of the language of the archive itself. His research anticipated the work of literary theorists and historical geographers who have used accounts (as also fictions) of the mutiny-rebellion to examine closely the ideological and discursive bases of empire. They focused especially on exaggerated reports of rebels' sexual violation of British women to show how colonial accounts of the revolt might be understood as a necessary moment in colonial chivalry, an intervention required for the protection of British honour and prestige, and therefore as one aspect to the gendering of empire.[36]

A final corpus of work on the mutiny-rebellion has coalesced around the issue of governance. Though in many ways British administration after 1857–8 continued with long-term trends, there were a number of tangible developments. Politically, of course, the most immediate effect was the almost complete dissolution of the East India Company on 1 November 1858 and the transition to the direct rule of India from London. The colonial state acquired greater *de facto* influence in the supposedly independent native states. Socially, government reinstated old aristocracies and elites. It co-opted Indian intermediaries into the bureaucracy of government, where they sat on the viceroy's and other councils, or it employed them as low-level administrators. Economically, the government made conservative efforts to rebalance the policy on land to favour landlords and cultivators, and largely switched to a system of direct taxation. Culturally, it propagated a policy of non-interference in religious affairs. It replaced traditional areas of army recruitment like Awadh and Benares with the apparently loyal Panjab, and to some extent Nepal, and divided the army by caste and religion. It also reshaped fundamentally what Bayly describes as 'the information order', particularly communications like the railways and telegraph. The British also made more concerted efforts to understand Indian society, and therefore possible sources of discontent, and so the production of colonial knowledge, notably anthropological or ethnographic understandings, took on new forms. These generated radical modes of social posturing and caste mobility among Indian communities who sought to use modified colonial categories to their own economic, social, and cultural ends. The social distancing of Europeans from Indians also deepened, among the middle classes at least, sowing the seeds of the social and economic degradation of the by then substantial Eurasian (British-Indian) community.[37]

Cultures of confinement in colonial South Asia

Despite the multidimensional nature of the revolt the prison became a target of attack in almost every area affected by rebellion, and this requires explanation. Though not a peculiarly colonial institution, the nature of confinement in early colonial India underwent what David Arnold has described as a fundamental shift in form and function under the East India Company's administration. Prisons had existed in the subcontinent since the third century B.C., but they were used mainly to confine political rivals or rebels whose execution was impolitic or to house pre-trial defendants. Discretionary punishments such as public disgrace (*tashir*), fines, banishment from a town, city or locality, amputation, and mutilation were all far more common expressions of social, cultural, or economic transgression.[38] The Company moved to replace these penal interventions with imprisonment and overseas transportation. It adapted old or constructed new buildings for the purpose of incarceration, mostly if not exclusively in Indian town centre or city locations. Further, it set up a series of penal settlements across the Indian Ocean: in Bengkulu (1787–1825), the Andaman Islands (1793–6), Pinang or Prince of Wales Island (1790–1860), Mauritius (1815–53), Melaka and Singapore (1825–60), and Burma (1828–62).[39] The move towards mainland or overseas confinement and its associated disciplinary manoeuvres, notably the performance of hard labour, as punishments in themselves were radical changes in penal practice, and the significance, nature, and perhaps most importantly the north Indian response to this shift is the first broad theme of this book.

As we will see in Chapter 2, during the first half of the nineteenth century northern jails were often the target of local campaigns against colonial interference into cultural practices, for they were places of unprecedented intervention into the Indian body politic. Prisons became sites of Indian resistance to and negotiation with the Company regime, and jail instability with regard to the disciplinary issues of penal work, the award of privileges, and most significantly dietary rationing continued from the end of the eighteenth century into 1857–8. In many cases, prison rioting and general unrest, particularly around perceived assaults on religion, was either inspired or supported by urban dwellers. Sepoys too became entangled in penal controversies, especially in places that supplied troops for the Bengal army. This reveals much of the porousness that characterized penal institutions during the first half of the nineteenth century. However, sepoys and townspeople were concerned largely with prisoners of 'respectable' status, with regard to religion or social standing, and their anti-colonial sentiments did not unite them against broader social fissures. Although there is evidence that jails encouraged Hindu-Muslim syncretism amongst prisoners of status, they were also potential sites for the creation and consolidation of religious and caste difference. Further, if we accept the general claim that the mutiny-rebellion was unique in scale but not in form, for social and economic unrest characterized the first half of the nineteenth century, rebel activity around colonial prisons was not only an important element of the revolt itself but provides an important *entrée* into north Indian attitudes to colonial confinement. As suggested above, though historians have focused closely on uprisings in the countryside, the urban context of the revolt remains relatively hazy. The colonial prison is an important means of understanding the nature of unrest in towns and cities, and jail-breaking, the second theme of the book, at least partly redirects attention towards the urban context (Chapters 3 and 4).

With some important exceptions contemporary, nineteenth-century, and post-colonial British historiography of the mutiny-rebellion is drawn from a peculiarly constituted colonial archive that centralizes European eye-witness accounts and observations and the so-called 'mutiny narratives' (local diaries). That is not to say that such literature should be dismissed out of hand or that it is necessarily unsympathetic to the rebel cause. Though some historiography focuses squarely on Indian atrocities or belittles a supposedly ignorant peasantry, other accounts present the rebel-mutineers as communities under extreme economic and social pressure. Perhaps surprisingly, however, relatively few historians writing in English have turned to mutineer/rebel-centred or to vernacular accounts as a basis for unpicking the complexities of the revolt.[40] This book will attempt to break some ground with regard to jail-breaking and its aftermath, drawing upon Indian sources like first-hand accounts recorded in colonial archives and newspapers, vernacular pamphlets, and poetry. Historians working on colonial imprisonment in other contexts have shown how remnants of material culture might be used in the reconstruction of convict lives, or convict bodies themselves placed at the centre of analyses of the relationships between subject peoples and the state.[41] Despite the constraints that technologies of colonial power and the politics of archival survival bring to the table, the recorded words of prisoners and convicts buried within official colonial documents also comprize important penal tales. These narratives have yet to be exploited fully.[42] They survive mainly in reports of government consultations and proceedings as well as in trial records. With the exception of vernacular petitions, they appear mainly in English translation. The usual limitations of this linguistic transformation must be considered, especially when it involved multiple translations. Moreover, convict words were not usually spontaneous for they were spoken within and mediated by the peculiarities of the colonial administration. Yet they are extremely valuable fragments of empire. They are not nearly as rare as one might imagine and have the further advantage of placing that most subaltern of subalterns, the illiterate and usually unnamed convict, into the frame.[43] These are what James C. Scott has described famously as the 'hidden transcripts' embedded in the colonial archive.[44] Another historian researching in this area has dubbed such verbal traces 'high-density micro-narratives'.[45]

This methodological underpinning represents an effort to shift the focus of analysis towards the negotiations and perceptions of mutineer-rebels around and about colonial modes of punishment. Such an approach is particularly pertinent to this project, for while commonly British contemporaries and post-colonial historians explore the cultural provocations invoked by colonial interventions into Hindu widow remarriage, inheritance legislation, and fears about forced conversion to Christianity more generally, most do not mention the extent or depth of feeling invoked during the cultural confrontations that played out in north Indian jails in the years leading up to and during the revolt. As we will see, the colonial prison assumes a much more central role in Indian accounts than it does in European ones. This stark contrast perhaps belies the extent to which some north Indian communities felt acutely the prison as both a socially and culturally alien institution and as a symbol of the broader wrongs of the British colonial administration. As such prisons were not only sites of rebellious activity but assumed a dynamic place in the discursive and symbolic elements of the events of 1857–8.[46]

Yet the mutiny-rebellion did not spread beyond the Gangetic plains and jails in the Madras and Bombay presidencies did not become sites of revolt. Even the feared Indian rising in the penal settlements in Southeast Asia, where large numbers of Bengal convicts were held under sentence of transportation, never materialized, despite the fact that they overwhelmingly came from the regions most affected by the mutiny-rebellion. The regional dynamics and spatial limitations of the 1857–8 uprising seem to inform broader arguments about the uneven cultural, social, and economic impact of Company rule, especially with relation to land settlement, trade, and annexation, though this is far from settled issue. Moreover, the spatial limitations of the uprising suggest that in places affected by the mutiny-rebellion the prison was not so much the genesis of revolt as a space around which other social, cultural, and economic grievances coalesced. This has potentially interesting implications for our understanding of the relationship between jail-breaking and the revolt as also broader studies of divergent Indian views about, rather than the more usual focus on the nature and impact of, colonial innovations and interventions more generally.

The revolt left a serious penal crisis its wake, especially in the North-West Provinces where the rebels set thousands of prisoners free and damaged or destroyed dozens of jails. The third theme of the book addresses how the government of India, prisoners, and mutineer-rebels alike coped with the consequences of jail-breaking. Chapter 3 will examine colonial strategies for the recapture or pardon of escapees and mutineer-rebels. Chapter 4 will discuss the issue of jail overcrowding and prisoner transfers, the response of penal administrators in the Straits Settlements and Burma to the prospect of the overseas transportation of thousands of apparently dangerous offenders, and the reaction of prisoners and convicts themselves. The chapter will show that although there were only limited changes in the architecture of mainland confinement, the mutiny-rebellion gave new forms of confinement and discipline greater urgency, forcing the government's hand with regard to the settlement of the Andaman Islands as a penal colony. Chapter 5 will focus on the early years of convict settlement there.

Since Indian independence, the Andamans have assumed a central place in post-colonial discourses of the freedom struggle. Because in the early decades of the twentieth century it was a place for the transportation and punishment of nationalists, the Islands have been transformed both imaginatively and figuratively into a site of valiant anti-colonial struggle and martyrdom. It is therefore somewhat anomalous that English language accounts rarely draw on the rich material recorded or produced by convicts shipped to the Islands in the aftermath of revolt.[47] This presents a stark contrast to their general focus on the brutalities and indignities of the penal colony's disciplinary regime and more particularly its notorious cellular jail as described in widely published early twentieth-century convict memoirs.[48] In a recent intervention on the representation of convicts transported to the Indian penal colony in the Andaman Islands during the nineteenth century, Satadru Sen has noted that the problem for historians is that there is an acute lack of first-hand accounts by convicts themselves. To this end he has rehabilitated a narrative account produced by *Wahabi* convict rebel Maulana Muhammad Ja'far Thanesari, who was transported to the Andamans in 1866 for conspiring to smuggle funds to Afghan *mujahideen*. He served nearly eighteen years in the colony and subsequently wrote an autobiography.[49]

And yet there are other such narratives. This book will unravel the writings of two convicts transported in the aftermath of the mutiny-rebellion. The first is Fazl-i-Haq Khairabadi (1797–1861), an Awadhi scholar of Islamic theology, literature, and languages who was alleged to have joined the revolt, proclaimed his loyalty to Bahadur Shah, and drawn up the constitution of liberated Delhi.[50] He turned himself in, believing that he would be pardoned under the British amnesty, but instead was convicted of instigating rebellion, propounding doctrines 'calculated to encourage murder', and taking a prominent part in the 'council of rebels'. In 1859 the government confiscated his property and shipped him to the Andamans under sentence of transportation for life.[51] Fazl-i-Haq Khairabadi wrote in Arabic both an eyewitness account of the 1857–8 uprising and about his experiences as a convict in the Andamans.[52] The text bears the traces of its production, for it remains elusive in the identification of rebels. It was smuggled out of the Islands on pieces of torn cloth through a released convict, Mufti 'Inayat Ullah Kakorwi, who gave it to Fazl-i-Haq's son, 'Abd al-Haqq, to edit. Fazl-i-Haq did not give his narrative a title. Only later was it called *Risala Ghadariyya* (*Book of Mutiny*), *al-Fitna al-Hindiyaa* (*The Indian Intrigue*), or *Bagh-i-Hindustan (Rebel India)*. A further Urdu translation appeared as *Saurat-ul-Hindya (Indian Revolution)*, followed shortly afterwards by an English translation, *The Story of the War of Independence*.[53] Within this process of collation, editing, and translation we see a shift in the meaning of the narratives that reflected contemporary concerns, for the 'mutiny' or 'intrigue' was transformed into 'war of independence'. Despite this political deployment astonishingly until very recently Fazl-i-Haq has been ignored in the English historiography of the revolt, though he figures frequently in the Urdu literature.[54]

The second convict to leave narrative traces of his experiences in the Andamans is Sayyid Ismail Husain Shikohabadi (1819–81), an Urdu poet of the Lakhnao School who wrote under the pen name 'Munir'. In 1860 the government transported him to the Andamans on a charge of conspiracy to murder a courtesan. He maintained that this was a trumped-up charge that masked the real reason for his transportation: he was the poetic master (*ustad*) of the rebel *Nawab* of Banda. During the mutiny-rebellion the *nawab* expressed loyalty to the anti-British leader Nana Sahib and the Mughal Emperor, and was on friendly terms with the rebel Farrukhabad court.[55] After his shipment to the Andamans, Munir wrote several poems about his experiences of imprisonment and transportation.[56] Because he was sentenced for the murder of a courtesan Munir was not a political offender *per se*. Nevertheless in his poetry he associated his sentence directly with the mutiny-rebellion. Munir's social marginality as a convict is reflected in his current literary and historiographical standing. He is a minor figure in most Urdu literary histories. Moreover, historians have made only passing mention of the immense significance of his work.[57] It is his historical significance that concerns us here, for even if his poetry did not display remarkable technical skill and ingenuity (which it does), the verses are important expressions of an individual convict's experience of the social, economic, and cultural dislocation of revolt and transportation.

Moreover, both texts are the earliest known examples of Indian convict writing in narrative form. The accounts and poetry of Fazl-i-Haq and Munir Shikohabadi thus provide unique and original insights into the causes, nature, and trajectory of the mutiny-rebellion and into life in the early colonial Andamans – the focus here - where the men became companions. In this sense their work can be read in parallel with *Wahabi* rebel Thanesari's later manuscript *In Exile*. However, the texts should not be seen as somehow representative of Indian attitudes to the prison, penal colony or 1857–8 uprising more broadly. As Sen points out in relation to Thanesari's narrative, such sources must be treated with caution for their very existence belies their typicality.[58] Moreover, as Jamal Malik argues, jail literature more generally inspires solidarity among prisoner authors and their readers. It constructs what he describes as a liminal space that assumes interesting meanings with regard to the construction of history and identity formation when it is smuggled out of the jail and read in the outside world.[59] Nowhere is this process more evident than in the continued renaming of Fazl-i-Haq's memoir.

Notwithstanding the widening of the archive of revolt that these narrative accounts represent, sources of all kinds remain almost completely silent on the fate of female prisoners. This perhaps in part reflects the more general absence of subaltern women from mutiny records, except perhaps when they appear in the guise of the loyal European *ayah* (nursemaid). Women like the extraordinary Rani of Jhansi, Hazrat Mahal (the mother of the deposed *Nawab* of Awadh), and Zinat Mahal (wife of Bahadur Shah) of course played an important role in the revolt, and their historical presence has been acknowledged and explored in a number of accounts, both contemporary and historical.[60] Undoubtedly, however, contemporaries and historians have gendered both the instigation and pattern of the mutiny-rebellion in such a way as to exclude women who lacked political or social clout. It is extremely unlikely that civil revolt was an exclusively male preserve. Guha for instance has pointed to the involvement and incarceration of Santal women for their part in the 1855 *hul*.[61] And yet only the faintest trace of ordinary female rebels remains, and we know almost nothing of the fate of women prisoners in the wake of the rebels' mass liberation of the jails.

In the aftermath of revolt the prison remained a socially dynamic institution, and during the second half of the nineteenth century imprisonment and transportation continued to provoke and to inspire Indian communities in conceptualizing and expressing their relationship with the colonial regime. By the 1920s, both the jail and the penal colony had become well-established and central tropes in the playing out of political struggles.[62] Moreover, by this time nationalists viewed India itself as a vast prison, ensuring that incarceration and transportation took on important new symbolic meanings.[63] Beyond fleeting glimpses of Governor-General (later Viceroy) 'Clemency' Canning, so called because of his supposed leniency in dealing with mutineer-rebels, or the notion of the Andamans Islands as a place of martyrdom (a theme discussed in Chapter 5), historians have not examined systematically the broader impact of the mutiny-rebellion in these respects. The conclusion centres on this historiographical breach, repositioning jails and penal colonies as spaces of cultural intervention and resistance with long material and symbolic histories. In rethinking those histories we shall turn first to a discussion of the inception of the colonial jail as a space of penal confinement and cultural negotiation.

Notes

1. Henry Scholberg, *The Indian Literature of the Great Rebellion*, New Delhi, Promilla, 1993, 115. *Feringi* = foreigner (Christian westerner).
2. There is a massive literature on the mutiny-rebellion. Contemporary and later nineteenth-century British writing is too extensive to detail here, though the classic account remains *Kaye's and Malleson's History of the Indian Mutiny of 1857–8* (6 vols), London, W.H. Allen, 1888–9 (henceforth 'Kaye and Malleson'). J.W. Kaye wrote the first three volumes, and after his death G.B. Malleson produced volumes IV - VI, also revising substantially volume III. Kaye's original three volumes were entitled *A History of the Sepoy War in India, 1857–8*. (I thank Doug Peers for this insight). For a useful recent overview of events see C.A. Bayly, *The New Cambridge History of India II.i: Indian society and the making of the British Empire*, Cambridge, Cambridge University Press, 1988, ch. 6. Other good starting points include: David Baker, 'Colonial Beginnings and the Indian Response: The Revolt of 1857–58 in Madhya Pradesh', *Modern Asian Studies*, 25, 3 (1991), 511-43; E.I. Brodkin, 'The Struggle for Succession: rebels and loyalists in the Indian Rebellion of 1857', *Modern Asian Studies*, 6, 3 (1972), 277-90; Haraprasad Chattopadhyaya, *The Sepoy Mutiny, 1857: a social study and analysis*, Calcutta, Bookland Private Ltd, 1957; S.B. Chaudhuri, *Civil Rebellion in the Indian Mutinies*, Calcutta, World Press, 1957; P.C. Joshi (ed.), *Rebellion 1857: A Symposium*, New Delhi, People's Publishing House, 1957; Rudrangshu Mukherjee, *Awadh in Revolt 1857–1858: a study of popular resistance*, New Delhi, Oxford University Press, 1984; Tapti Roy, 'Visions of the Rebels: A Study of 1857 in Bundelkhand', *Modern Asian Studies*, 27, 1 (1993), 205-28; Tapti Roy, *The Politics of a Popular Uprising: Bundelkhand in 1857*, New Delhi, Oxford University Press, 1994; S.N. Sen, *Eighteen Fifty-Seven*, New Delhi, Publications Division, Ministry of Education and Broadcasting, Government of India, 1957; E.T. Stokes, *The Peasant and the Raj: Studies in Agrarian Society and Peasant Rebellion in Colonial India*, Cambridge, Cambridge University Press, 1978; E.T. Stokes (ed. C.A. Bayly), *The Peasant Armed: the Indian Revolt of 1857*, Oxford, Clarendon, 1986; and the special edition of *Social Scientist*, 296-9 (1998) (henceforth *SS*).
3. Irfan Habib, 'The Coming of 1857', *SS*, 7.

4. S.A.A. Rizvi and B. Bhargarva, *Freedom Struggle in Uttar Pradesh*, Lucknow, Publications Bureau, Information Department Uttar Pradesh, 1957–60 (henceforth *FSUP*), *vol. I*, 293-300.

5. Avril A. Powell, *Muslims and Missionaries in Pre-Mutiny India*, London, Curzon, 1993, 263 (quote), 278-9.

6. E. Daniel Potts, *British Baptist Missionaries in India 1793–1837: the history of Serampore and its missions*, Cambridge, Cambridge University Press, 1967, 220.

7. Sayyid Ahmed Khan, *The Causes of the Indian Revolt, written by Syed Ahmed Khan Bahadur in Urdu in the Year 1858, and translated into English by his two European friends*, Benares, Medical Hall Press, 1873; Fazl-i-Haq Khairabadi, *Saurat-ul-Hindya (The Indian Revolution)*, Lahore, Maktabah-yi Qādriyah, 1974; S. Moinul Haq, 'The Story of the War of Independence, 1857–8 (being an English translation of Allamah Fadl-i-Haqq's Risalah on the War)', *Journal of the Pakistan Historical Society*, 5, 1 (1957), 23-57 (an early annotated draft of this article is located in the P.C. Joshi Collection of JNU Library). See also OIOC P.146.12H (BJP 25 Feb. 1858): J. Rattray, commandant Bengal police battalion, to Young, 31 Jan. 1858, enc. A few words relative to the late Mutiny of the Bengal Army, and the Rebellion in the Bengal Presidency, by Shaik Hedayut Ali, Subadar and Sirdar Bahdoor, Bengal Sikh Police Battalion commanded by Captain T. Rattray, who has translated this paper from the original Oordoo (henceforth 'A few words relative to the late mutiny'). Unfortunately the original Urdu pamphlet does not survive, though there is a copy of the published English document in the British Library and in PP 1857–58 (2449): Papers relative to mutinies in East Indies. The Bengali press at the time also noted the 'dissatisfaction' caused by legislative interventions, such as into Hindu widow remarriage. OIOC P.188.52 (BPP 30 Apr. 1858): Translation from the Bengali newspaper "Bhaskar", 20 Mar. 1858. The theme of religious infringement further emerges from the magnificent collection of contemporary source material in English (some of it translated from the original vernacular) in the five volume series *FSUP*.

8. Ranajit Guha, *Elementary Aspects of Peasant Insurgency in Colonial India*, New Delhi, Oxford University Press, 1983, 251-68.

9. Kenneth W. Jones, *The New Cambridge History of India III.i: Socio-religious reform movements in British India*, Cambridge, Cambridge University Press, 1989.

10. Roy, 'Visions of the Rebels', 213.

11. Gyanendra Pandey, *The Construction of Communalism in Colonial North India*, New Delhi, Oxford University Press, 1990, 81.

12. Rajat Kanta Ray, 'Race, Religion and Realm: The Political Theory of "The Reigning Indian Crusade", 1857', in Mushirul Hasan and Narayani Gupta, eds, *India's Colonial Encounter: essays in memory of Eric Stokes*, New Delhi, Manohar, 1993, 133-82 (quote 145).

13. Mukherjee, *Awadh in Revolt*, 152. On religion, see also Chattophadhyaya, *The Sepoy Mutiny*, 29-33.

14. Joyce Lebra-Chapman, *The Rani of Jhansi: a study in female heroism*, Honolulu, University of Hawaii Press, 1986; K.K. Datta, *Biography of Kunwar Singh and Amar Singh*, Patna, K.P. Jayaswal Research Institute, 1957; Pankaj Rag, '1857: Need for Alternative Sources', *SS*, 113-47; Roy, *The Politics of a Popular Uprising*; S.K. Sinha, *Veer Kuer Singh: The Great Warrior of 1857*, New Delhi, Konark Pubishers, 1997.

15. Qeyamuddin Ahmad, *The Wahabi Movement in India*, Calcutta, Firma K.L. Mukhopadhyay, 1966, ch. 7. On the effect of British rule on Muslims before 1857

and the fate of Muslims during the revolt, see P. Hardy, *The Muslims of British India*, Cambridge, Cambridge University Press, 1972, chs 3, 4.

16. For a recent literary reading of Muslim participation in the mutiny-rebellion, see Alex Padamsee, *Representations of Indian Muslims in British Colonial Discourse*, Basingstoke, Palgrave Macmillan, 2005, esp. part II.

17. Peter Robb, 'The impact of British rule on religious community: reflections on the trial of Maulvi Ahmadullah of Patna in 1865', in Peter Robb (ed.), *Society and Ideology: Essays in South Asian History, presented to Professor K.A. Ballhatchet*, New Delhi, Oxford University Press, 1993, 142-76.

18. Ray, 'Race, Religion and Realm', 151.

19. Faruqui Anjum Taban, 'The Coming of the Revolt in Awadh: The Evidence of Urdu Newspapers', *SS*, 17.

20. K.S. Singh, 'The "Tribals" and the 1857 Uprising', *SS*, 81-4. P.C. Roy Choudhury in contrast argues that the 1857 mutiny-rebellion 'followed absolutely' the 1855 Santal *hul*: *1857 in Bihar (Chotanagpur and Santhal Parganas)*, Patna, Gazetteers' Revision Office, Revenue Department, 1957, 121.

21. Muslims comprized 38 per cent of the urban population of the North-West Provinces, and were a demographically significant community in cities in Bihar: Jones, *Socio-religious reform movements*, 48. Almost a quarter of the population of Patna was, for instance, Muslim: Sinha, *Veer Kuer Singh*, 53.

22. On urban weaver communities, see Pandey, *The Construction*, ch. 3.

23. V.D. Savarkar, *The Indian War of Independence, 1857*, Bombay, Phoenix Publications, 1947 (first authorized Indian edition; first published in England 1909). See also V.D. Savarkar, *The Story of My Transportation for Life*, Sadbhakti Publications, Bombay, 1950; Harindra Srivastava, *Five Stormy Years: Savarkar in London, June 1906 – June 1911*, New Delhi, Allied Publishers, 1983.

24. See, for instance, Chattopadhyaya, *The Sepoy Mutiny*; R.C. Majumdar, *The Sepoy Mutiny and the Revolt of 1857*, Calcutta, S.S. Chaudhuri, 1957.

25. Sen, *Eighteen Fifty-Seven*.

26. Rag, '1857', 142-4.

27. Bayly, *Indian society*, 170.

28. An important exception, focusing on peasant action, is Guha, *Elementary Aspects*.

29. On the complexities of the status of 'loyalty' and 'rebellion', see Brodkin, 'The Struggle for Succession'.

30. Roy has called for more rigour in charting actions and events: 'Visions of the Rebels', 206.

31. Rag, '1857', 129-37.

32. *Ibid.* See also S.B. Chaudhuri, *Civil Disturbances during the British Rule in India, 1765–1857*, Calcutta, World Press, 1955; Guha, *Elementary Aspects*.

33. Nicholas B. Dirks, *Castes of Mind: colonialism and the making of modern India*, Princeton, University of Princeton Press, 2001, ch. 9; Sandria Freitag, 'Crime in the Social Order of Colonial North India', *Modern Asian Studies*, 25, 2 (1991), 227-61; Radhika Singha, '"Providential" Circumstances: The Thuggee Campaign of the 1830s and Legal Innovation', *Modern Asian Studies*, 27, 1 (1993), 83-146; Radhika Singha, *A Despotism of Law: Crime and Justice in Early Colonial India*, New Delhi, Oxford University Press, 1998; Anand A. Yang (ed.), *Crime and Criminality in British India*, Tucson, University of Arizona Press, 1985.

34. Rag, '1857'; Roy, 'Visions of the Rebels'; Roy, *The Politics of a Popular Uprising*; Singh, 'The "Tribals"'.

35. Gautam Bhadra, 'Four Rebels of Eighteen-Fifty-Seven', in Ranajit Guha (ed.),
     Subaltern Studies IV: Writings on South Asian History and Society, New Delhi, Oxford
     University Press, 1985, 230; Guha, *Elementary Aspects*, 13. See also Mukherjee's new
     introduction to the second edition of *Awadh in Revolt*, New Delhi, Permanent Black,
     2002.

36. Alison Blunt, 'Embodying war: British women and defilement in the Indian
     "Mutiny", 1857–8', *Journal of Historical Geography*, 26, 3 (2000), 403-28; Gautam
     Chakravarty, *The Indian Mutiny and the British Imagination*, Cambridge, Cambridge
     University Press, 2005, 38-9; Indira Ghose, *Women Travellers in Colonial India: the
     power of the female gaze*, New Delhi, Oxford University Press, 1998, ch. 5;
     Rudrangshu Mukherjee, '"Satan Let Loose Upon Earth": The Kanpur Massacres
     in India in the Revolt of 1857', *Past and Present*, 128 (1990), 92-116; Upamanyu
     Pablo Mukherjee, *Crime and Empire: The Colony in Nineteenth-Century Fictions of Crime*,
     Oxford, Oxford University Press, 2003, 138-41; Nancy L. Paxton, 'Mobilizing
     Chivalry: rape in British novels about the Indian Uprising of 1857', *Victorian Studies*,
     36, 1 (1992), 5-30; Nancy L. Paxton, *Writing under the Raj: Gender, Race, and Rape in the
     British Colonial Imagination, 1830–1947*, New Brunswick, Rutgers University Press,
     1999, 4-11, ch. 3; Laura Peters, '"Double-dyed Traitors and Infernal Villains":
     Illustrated London News, Household Words, Charles Dickens and the Indian Rebellion',
     in David Finkelstein and Douglas M. Peers (eds), *Negotiating India in the Nineteenth-
     Century Media*, Basingstoke, Macmillan, 2000, 110-34. On post-revolt literary
     representations of India see also Hyungji Park, '"The Story of Our Lives": *The
     Moonstone* and the Indian Mutiny in *All the Year Round*', in Finkelstein and Peers
     (eds), *Negotiating India*, 84-109. Important new work on gender and empire includes
     the collection of essays edited by Philippa Levine, *Gender and Empire (Oxford History of
     the British Empire Companion Series)*, Oxford, Oxford University Press, 2004.

37. C.A. Bayly, *Empire and Information: intelligence gathering and social communication in India,
     1780–1870*, Cambridge, Cambridge University Press, 1999, ch. 10; Susan Bayly,
     Caste, Society and Politics in India from the Eighteenth Century to the Modern Age, Cambridge,
     Cambridge University Press, 1999, ch. 3; Bernard S. Cohn, *Colonialism and Its Forms
     of Knowledge: The British in India*, Oxford, Oxford University Press, 1997; Dirks, *Castes
     of Mind*; Thomas R. Metcalf, *The Aftermath of Revolt: India, 1857–1870*, Princeton,
     University of Princeton Press, 1964; David Omissi, *The Sepoy and the Raj: The Indian
     Army, 1860–1940*, Basingstoke, Macmillan, 1994.

38. David Arnold, 'The Contested Prison: India 1790–1945', in Frank Dikotter and
     Ian Brown (eds), *Cultures of Confinement: a history of the prison in global perspective*,
     London, Hurst, 2007, 147-84. See also Sumit Guha, 'An Indian Penal Regime:
     Maharashtra in the Eighteenth Century', *Past and Present*, 147 (1995), 100-26;
     Singha, *A Despotism of Law*.

39. Clare Anderson, 'Sepoys, Servants and Settlers: convict transportation in the
     Indian Ocean, 1787–1945', in Dikotter and Brown (eds), *Cultures of Confinement*,
     185-220; Clare Anderson, *Convicts in the Indian Ocean: transportation from South Asia to
     Mauritius, 1815–53*, Basingstoke, Macmillan, 2000; Arnold, 'The Contested Prison';
     David Arnold, 'The Colonial Prison: Power, Knowledge, and Penology in 19th-
     Century India', in David Arnold and David Hardiman (eds), *Subaltern Studies VIII,
     Essays in Honour of Ranajit Guha*, New Delhi, Oxford University Press, 1994, 148-87;
     John Furnivall, 'The Fashioning of Leviathan', *Journal of the Burma Research Society*,
     29, 1 (1939), 36-43; Anoma Pieris, 'Hidden Hands and Divided Landscapes: Penal
     Labor and Colonial Citizenship in Singapore and the Straits Settlements, 1825–
     1873', PhD in Architecture, UC Berkeley, 2003; Anoma Pieris, 'On Dropping

Bricks and Other Disconcerting Subjects: unearthing convict histories in Singapore', *Fabrications*, 15, 2 (2005), 77-94; Rajesh Rai, 'Sepoys, convicts and the "bazaar" contingent: the emergence and exclusion of "Hindustani" pioneers at the Singapore frontier', *Journal of Southeast Asian Studies*, 35, 1 (2004), 1-20; Singha, *A Despotism of Law*; C.M. Turnbull, 'Convicts in the Straits Settlements, 1826–67', *Journal of the Malay Branch of the Royal Asiatic Society*, 43, 1 (1970), 87-103; Anand A. Yang, 'Indian convict workers in Southeast Asia in the late eighteenth and early nineteenth centuries', *Journal of World History*, 14, 2 (2003), 179-208. For a contemporary account of the convict system in Southeast Asia, see J.F.A. McNair, *Prisoners Their Own Warders: A Record of the Convict Prison at Singapore in the Straits Settlements established 1825, Discontinued 1873, together with a Cursory History of the Convict Establishments at Bencoolen, Penang and Malacca from the Year 1797*, Westminster, Archibald Constable and Co., 1899.

40. An important exception here is the collection of articles in *SS*. See also William Dalrymple, *The Last Mughal: the fall of a dynasty, Delhi, 1857*, London, Bloomsbury, 2006; Husain, 'Fazle Haq'; Sumit Guha, 'Surviving the maelstrom: the north Indian adventures of Vishnubhat Godse, 1857–1858', paper presented at British Association of South Asian Studies annual conference, Birkbeck College, University of London, Apr. 2006. On 1857 folk songs see William Crooke, 'Songs of the Mutiny', *The Indian Antiquary*, 40 (1911), 123-24, 165-69; Joshi, '1857 in Folk Songs', in Joshi (ed.), *Rebellion 1857*, 271-87. The *FSUP* volumes are also invaluable as a source of mutineer-rebel proclamations, correspondence, and statements. There is just one published account by an Indian sepoy from this period: James Lunt (ed.), *From Sepoy to Subadar being the life and adventures of Subedar Sita Ram, a Native Officer of the Bengal Army written and related by himself, translated and first published by Lieutenant-colonel Norgate, Bengal Staff Corps at Lahore, 1873*, London, Routledge and Kegan Paul, 1970. In 1959, a senior British officer in the Indian army reconstructed Sitaram's career and concluded that the account is authentic. See Patrick Cadell, 'The Autobiography of an Indian Soldier', *Journal of the Society for Army Historical Research*, 37 (1959), 3-11, 49-56. (I thank Doug Peers for this reference).

41. Clare Anderson, *Legible Bodies: race, criminality and colonialism in South Asia*, Oxford, Berg, 2004; Eleanor Conlin Cassella, '"Doing Trade": a Sexual Economy of 19th Century Australian Female Convict Prisons', *World Archaeology*, 32, 2 (2000), 209-21; Eleanor Conlin Casella, 'Landscapes of Punishment and Resistance: a Female Convict Settlement in Tasmania', in Barbara Bender and Margo Winer (eds), *Contested Landscapes; Landscapes of Movement and Exile*, Oxford, Berg, 2001, 143-59; Eleanor Conlin Casella, 'To Watch or Restrain: Female Convict Prisons in 19th Century Tasmania, Australia', *International Journal of Historical Archaeology*, 5, 1 (2001), 45-72; Pieris, 'On Dropping Bricks'; Anand A. Yang, 'The Lotah Emeutes of 1855: Caste, Religion and prisons in North India in the Early Nineteenth Century', in James H. Mills and Satadru Sen (eds), *Confronting the Body: the politics of physicality in colonial and post-colonial India*, London, Anthem, 2004, 102-17.

42. Lucy Frost and Hamish Maxwell-Stewart, 'Introduction', in Lucy Frost and Hamish Maxwell-Stewart (eds), *Chain Letters: narrating convict lives*, Melbourne, Melbourne University Press, 2001, 3.

43. On the erasure of subaltern names in colonial archives, see Durba Ghosh, 'Decoding the Nameless: gender, subjectivity, and historical methodologies in reading the archives of colonial India', in Kathleen Wilson (ed.), *A New Imperial History: Culture, Identity, and Modernity in Britain and the Empire, 1660–1840*, Cambridge, Cambridge University Press, 2004, 297-316.

44. James C. Scott, *Domination and the Arts of Resistance: hidden transcripts*, New Haven, Yale University Press, 1992.

45. Ian Duffield, '"Stated this Offence": high-density convict micro-narratives', in Frost and Maxwell-Stewart (eds), *Chain Letters*, 119-35. Megan Vaughan too has used records of criminal investigations and proceedings to explore ethnicity, gender, sexuality, and language in eighteenth-century Ile de France (Mauritius): *Creating the Creole Island: Slavery in Eighteenth-Century Mauritius*, Durham, Duke University Press, 2005.

46. On this point see also Rag, '1857', 117.

47. Indian accounts situating the Andamans firmly within the Indian freedom struggle include: S.N. Aggarwal, *The Heroes of Cellular Jail*, Patiala, Publication Bureau, Punjabi University, 1995; N. Iqbal Singh, *The Andaman Story*, New Delhi, Vikas, 1978; R.C. Majumdar, *Penal Settlement in Andamans*, New Delhi, Gazetteers Unit, Department of Culture, Ministry of Education and Social Welfare, 1975; L.P. Mathur, *Kala Pani: History of Andaman and Nicobar Islands with a study of India's Freedom Struggle*, New Delhi, Eastern Book Company, 1992. A more nuanced account that focuses on ordinary convicts during the nineteenth century is Satadru Sen, *Disciplining Punishment: Colonialism and Convict Society in the Andaman Islands*, New Delhi, Oxford University Press, 2000.

48. Contemporary writing in English includes: Barendra Kumar Ghose, *The Tale of My Exile*, Pondicherry, Arya Office, 1922; B. Parmanand, *The Story of My Life*, New Delhi, S. Chand and Co., 1982; Savarkar, *The Story*; Bejoy Kumar Sinha, *In Andamans, the Indian Bastille*, Kanpur, Profulla, C. Mitra, 1939. See also David Arnold, 'The Self and the Cell: Indian Prison Narratives as Life Histories', in David Arnold and Stuart Blackburn (eds), *Telling Lives in India: Biography, Autobiography, and Life History*, Bloomington, Indiana University Press, 2004, 29-53.

49. Satadru Sen, 'Contexts, Representation and the Colonized Convict: Maulana Thanesari in the Andaman Islands', *Crime, History and Societies*, 8, 2 (2004), 117-39.

50. Fazl-i-Haq was a contemporary of Ghalib, who sought news of his fate after his transportation to the Andamans. See *Ghalib, 1797–1869, Life and Letters*, translated and edited by Ralph Russell and Khurshidul Islam, New Delhi, Oxford University Press, 1994, 263-4.

51. OIOC L.PS.6.466 no. 59: Trial of *Rajah* Lonee Singh of Methowlee and Moulvee Fuzl Huk &c; OIOC P.206.62 (IJP 6 Jan. 1860): J.C. Haughton, Superintendent Port Blair, to W. Grey, Secretary to Government of India, 13 Nov. 1859.

52. Though his text was in *qasida* (poetic) form, the translation used here is presented as narrative text.

53. Haq, 'The Story', 23, n. 1; Mahdi Husain, *Bahadur Shah II and the war of 1857 in Delhi with its unforgettable scenes*, New Delhi, M.N. Publishers, 1987, 298, 372-92; Jamal Malik, 'Letters, prison sketches and autobiographical literature: The case of Fadl-e Haqq Khairabadi in the Andaman Penal Colony', *Indian Economic and Social History Review*, 43, 1 (2006), 77-100.

54. Malik, 'Letters, prison sketches and autobiographical literature', 77.

55. Abu Muhammad Sahar (ed.), *Intikhab-e qasa'id-e urdu*, Lucknow, Nasim Book Depot, 1975, 358.

56. Christopher Shackle, 'Munir Shikohabadi on his imprisonment', forthcoming in Shobna Nijhawan (ed.), *Writings in Hindu and Urdu on Indian Nationalism*, New Delhi, Permanent Black, 2007; other unpublished English translations in the possession of Christopher Shackle. On the forms of Urdu poetry, see Stefan Sperl and Christopher Shackle (eds), *Qasida poetry in Islamic Africa and Asia*, Leiden, Brill, 1996.

57. Riaz ud Din (ed.), *Intikhab-e kalam-e Munir Shikohabad*, Lucknow, Uttar Pradesh Urdu Academy, 1982, 88-90; Siraj ul Haq Qureshi, *Munshi Sayyid Ismail Husain Munir Shikohabadi aur unki sha'iri*, Karachi, Academic Publishers, 1989, 33-5; R.B. Sakasena, *A History of Urdu Literature*, Allahabad, Ram Narain Lal, 1927, 110-11.
58. Sen, 'Contexts', 118-9.
59. Malik, 'Letters, prison sketches and autobiographical literature', 89-91. Peter Zinoman has shown similarly that communist prison narratives from colonial Vietnam provide more insight into political culture than the colonial jail: *The Colonial Bastille: a history of imprisonment in Vietnam, 1862–1940*, Berkeley, University of California Press, 2001, 1, 9-12, 294, 301-2.
60. Chapman, *The Rani of Jhansi*. On female *jihadis*, see also Ray, 'Race, Religion and Realm', 139-40.
61. Guha, *Elementary Aspects*. 130-2.
62. Ujjwal Kumar Singh, *Political Prisoners in India*, New Delhi, Oxford University Press, 1998, ch. 6.
63. Arnold, 'The Self and the Cell', 39-46.

CHAPTER 2
THE PRISON IN COLONIAL NORTH INDIA

Introduction

Contemporary observers claimed frequently that religion was an important cause of the Indian mutiny-rebellion of 1857–8. They viewed missionary activities, inappropriate legislative interventions into religious affairs, and the alleged introduction of cartridges greased with animal fat into the Bengal army as significant reasons for revolt. A number of nineteenth-century writers and historians have taken up this perspective to argue that the uprising was at least partly a cultural arena in which north Indian communities responded to perceived colonial assaults on religious practices. As we have seen, other military, social, and economic concerns fuelled and sustained widespread unrest. However, this chapter will focus on a further dimension to the cultural background to revolt: the colonial jail in north India. Accounts detailing the run-up to the mutiny-rebellion sometimes mentioned local hostility to prisons, for jails were newly constituted colonial spaces in which Indian bodies were confined, controlled, and disciplined in unprecedented ways. Penal practices often transgressed Indian social norms, particularly with regard to religion and caste. In this reading, jails both embodied and symbolized broader social fears about colonial interference in religious affairs and forced conversion to Christianity.

In the pages that follow we will examine the penal practices that invoked these concerns, discussing north Indian responses to and negotiations with colonial innovations in imprisonment during the first half of the nineteenth century. Now it is historiographically well established that prisons were sites in which essential colonial social categories were reflected, institutionalized, and embedded.[1] The chapter will suggest further that during the unravelling and reconstitution of an array of apparently culturally complex practices, the British penal regime endowed prisoners with both a sense of shared grievance and a vehicle for the formation and consolidation of their own social and religious categories. This leaked out of the jail walls and fused with 'respectable' community concerns about broader changes in their social, economic, and cultural lives.

Confinement in colonial north India

After 1790 the East India Company began to use imprisonment as a punishment both extensively and systematically. It converted existing buildings including military forts and barracks into prisons, and purpose-built dozens of new institutions. It placed them under the control of district magistrates. The Company also established a series of penal settlements in Bengkulu, the Andaman Islands, the Straits Settlements, Burma, and Mauritius. Penal settlements were particularly significant with regard to the punishment of serious offenders who formed a relatively small proportion of mainland prisoners but an overwhelming majority of transportation convicts.[2] Imprisonment and transportation supplemented discretionary penal interventions like exile and mutilation common in pre-colonial India. Under the Company regime banishment to distant jails, flogging, penal tattooing, and capital punishment all persisted in and were even extended by the penal repertoire.[3]

By 1857 there were 40 jails in the North-West Provinces and 55 in the Bengal Presidency.[4] Though there were a few large jails, notably Alipur near Calcutta and Allahabad and Agra in the North-West Provinces, typically these prisons did not resemble the sort of closed institutions prevalent towards the end of the second half of the nineteenth century. Most jails were simple constructions of mud and thatch holding a few hundred prisoners; some had no secure walls or gates. On the eve of the mutiny-rebellion Bengal's Lohardaga jail was in the middle of the town bazaar.[5] A further factor in the spatial dynamics of incarceration was the location of prisons in towns and cities. Company officials expressed repeated anxiety about this during the first half of the nineteenth century. In 1855, the inspector of prisons in Bengal, F.J. Mouat, reported that the district of Behar's jail was in Gaya, an important site of religious *melas* (fairs). It accommodated, he wrote, 'a bigoted [sic], unruly and impracticable race' and occasionally it 'swarmed with pilgrims'. The government had already condemned the site; Mouat expressed his desire that the town should not have a jail at all.[6] Historically the jail had extraordinarily high escape rates, no doubt due to the sympathy of outsiders. All prisons, Mouat added, should be as isolated as possible.[7] The public works attached to another jail in Sylhet district at about the same time were close to a colony of prostitutes. This outraged Mouat, who wrote that it would hardly help to mend the morals of the prisoners.[8] When a jail was first built at Agra, the town was a relatively small civil station, but by the 1850s it was the principal city in the North-West Provinces. The jail almost doubled in size between 1849 and 1855, by which time it held the astonishingly high daily average of 3,589 prisoners. The inspector of prisons in the North-West Provinces, C.B. Thornhill, felt that this caused 'serious inconveniences' to the surrounding neighbourhoods. Though the government agreed in principle that the jail should be rebuilt outside the city it was constrained by the considerable cost involved.[9]

In addition to the urban location of most prisons, there was a constant movement of prisoners and other communities in and out of jails, for throughout the first half of the nineteenth century most prisoners worked and often slept outdoors on public road labour. Generally prisoners preferred the freedoms of outdoor work because it gave them the chance to see friends and relatives and to obtain forbidden articles. Reproducing a common colonial representation of the road gang, the *Calcutta Review* noted in 1846: 'We would ask any one who has seen a gang of convicts at work on the roads, whether he ever saw a happier set of labo[u]rers at work? One half of them are, probably, smoking, and the other half pretending to work; singing, laughing, joking, and only waiting their turn to exchange the Spade for the Húka (pipe)'.[10] Adding to the spatial fluidity afforded by outdoor labour was the transfer of prisoners between jails, the ingress and egress of contractors from whom some prisoners bought food and other consumables with their money allowances, the sentencing of most prisoners (especially habitual offenders) to short jail terms, and the recruitment of guards locally. The spread of information about and between jails was considerable, and prisoners were strongly aware of variable discipline in different jails. As Mouat recorded in 1856, he rarely heard a prisoner's appeal without reference to practices in other prisons.[11] Indeed, local knowledge about the preferential treatment of prisoners in jails elsewhere resulted in episodic unrest, for instance an 1855 attack on the *daroga* (Indian jailer) by inmates of Mithapur jail (Patna) unhappy about being kept at indoor labour.[12]

Despite local unwillingness to invest large amounts of money in prisons, from the 1820s when magistrates began to employ some prisoners indoors there was a gradual move towards building jails with brick or stone. Such constructions were architecturally alien to many Indian communities. As late as 1857 prisoners in Bhagalpur, many of whom were from *adivasi* communities, refused to go up a flight of stairs to the jail's second floor, preferring instead to sleep in a damp shed outside in the yard.[13] Indoor employment was partly the result of government injunctions against disgracing 'respectable' prisoners through public exposure within their communities, but it was also related to high death-rates among outdoor workers.[14] In 1836, provoked by the issue of how to punish prisoners of status, but perturbed by mortality figures associated with road labour, the government of Bengal began an investigation into prison work, appointing a Committee of Convict Labour. With regard to high death-rates, the committee was hampered by its inability to differentiate between prisoners who slept in or out of jail. Neither did it have comparative statistics for local free populations. Nevertheless, it concluded that prisoners employed outdoors suffered an excess rate of mortality of at least three per cent. Ideally, it recommended, prisoners should be put to work inside jails, but as there was no proper system of prison management they could continue to work outside. The committee also considered the relationship of road gangs to free labour, concluding that as prisoners would have been in competition with other workers if they had not been in jail, road gangs did not displace the labour of local populations. Third, it looked at the relationship between punishment and public disgrace, concluding that working prisoners on the roads had a 'very slight and inconsiderable' effect. Rather, lax supervision gave prisoners certain advantages, notably the opportunity to see their kin and to acquire food and tobacco.[15] By the time the committee presented its final report, death-rates among prisoners working on the roads had risen even more. The government therefore resolved that all prisoners would be kept at work in their districts rather than on distant public works. In the meantime, the report was forwarded to a group of Calcutta officials, the Prison Discipline Committee, by then considering the broader question of jail management.[16]

The government established the Prison Discipline Committee in 1836, two years after a group of prisoners murdered the district magistrate and superintendent of Alipur jail, Thomas Richardson. Alipur incarcerated the most hardened district prisoners from across the Bengal Presidency together with convicts awaiting transportation to overseas penal settlements, all of whom had been convicted of serious offences like aggravated robbery, dacoity (gang robbery with violence) or murder. On 5 April 1834, shortly after his morning ride, Richardson went into a jail work shed where just over two hundred prisoners were engaged in spinning and twisting twine. He started to speak to one of the prisoners, Dirkpal Sing, a prisoner of 'respectable' status whom the other prisoners addressed as *'rajah'*.[17] Almost instantly Dirkpal Sing attacked Richardson on the side of the head, transforming his *lota* (brass drinking vessel) into a lethal weapon through the attachment of a long string around its neck. A dozen or so prisoners joined him, some armed with *lota*s and others with clubs. Within three minutes

Richardson was dead. Some of the prisoners returned to their work stations; others left the shed to mingle with the uninvolved prisoners. Remarkably the European jailer Sergeant Hornby, also himself attacked by a second prisoner wielding a *lota*, and the Indian guards managed to restore order. Fourteen convicts were later arrested. They were brought to trial on a charge of murder, five men as principals and nine as accomplices. The *nizamat adalat* (supreme criminal court) sentenced three men including Dirkpal Sing to death, and nine others to life transportation.

The authorities hanged the capitally condemned men in front of the prison work shed in a carefully orchestrated disciplinary ritual watched by the prisoners. The officer by then in charge of the jail reported the 'entire absence of any disposition to disorder or tumult' during this penal display, adding that he expected the hangings to promote the regulation and discipline of the jail.[18] Tattooists gave the prisoners sentenced to transportation the penal mark of *godna* on the forehead, and the authorities shipped them to penal settlements in Burma.[19] We know relatively little about their fate, though three later escaped.[20] According to a later jail superintendent, H. Fergusson, a fourth prisoner involved in the attack, Sheik Meerash, led subsequently every disturbance in Alipur. He even pretended to be blind as a means of evading labour. Fergusson wrote in 1856: 'He never was blind until his work was increased, and he recovered wonderfully when it was again diminished. It is well known to all the convicts in the Jail.'[21]

The investigation into Richardson's death reported that canvas manufacture had been introduced into the jail six weeks before the attack. The associated tasks required 'more skill and attention' than the prisoners' previous employment (the manufacture of gunny bags) and at the same time officials expected a greater output. They punished prisoners who lacked the aptitude for the task, found it difficult to concentrate or displayed 'wilful neglect' through the imposition of overtime or a reduction in the money allowance for food. The new arrangements caused great discontent among prisoners, and it was clear that the attack was a premeditated attempt at a more general rising on the part of the 1,200 prisoners then in Alipur. Indeed, a life prisoner had informed personally both Richardson and Hornby of a conspiracy headed by Dirkpal Sing, though fatally for Richardson they did not act on his information. The report into Richardson's death concluded that the prisoners should have been better managed, the task should have been 'mitigated' to take account of prisoners' concerns, and the guards should have been more numerous and properly armed. At the time there were just 14 Indian guards and European jailer

Hornby in charge of the 396 prisoners in the work shed. They had no muskets and were armed only with *lathis* (bamboo sticks). The report advised that in future changes to working regimes should be accompanied by 'patient instruction and supervision', and only moderate punishments inflicted for prisoner non-compliance.[22]

With Alipur holding the most serious offenders from across the Bengal Presidency, most sentenced for life, the attack on Superintendent Richardson was part of a long history of prisoner resistance in the jail. Indeed, the assistant commissioner of the Tenasserim Provinces, T. de la Condamine, wrote later that the worst behaved convicts transported to the penal settlements in Burma were known by others as 'Allypore men'.[23] Just five years after Alipur was built Superintendent John Eliot wrote of his difficulties in controlling prisoners who were constantly trying to escape.[24] Riots had broken out after a prisoner had stabbed the *subadar* (captain) of the guard while he was at prayer. Prisoners had tried to kill Eliot himself on two occasions. Prisoners destined for transportation overseas insisted that they were exempt from labour and so refused to work.[25] A visiting official later wrote that during the jail riot European troops had fired on the prisoners in the yard from the top of the jail walls, killing and wounding many of them.[26] In 1815 Alipur prisoners became aware that their money allowance was lower than that of prisoners in other jails and so once again refused to work.[27] In 1816 Eliot reported his repeated detection of chisels, which prisoners used to try and force open the windows and main gate. The ventilation holes between wards allowed prisoners to communicate and to plan escape attempts.[28] Later that year over 200 convicts under sentence of transportation again refused to work.[29]

Such episodes continued unabated in the decades that followed. In 1833 the authorities constructed a dozen solitary cells in an attempt to find an effective means of punishing prisoners who seemed unaffected by reduced rations or flogging. The immediate spur was the death of a prisoner in a fight.[30] The European superintendent placed one *Brahmin* inmate, Hurree Pandee, frequently in such cells. He refused to work over a period of many years, despite being punished with heavy fetters, reduced rations, and flogging. Each time he was placed in solitary confinement he went on hunger strike, a seemingly common response to imprisonment during this period, and was apparently able to survive for 21 days without food. He claimed that he was unable to eat the food brought to his cell though it had been prepared by a man he called his brother, also a prisoner in the jail. Superintendent Eliot gave an indication of the prisoner's social standing when he wrote:

The moment he is released he dances and sings all day long and enriches himself by a system of oppression on other less clever convicts and teaches others to defy authority ... I see no hope of keeping the jail in order if I am obliged to give in to this obstinacy. He will not weave cloth or gunny bags or blankets. He will not spin twine nor thread, he will not rub blankets, he will not grind flour, he will not card wool. His uniform reply is that he will do anything he <u>can</u> do but the result is and has been all the years he has been in jail that he does nothing.

Seven prisoners joined Hurree Pandee's hunger strike, and the superintendent was convinced that they would rather die than work. Though he believed that he should be left to his fate, the secretary to government disagreed and ordered Eliot to force feed the man. He argued that Pandee should neither be made a martyr nor be allowed to say that his caste had been compromised. Therefore, the superintendent should use 'brahmins or persons of his own caste to force him to swallow'.[31]

It was in the aftermath of the death of Superintendent Richardson that the Bengal authorities set up a Prison Discipline Committee to report on conditions in jails and to make recommendations for improvements in management. At the time there were about 24,000 prisoners in Bengal and just over 18,000 in the North-West Provinces. A further 2,000 convicts from the Bengal Presidency and North-West Provinces were serving out sentences of transportation in the Straits Settlements and Burma.[32] Notwithstanding the passing through the jail gates of a larger number of prisoners sentenced for short terms only in any given year, the jail population was only a tiny proportion of a population estimated at 90 million.[33] The committee gathered information from prisons and penal settlements across India and its associated territories, publishing a major report in 1838. It made a series of recommendations, the main two being the replacement of road labour with 'dull wearisome and disgustful' intramural work such as the treadmill, and the enforcement of the separate (cellular) system. Additionally, it recommended that officers classify prisoners more systematically, substitute money allowances or food rations for common messing, deny prisoners all luxuries, use solitary confinement more as a form of secondary punishment, construct central jails for the incarceration of long-term prisoners, and appoint inspectors of prisons for each province. They should treat prisoners under trial with greater leniency, abolish heavy fetters, and ban prison visits. The committee also urged the adoption of rules for the better management of convicts in the penal settlements, after which government should consider the question of whether to transport overseas all prisoners sentenced to imprisonment for life.[34]

As Radhika Singha has suggested, the committee's recommendations in practice advocated 'experiments already in progress.'[35] However, due to financial constraints and worries about the impact of differences in climate and culture on prison reforms and despite the widespread circulation of the report, the government of Bengal made few decisive changes during the years that followed. It was keen to enforce some measures, notably the restriction on prison visits, the prohibition of luxuries, and the introduction of rations. However, it was less sure about the cessation of outdoor labour or the replacement of indoor work with non-productive tasks.[36] The government resolved that it would not build the proposed experimental central penitentiary near Calcutta, but that it would instead trial the separate system in the presidency's district jails. It cited as factors in its decision the increased death-rates that experience showed would result from the transfer of prisoners from across the presidency to Calcutta and the uncertain effect that the tropical climate would have on prisoners in cells.[37] Ambivalence about the committee's recommendations was also reflected in an only gradual shift towards working prisoners indoors. Almost twenty years later, about a quarter of Bengal labouring prisoners fit for work was still employed on the roads.[38] Treadmills and cranks were introduced briefly in Calcutta and Digha (near Patna), but they fell into disuse after the machinery kept breaking down.[39] By 1857 only a few prisons had means of enforcing non-productive penal labour for the secondary punishment of refractory prisoners. They were put to work on oil mills or in *surkhi* (brick) making or pounding.[40] In practice, as the *Calcutta Review* pointed out later on, the Prison Discipline Committee's report was left to languish in a government office 'enveloped in cobwebs and dust'.[41]

The first radical initiatives in north India's architecture of confinement were instigated seven years later, not in Bengal but in the North-West Provinces under the new inspector of prisons, W.H. Woodcock. In 1845, the government instructed him to introduce a stricter system of classification, management and discipline, to reduce expenditure, and to make prison labour profitable. The monies saved and earned would be used in the construction of new prisons and the alteration and repair of old ones. Subsequently, Woodcock was able to attempt some classification, notably total separation at night, though he was limited by the architecture of existing jail buildings. Where he was able to adapt buildings or build new cells, such as in Agra, Allahabad, Bareilly, Delhi, Benares, and Gorakhpur, he imposed a sort of mixed system. Woodcock constructed also places of solitary confinement in Bareilly, Allahabad, and Delhi.[42] Woodcock's successor C.B. Thornhill continued this programme of innovation with

single occupancy cells and radiating barracks, for instance in Bareilly and
Allahabad, which also had a central watchtower. He also extended
Woodock's earlier experiment in 'moral improvement' through instruction
in reading and writing.[43] Gradually, he took prisoners off outdoor labour
and put them to work at indoor manufactures. According to Thornhill,
prisoners regarded this as more severe punishment, making indoor labour
an important means of invoking public dread of confinement.[44] In 1854, the
government decided to set up six central jails for long-term prisoners, at
Agra, Allahabad, Bareilly, Benares, Meerut, and Jubbulpur. Lahore in the
Panjab also had a large central jail. At the time of the mutiny-rebellion Agra
held over 3,000 prisoners, and with its mixed design including some
radiating barracks was the largest jail in the world.[45] The Bombay inspector-
general of prisons, C.G. Wiehe, wrote in 1865 that radiating prisons were
the most desirable form of confinement, for they secured the 'economical
and efficient supervision' of prisoners and the free circulation of air.[46]

While experiments in jail construction on cellular principles characterized
penal innovations in the North-West Provinces, in direct opposition to the
thrust of the recommendations of the reports on convict labour and prison
discipline, Bengal jails became renowned not for their non-productive
labour but for their indoor manufactures.[47] Prisons in the North-West
Provinces did produce industrial goods, including carpets and even
lithographed and coloured papier-mâché globes,[48] but not to the extent of
those in Bengal. Innovations in indoor labour began under Inspector of
Prisons T.C. Loch, and gathered pace when F.J. Mouat took over the post
in 1855 and became inspector-general. At that time, Alipur, Patna, Hughli,
Munger, Jessore, Nadia, and Sylhet were best known for their industrial
goods, many of which were exhibited at the first exhibition of prison
manufactures, organized by Mouat and held in Calcutta in November 1856.
Most prisons in Bengal and a few in the North-West Provinces sent goods
for exhibition. Manufactures included: fine and coarse cloth; towelling;
carpets; rugs; blankets; saddlery; carpentry; iron work; bricks and tiles;
paper; shoes; and fabrics made from bamboo, rattan, and reed. With a view
to ascertaining the commercial value of these products Mouat asked the
chamber of commerce to report on the exhibition. It suggested the opening
of an office in Calcutta to manage the sale of jail manufactures.[49] Alipur jail
even had its own shop for the sale of prison-made goods, and a printing
press. For Mouat, prison industry was an important means of promoting
prisoner reformation and the self-sufficiency of the jails. Indeed, by 1862
Bengal recouped about one-seventh of the cost of maintaining prisoners
from prison labour. Alipur and Hughli jails were so productive that they

repaid the entire cost of prisoner maintenance.[50] Mouat believed that because of the potential productivity of jails, efforts in the North-West Provinces to teach prisoners basic literacy were a waste of time.[51] However, architecturally Bengal jails lagged far behind those of the North-West Provinces, particularly with respect to the separation of prisoners. There was no systematic use of solitary confinement, and there were no central or radiating jails.[52] Indeed, writing in 1856 Mouat claimed that Bengal's prison design encouraged escape, prevented classification, made penal servitude impossible, in short 'unite[d] every quality that is undesirable in a place of incarceration.'[53]

Though efforts were made in some jails in the North-West Provinces with regard to the classification and in some cases the separation of prisoners, during this period most prisoners were still held in large wards. It was not unusual for several hundred prisoners to sleep in one place. Although some wards were divided into smaller rooms, the barred doorways left open for the purpose of ventilation allowed prisoners to communicate with each other. When prisoners were unlocked in the morning, during meal times, and before the nightly lock-up, they congregated in the general yard. The magistrate of Bhagalpur, W.J. Tucker, declared in 1858 that at such times 'the greatest confusion prevails' and the noise was deafening. Prisoners and their overseers, he said, lost sight of each other and neither knew what the other was doing.[54]

The prisoner resistance that had precipitated the setting up of the Prison Discipline Committee was an important feature of the jail regime during the first half of the nineteenth century. In ameliorating the effect of colonial innovations or in subverting them altogether, prisoners challenged and shaped prison management in important ways. As in the spur to the murder of Superintendent Richardson, labour was a key focus of discontent. Prisoners sometimes tried to invalid themselves, using poisons like arsenic trioxide meant for the control of vermin to produce or to enlarge sores.[55] Prisoners protested against the introduction of hand-mills in Benares jail in 1842 by going on hunger strike and by attacking the jail *daroga* with their mills and *lotas*.[56] Prisoners in Agra and elsewhere broke the machinery associated with the introduction of flour milling into jail.[57] When in 1846 the superintendent of Alipur jail, R.H. Mytton, increased the prisoners' spinning and weaving task, many refused to work and went on hunger strike. Mytton called the district judge to the jail to hear the prisoners' complaints, but when he saw them as unfounded Mytton threatened the withdrawal of the usual *Holi* festival holiday. The weavers went back to work but the spinners did not. The government granted Mytton a guard of 100 men while he flogged the striking prisoners a dozen at a time, in a desperate attempt to restore order.[58]

Rationing, common messing, *lotas*

Though changes in the working regime were a source of unrest within prisons, innovations in rationing resulted in prisoner resistance that was to at least some degree supported by free communities and, in an ominous precursor to what lay ahead, by sepoys outside the jail walls. At the time of the Prison Discipline Committee, most prisoners were given cash averaging just under a penny per day to buy food from shopkeepers, who were permitted access to the jails. The committee was uncomfortable with the issue of money allowances to prisoners because it believed that this system allowed them to enjoy a standard of living unparalleled in equivalent communities outside the prison, and to acquire narcotics and other illicit substances. This contravened the principle of less eligibility crucial to the penal intent of incarceration. Moreover, it believed that cash allowances created an undesirable alignment between free and prison labour, for it allowed prisoners to save money or to support their families financially while in jail.[59] The cooking of food also broke up the monotony of prison life and according to the committee this pleasure was incompatible with good prison discipline. 'The cooking of his dinner is, we believe, one of the greatest enjoyments of every individual amongst the lower orders in India,' it reported. '[C]onsequently this long operation must be the chief alleviation of the tedium of a prisoner's life. The privation of this enjoyment appears to us one of the most legitimate means of enhancing the effect of imprisonment'.[60]

After the Prison Discipline Committee published its report in 1838, the Bengal government moved quickly to adopt its preferred system, rationing.[61] It issued a first resolution on the issue in April 1839. It ordered that as soon as contracts to supply prisoners expired, magistrates should issue prisoners with 'such rations as they may think fit and sufficient, consulting the inclinations and habits of the prisoners as far as may be discreet, humane and within the limits of a just economy'. It cautioned them against distributing luxuries, on the grounds that they were out of the reach of ordinary labourers and unnecessary for the maintenance of good health. Further, the government ordered that prisoners should be discouraged or even prevented from cooking their own rations and encouraged to form common messes. Cooks should be supplied from among the prisoners or from outside the jail 'as may seem practicable and proper'. Finally, prisoners would no longer be allowed to bring money into jail.[62] Despite the plea for local considerations to be taken into account, in effect the *per diem* rations scale amounted to two pounds of uncooked rice (some of which could be exchanged for condiments), a pound of wood for cooking, and a small quantity of tobacco.

Prisoners in a number of jails contested violently the introduction of the rations system. The superintendent of Alipur, J.H. Patton, wrote of the difficulties he faced when confronted with 'creatures of habit ... tenaciously attached to customs and usages.'[63] Some prisoners refused to accept rations because they did not include fish or *masala* (a blend of spices), and ate instead boiled roots and leaves. One prisoner died; the remainder told the jail's European doctor that they would rather suffer the same fate than accept insufficient supplies.[64] It was not long before the jail administration decided to grant prisoners money allowances once again and government exempted Alipur from the 1839 order altogether.[65] Patton wrote: 'I verily believe that many of them would die rather than submit to the innovation.'[66] Prisoner complaints were not simply grounded in concerns about the quantity of food, but in the dietary preferences of men from across north India. With money allowances, each could buy their preferred foodstuffs, notably for up-country prisoners from the areas north of Patna wheaten flour in lieu of rice.[67]

In 1840 the government ordered once more the introduction of the rations system in Alipur. Again Superintendent Patton urged a reconsideration of the issue, writing that the measure would lead to prisoner discontent and resistance. He claimed that he had run the jail using a system of incentives and punishments, transforming it into a 'model of order and regularity', and increasing prisoner productivity by one thousand per cent. He wrote: '[T]he alacrity with which they now perform their daily task is most remarkable and leads one almost to imagine, that they viewed it rather as a relief to break the monotony and tediousness of their life than an irksome duty they were compelled to discharge.' This was not an appropriate time to create 'unmitigated disaffection' in jails. He persuaded the government not to intervene, and money allowances persisted in Alipur for some years to come. The government asked Patton, however, to introduce rations gradually for new district prisoners.[68] Although most had received rations before their transfer to Alipur, the measure caused the predicted discontent. A new officiating superintendent wrote that because all Alipur prisoners worked indoors, cooking was a welcome form of employment because most finished their tasks by noon. With nothing else to do, prisoners engaged in 'gambling, quarrelling and other probable [sic] worse vices.'[69]

Despite prisoner resistance in Alipur, by 1840 the government had largely introduced the ration system elsewhere across Bengal. At this time it was agreed that due to the limitations of the original scale, vegetables, fish, and meat would be introduced into prison diets. After concerns that even this was inadequate, in 1843 the authorities adopted an increased scale that included also *ghee* (clarified butter), *dhal* (lentils), and flour instead of rice for up-country prisoners. This allowance gave prisoners enough food for two cooked meals per day and the opportunity to exchange rations for preferred items like milk and flour. In 1851, however, prison administrators decided that this diet was far too generous and reduced the ration scale to its prior level.[70] In effect, this put a stop to the procurement of other foodstuffs, and 'respectable' inmates were incensed by the change. A group of Hughli prisoners claiming 'noble birth' petitioned against it, arguing that they were unable to take a cooked evening meal or swap part of their rice allowance for flour. 'Particularly it is highly deplorable', they wrote, 'that the Magistrate together with his under officers should blot out all other human feelings to undertake artificially the death of these wretched persons … in annulling a custom, which has in some measure (without any injury to the Government) tolerated our condition.'[71]

The government of Bengal's 1839 resolution called also for the introduction of common messing. This innovation was far more controversial than the simple substitution of money allowances with rations because potentially it forced prisoners of all religions and castes to prepare food and eat together, so compromising ritual purity. The Bengal government had tried to implement common messing in jails over 40 years earlier, in 1796, but their attempts had failed. District magistrates found it difficult to procure high-caste Hindu *Brahmins* to cook for prisoners; they claimed that such employment would compromise caste.[72] In some jails, prisoners refused to eat the prepared food, telling the district magistrates that if they did so after release their communities would refuse to eat with or to marry them. In an indication of the nature and extent of shared cultural practices relating to the preparation and consumption of food, Hindus and Muslims were said to be equally resistant to the measure.[73] Prisoners even agreed to a reduced money allowance in preference to the continuance of the messing system.[74] The withdrawal of money allowances had a broader social impact too, for formerly prisoners had used their cash to support their families. In one jail, the measure caused such distress to prisoners' wives and mothers that the district magistrate employed them as cooks.[75] As the extent of the difficulties in enforcing common messing became clear, the governor-general suspended the order.[76]

As memories of this dismal failure faded, in 1841 the Bengal government drew attention to its earlier resolution on common messing, ordering that all labouring prisoners should eat in group messes. Non-labouring prisoners were exempt from the order. Ideally, government resolved, prison messes should be composed of 20 men with one cook, but they could be varied according to local needs. By this time administrators had already introduced common messes into some jails and in others prisoners themselves had formed messes. However, the continued employment of prisoners at outdoor labour, the architectural limitations of many prisons, the large number of castes (and what officials regarded as their seemingly endless permutations), and the antipathy of prisoners to the measure had precluded its widespread introduction. It was difficult to procure identical foodstuffs and to set up messes for prisoners sleeping out of jails. Moreover, it was not always possible to find suitable sites for cookhouses, and where they did exist often they were an inadequate fire hazard.

These difficulties were reinforced in areas such as Bihar where high-caste prisoners formed a relatively large proportion of the jail population. In 1841 the magistrate of Shahabad reported that a third of the prisoners in the district jail at Arrah were 'respectable' Rajputs or *Brahmins*. Prisoners protested that they were mainly in jail for affrays caused by disputes over land and that common messing would enhance their punishment unfairly. The magistrate agreed with them.[77] Other magistrates were more determined to enforce the measure, even in other places in Bihar like Chuprah in Saran district which imprisoned similar types of offenders. In response to the introduction of common messing in 1842, the prisoners in Chuprah drew up an extensive list of messes, but the magistrate rejected it and appointed 52 cooks for 630 working prisoners instead. The prisoners asserted that this would impact negatively on their character and family honour and the first of a series of jail riots broke out. One morning after the prisoners went outdoors to work all but ten of the cooks refused to prepare their meal. When the prisoners returned that evening they rose against their guards. Some of them were influential landholders and they were supported in their protest by relatives and friends. It was not long before over 3,000 townspeople had gathered outside the jail, throwing earth and shouting abuse at the magistrate, judge, and collector. The magistrate resolved to suspend the order, on the grounds that the prisoners' objections were 'sincere and genuine'. The government agreed that the rules on common messing were intended not as a punishment but as an improvement in discipline, and so prisoners should not be forced to adopt them.[78] As Anand A. Yang has argued, in ordering the enforcement of common messing colonial administrators had not engaged with the fact that the preparation and consumption of food were ritual and social acts through which caste status was manifested.[79]

Despite their earlier reservations, three years later the authorities in Bihar tried once more to implement common messing. Again, violence broke out in the district of Saran, as also in Shahabad and Behar (at Gaya jail). The Gaya jail riot was perhaps the most serious. After the magistrate attempted to enforce messing the prisoners barricaded themselves into the jail for five days. Eighteen prisoners were killed during the protest. The magistrate was only able to re-enter the jail when military reinforcements arrived. In 1845, however, the government was more determined to enforce messing and less accommodating to prison protests. The judicial authorities later tried sixteen of the riotous Shahabad (Arrah) prisoners, for instance, and sentenced them to transportation.[80] It became apparent that though not generally concerned with jail inmates, in many places townspeople and prison guards were sympathetic to 'respectable' prisoners sentenced for offences like affray.[81] Indeed, jail messing formed the background to the 1845–6 'Patna Conspiracy', an anti-British alliance with wide social support.[82] Six thousand townspeople showed up in support of the Chuprah jail (Saran district) riot, and when the measure was enforced in Arrah sympathetic supporters even set fire to the court-house, destroying the witness statements against the rebellious prisoners. In jails where fewer prisoners were of 'respectable' class, community support was less apparent. This was the case in Gaya, where most prisoners were either low caste or 'desperate characters'.[83] The prisons remained unstable into the spring of 1846 when it was rumoured that prisoners in Gaya, Chuprah, and Patna (Mithapur jail) would resist further attempts to enforce common messing and break open the jail gates. Again, the townspeople came out in support of 'respectable' prisoners who claimed that on their release they would be shunned by their communities.[84] Prisoners won a major concession when the government of Bengal decided that in addition to the exemption of prisoners awaiting trial or sentenced to simple imprisonment (without labour) from common messing, prisoners could exempt themselves by paying a fine.[85]

Fears about the potentially wider significance of jail messing can be viewed through the lens of the rumours that began to circulate around the towns during the riots. Whispers in the streets and bazaars propagated the belief that common messing was the beginning of new cultural arrangements in which hundreds of children would be kidnapped and sacrificed, circumcision would be abolished, and all people made to eat together and forced to become Christians. The Bhojpuri speaking areas of

Bihar were traditional recruiting grounds for the Bengal army and many prisoners were connected to sepoys by kin or community. By the 1840s there were important parallels between military and penal discipline with regard to the lodging, mustering, superintendence, and punishment of soldiers and prisoners. Sepoys apparently believed that it was a matter of time before they too were forced into mealtime messes and converted forcibly to Christianity.[86] A letter written by sepoys to the Shahabad prison rebels is strongly suggestive of military solidarity with high-caste prisoners. '[T]he day on which the English shall attempt to destroy our religion', they wrote, 'every Regiment will revolt.' The letter ended with a show of support from 'Brahmins' and 'Rajpoots'.[87]

The government of the North-West Provinces was cautious in introducing common messing, first seeking advice from its counterparts in Bengal.[88] By 1846 it had been able to implement the system in only half of its prisons. It was widely acknowledged that the measure was as unpopular outside the prisons as it was within it.[89] In September 1846, for instance, there was a riot over the issue in Allahabad jail. Four prisoners died and many more were seriously injured.[90] An 1848 description of common messing in the provinces is instructive. The system was compared to the serving of food at marriages or other large gatherings. Meals were prepared in the jail yard. Inner and outer circles were then traced on the ground. Prisoners sat down in their own individual eating places, which they plastered daily. Cooks brought the food along plastered paths running beside each circle. In this way, up to a thousand prisoners were able to eat together, as the inspector of prisons described it 'in silence and without confusion'.[91] Despite this apparent cultural sensitivity prisoner objections to common messing continued and by 1854 two jails in the North-West Provinces still had not enforced the measure.[92] Given their earlier experiences also the authorities in Bihar remained nervous about implementing it fully. By 1856 common messing had been introduced to only a limited extent. Gaya prisoners for instance continued in their daily trips to town, which gave them the opportunity to procure forbidden foodstuffs and other goods. This, Mouat reported with disgust, was 'preposterous'.[93]

In a vehement critique of colonial policy on messing in jails, in 1846 the *Calcutta Review* claimed that the Prison Discipline Committee did not realize how great opposition to the proposed system would be or it would have devoted more time to the issue. It was indicative of this neglect that the committee had not mentioned rations, cooking or messing in its circular calling for opinions on jail management. The *Review* noted that even the most educated Indians were at a total loss to understand the reasoning behind the measure. The *Review* lamented: '[A]re we to run the risk of corrupting the fidelity of our Native Army – are we to cause ourselves to be looked upon as a set of tyrants – as the poor man's persecutor?' 'The Messing system,' it went on, 'is a perpetual blister, an irritating ulcer, which time will not heal, nor years serve to assuage.'[94] These were to be strangely prophetic words.

There were further jail riots in Bihar in 1855 after the first inspector of jails in Bengal, Thomas Loch, in a bid to establish a 'uniform scale of personal necessities' ordered that a number of prisoners' possessions be removed. These included writing materials, excess clothing and bedding, hookahs, books (unless of 'moral character'), and musical instruments. He did not mention *lotas*, brass drinking vessels of the type prisoners used in the murder of the superintendent of Alipur jail twenty years before. However, Loch clearly desired their removal, for he prescribed the use of *katoras* (earthen vessels) only for drinking.[95] Not all prisoners had *lotas*. They tended to be brought into jail by high-caste Hindu and 'respectable' Muslim prisoners. Prisoners who were admitted without them were issued with the *katoras* preferred by Loch. Equally, in some prisons due to what one magistrate described as 'frequent thefts ... and quarrels' officers had already replaced *lotas* with earthen cups or *toomras* (dried gourd shells).[96] The explicit removal of *lotas* was nevertheless controversial because they were made of brass, a material which could be purified ritually and therefore reused. *Katoras* and *toomras*, on the other hand, became impure after use and so high-caste prisoners would use them once only. It was not at all clear that Loch's order allowed for their constant renewal. Moreover, officials removed the *lotas* (and other forbidden articles) with no prior warning while the prisoners were out at work.

Subsequent to the sudden enforcement of the removal order there were outbreaks in two district jails, Arrah and Tirhut (Muzzaffarpur jail). Just as they had supported prisoners during the messing riots of the 1840s, townspeople and jail guards came out in sympathy against the *lota* order. In Muzzaffarpur, thousands of opium *raiyats* (cultivators) in town for the weighing season arrived at the jail bearing *lathis* and pieces of wood. If the district magistrate is to be believed, unrest was fanned by 'rich natives' and 'mulahs' who feared forcible conversion to Christianity.[97] Officials in the town were worried about the security of the prison as well as the neighbouring opium stores (they suspended weighing temporarily), court-house, and treasury. Far from inducing concessions, the unrest made the government even more determined to implement the order. 'The government,' wrote the sessions judge Robert Forbes, 'will not concede to popular violence'.[98]

Rioting over the removal of prisoners' *lotas* became enmeshed in former unrest about common messing. The leader of the prisoners in Muzzaffarpur jail, Kalichurrun, sought reassurance from the magistrate that low-caste prisoners would be kept out of his cooking place. District Magistrate J.B. Drummond lamented that he could not understand the request as this was already the case, but it becomes comprehensible when it is seen in the context of the wider rumours about forced conversion by then circulating.[99] In Arrah, the outbreak was so serious that the magistrate and the surgeon were forced out of the jail when the prisoners pelted them with tiles, earth, and bricks. They asked several influential local landowners, including Kuer Sing who later became an important leader of the 1857 revolt in Bihar, to plead with the prisoners on their behalf. Muslim prisoners claimed that they had nothing to do with the riot, but a number of Hindus refused to eat or drink for some days. Apparently, like prisoners in Muzzaffarpur they shared a belief with the townspeople that they would all be made Christians. Rumours to this effect flew around the district. One army captain informed Magistrate Drummond that his *munshi* (clerk, translator) had even received a letter from his son in Bareilly claiming that the magistrate of that district had issued such an order.[100]

A number of prisoners in Arrah jail were still on hunger strike when the lieutenant-governor, F.J. Halliday, revoked Loch's order and ordered the return of the prisoners' *lotas*. Labouring under an attack of cholera it seems that Halliday had not been aware of what he described as an 'unjust, offensive, unpolitic and unnecessary' command. Grievances about the tightening of discipline were one thing, he wrote, but the violation of caste quite another.[101] Inspector of Prisons Loch was condemned for what Halliday saw as the capricious and unreasonable removal of effects 'closely and intimately connected with [prisoners'] religious notices and prejudices'.[102] Meanwhile, the Arrah prisoners received the news with what Drummond described as 'evident satisfaction'.[103] It was not long before the lieutenant-governor replaced Loch with F.J. Mouat, calling on him to revise the notorious *lota* circular. Mouat deplored its sudden introduction, writing with a perhaps misplaced optimism that had it been carefully explained to prisoners it could have been enforced peacefully.[104] Another official agreed, writing that because officials took the *lotas* without warning while prisoners were out at work, the prisoners felt tricked.[105]

Nevertheless, while some contemporary observers supported the government's later decision to respect the prisoners' cultural anxieties, others strongly disapproved of it. Scottish missionary Alexander Duff for instance wrote that as a result imprisonment had become 'a bed of luxurious repose':

That caste usages should be obsequiously yielded to in the case of otherwise well-behaved citizens, is bad enough; but that these should be so unworthily submitted to in the case of *felons or condemned criminals*, must surely be pronounced the very climax of sinful weakness! Verily, it is high time that caste should be *officially ignored in jail*, as well as everywhere else, - that the whole of the old system of caste regulation should everywhere cease ... Let it cease, and jail imprisonment will soon become, what it ought ever to be, an object of real terror, - fitted, not, as now, to encourage, but to scare away from the commission of crime ... Let it cease, and we at least shall no longer be guilty of fostering the fatal delusion that caste is character, - that a rigorous attention to its external observations alone constitutes respectability.[106]

The *Bengal Hurkaru* newspaper reported similarly the 'folly and wickedness' implied by the withdrawal of the *lota* order, and the '*pseudo*-philanthropy' that cared more for the religious prejudices of murderers and dacoits than the honest, industrious poor.[107]

Historians have presented unrest in jails over the issues of labour, rations, and messing as the expression of a confrontation between colonial power and prisoner resistance. Moreover, they have seen prisons as spaces in which the state could interrogate or understand Indian society, and have unparalleled access to prisoners' bodies for medical, ethnological or anthropometric purposes. Religion and caste were significant in these respects because they both informed the nature of colonial intervention and became weapons of prisoner subversion. Despite their claims about maintaining uniform discipline, research has shown unequivocally that the British authorities were forced by the demands of prisoners to take account of religion and caste.[108] Yet it seems that prisons had further significance with respect to cultural practices, for they gave inmates the opportunity to explore and extend their meaning. Therefore jails were not only spaces of discipline, punishment, and the complex and entangled threads of power and resistance. They were also places in which prisoners themselves generated and consolidated religious and caste distinctions and practices. As fears of forced conversion to Christianity surfaced from the 1840s on, this is of significance when considering the relationship between the prison and the 1857–8 revolt, as indeed the nature and meaning of the mutiny-rebellion itself. Not only was the prison a powerful symbol of unparalleled colonial intervention into Indian society, it also embodied and propagated new forms of religious and caste consciousness.

Before making legislative interventions, the colonial authorities commonly consulted *pandits* (learned Hindu *Brahmins*) and other supposedly respectable Hindus (notably *zemindars*) in attempting to make sense of what they viewed often as unintelligible social practices. In the aftermath of the *lota* jail riots, for instance, they requested and then reported evidence of religious sanctions on the purification of drinking vessels.[109] The interpretations of Indians of rank did not, however, always accord with the beliefs or practices of prisoners themselves. There is evidence of a strong sense of mobility by low-caste Hindu inmates, who in jail emulated the practices of their superiors in order to climb the social scale. Low-caste prisoners made impassioned claims against performing certain jail duties associated with inferior status, such as the removal of night soil, gunny weaving or laundry.[110] For jail officials like Mouat, this was evidence of their misunderstanding of caste, or at least of various Indian interpretations of its proper significance and performance. In 1856 he wrote that 'the most extravagant popular errors exist among the uneducated classes of Natives upon the subject of caste', claiming that most pleas for caste exemption from prison rules were 'untenable and erroneous.'[111] Indeed, Mouat asserted that he had a better understanding of 'the real nature of caste and its observances' than 'even highly educated and intelligent' Hindus.[112] These types of encounter might be interpreted not as an impartial correction of the mistaken claims of prisoners, but as part of a broader and more general struggle for higher social standing that was launched periodically by caste groups over time. The conceptual breach in the meaning of caste in jails was the result of its intense fluidity and the social mobility of communities who wished to imitate high-caste Hindus in their ritual practices.[113] Where but in jail could those of low caste or status have such good opportunities to observe and emulate the intimate cultural practices and rituals of their social betters?

Let us turn for a moment to the prisoners involved in the common messing and *lota* riots, for a close analysis of their caste backgrounds is instructive. Low-caste Ahir prisoners were central to riots over common messing in Digha penitentiary in 1845. The district magistrate sparked off unrest when he touched their food. Similarly, Dusadhs and other low-caste prisoners were an important element of the insurgency over the formation of jail messes in Gaya, which as we have seen explains the only limited support from the town.[114] The ambivalence surrounding caste perhaps explains why officials described Goalla prisoners, who were important leaders of the *lota* riots in Muzzaffarpur, both as 'low caste' and as 'respectable'.[115] Hindu *pandits* told colonial officials that Goallas like other lower castes had no grounds for refusing to drink from earthen vessels.[116] And yet the Goalla prisoners felt the removal of their *lotas* as a keen violation of their caste. Indeed, in their tenacious refusal to give up important material symbols of high caste, *lotas*, local officials described them as extremely influential in persuading other prisoners to resist government orders.[117] It is telling that Mouat described Goallas as 'that most troublesome of classes'.[118] In 1856 he reported that they were extremely vocal in their complaints. As well as demanding the issue of *lotas* they informed him that they would only eat food if they had cooked it themselves.[119]

As we have seen, Hindu and Muslim inmates and townspeople triggered off jail riots over common messing and the removal of prisoners' *lotas*. Their sense of shared grievance reveals seemingly widespread cultural sympathy between high-caste Hindus and 'respectable' Muslims in the preparation and consumption of food, and in the use of brass drinking vessels. Moreover, the threat that each intervention represented appears to have moved beyond community and caste to invoke more general anxieties and fears about forcible conversion to Christianity. In 1845, for instance, the magistrate of Saran decided to introduce common messing among the Muslim prisoners of Chuprah jail before extending the system to Hindus, in the belief that they could have no objections to it. He was sorely mistaken, for the Muslims all refused to comply.[120] However, the prison could also be a space in which Muslims could claim cultural separation from Hindus. In 1855, for example, some Muslim prisoners in Muzzaffarpur jail consciously distanced themselves from the *lota* riots. It is difficult to say to what extent this reveals a genuine lack of sympathy with high-caste Hindus or whether the move was a self-consciously communal attempt to procure remission of sentence. Indeed, the government halved the sentences of their leaders.[121]

During the first half of the nineteenth century it was common for the government to transfer rebellious prisoners to other district jails. This practice was evident in the aftermath of both the common messing and the *lota* riots. Eight prisoners concerned in the 1855 riots in Arrah were, for instance, transferred to half a dozen other jails, together with Muzzaffarpur rioters.[122] Officials saw the removal of disorderly inmates both as an important display of government strength and as a means to break the apparent unity between prisoners and townspeople.[123] While transfers perhaps realized successfully these goals, they had other unforeseen consequences, for they facilitated the development of new forms of consciousness in prison. Mouat noted in 1856 the extent of prisoners' knowledge about practices in other jails with some surprise: 'I scarcely enter a jail in which an appeal, or an argument, by a prisoner is not clinched by a reference to the practice of other jails, in which some of them have been.' One of the Muzzaffarpur rioters later told Mouat that prisoners were government servants working for the *'sircar'* (state), and therefore they were entitled to petition for better conditions.[124] According to Mouat, the prisoner described eloquently the disciplinary regime in other jails.[125] He further noted that after the Muzzaffarpur rioters were sent to Motihari jail, where *lotas* had been disallowed some years before Loch's infamous order, many prisoners petitioned earnestly for them.[126]

The fluidity of caste in prisons was also reflected in its shifting relationship to social practices outside the jail walls. Despite the fears expressed by some prisoners, they were not outcaste on release. As the inspector of prisons in the Panjab, H.M. Cannon, put it in 1856, what was viewed as a caste violation outside of jail was not so considered within.[127] This was because society saw prisoners as the victims of circumstances beyond their control. While in jail prisoners accepted the potential violations posed by the use of *katoras*, just as they did those caused by sleeping in communal wards, eating in messes or working at trades like weaving. After release, *Brahmins* paid priests to purify them, participating in ceremonies and ablutions that wiped out all ritual traces of pollution suffered in prison.[128]

Conclusion

During the first half of the nineteenth century, north Indian jails were spaces of colonial intervention into cultural practices relating to religion and caste, and of prisoner resistance against socially and often ritually intrusive measures. As colonial administrators tried to instil discipline on issues such as what, how, and with whom prisoners should prepare their meals and eat, how they should work, and what they should wear, jail controversies erupted and circulated around prisoners' bodies. Significantly, in some places the concerns of 'respectable' communities outside the jail, including sepoys, became fused with those of 'respectable' prisoners within. Jails were also socially fluid spaces in which prisoners were able to rethink and reconstitute religious or caste status.[129] As we will see in the following chapter on jail-breaking during the revolt of 1857–8, unrest in jails during the first half of the nineteenth century spilled over into the social unrest of the mutiny-rebellion. Prisons once again became sites of revolt, but this time on a much wider and more significant scale. This illuminates further north Indian attitudes to colonial cultures of confinement, and in replicating both solidarity and division between communities it also reveals the potentially socially fragile basis of revolt.

Notes

1. Arnold, 'The Colonial Prison', 170. See also Anderson, *Legible Bodies*; Arnold, 'The Contested Prison'; Anand A. Yang, 'Disciplining "Natives"': prisons and prisoners in early nineteenth century India', *South Asia*, 10, 2 (1987), 29-45; Yang, 'The Lotah Emeutes'.

2. For instance there were 1,246 life prisoners (six per cent of the total) in Bengal jails on 30 April 1856 and 1,286 Bengal convicts in the Straits Settlements at about the same time: F.J. Mouat, *Report on the Jails of the Lower Provinces of the Bengal Presidency for 1855–6*, Calcutta, John Gray, 1856 (henceforth Mouat's report, 1855–6); OIOC P.145.27 (BJC 8 May 1856): Extracts Returns of Convicts Straits Settlements, n.d.

3. This point is underlined by Arnold, 'The Colonial Prison' and Singha, *A Despotism of Law*. On penal tattooing, see Anderson, *Legible Bodies*, ch. 3.

4. The North-West Provinces had separated from Bengal in 1835.

5. OIOC P.145.73 (BJC 17 Sept. 1857): Inspector-General of Prisons F.J. Mouat's Memorandum on Lohardaga Jail, 22 Feb. 1857.

6. Mouat's report, 1855–6, 8, 69. On *melas* in nineteenth-century India, see Anand A. Yang, *Bazaar India: Markets, Society, and the Colonial State in Bihar*, Berkeley, University of California Press, 1998, ch. 3.

7. Mouat's report, 1855–6, 17, 167.

8. OIOC P.145.52 (BJC 4 Dec. 1856): Mouat's Memorandum on Sylhet Jail, 28 Oct. 1856.

9. OIOC P.234.35 (NWPJC 1-15 Mar. 1858): C.B. Thornhill, Inspector-General of Prisons North-West Provinces, to Right Reverend J. Persico, Roman Catholic Bishop of Agra, 18 Aug. 1856.

10. Anon., 'Prison Discipline in India', *Calcutta Review*, 12, 6 (1846), 471.

11. OIOC P.145.33 (BJC 21 Feb. 1856): Mouat's Memorandum on Champaran Jail, 29 Jan. 1856.

12. OIOC P.145.21 (BJC 1 Nov. 1855): G.D. Wilkins, Officiating Sessions Judge Patna, to W. Grey, Secretary to Government Bengal, 15 Oct. 1855.

13. OIOC P.145.66 (BJC 9 July 1857): S. Lushington, Officiating Magistrate Bhagalpur, to Mouat, 13 Mar. 1857.

14. Singha, *A Despotism of Law*, 253-65.

15. OIOC P.141.9 (BJC 14 March 1837): Second and Concluding Report of the Committee of Convict Labour, 28 January 1837, enc. 'Regulations under which the system of employing convict labour in large masses may be upheld in efficiency, and at the same time with a due regard for the health and lives of the convicts so employed' (henceforth Second Report CCL).

16. *Ibid.:* Resolution of Government, 14 Mar. 1837.

17. OIOC P.141.9 (BJC 14 Mar. 1837): J.H. Patton, Superintendent Alipur Jail, to R.D. Mangles, Secretary to Government Bengal, 28 Feb. 1837. *Rajah* = king; noble.

18. OIOC P.140.48 (BJC 7 Apr. 1834): E.R. Barwell, Commissioner Alipur, to C. Macsween, Secretary to Government Bengal, 5 Apr. 1834; OIOC P.140.50 (BJC 9 June 1834): Barwell (then Officiating Session Judge 24 Parganas) to J.F.M. Reid, Register *Nizamat Adalat*, 9 May 1834, enc. Court of Officiating Session Judge, Zillah 24 Parganas, Special Calendar April 1834, Extract Proceedings Court of *Nizamat Adalat*, 30 May 1834; Barwell to Macsween, 6 June 1834 (quote). See also *Bengal Hurkaru*, 7 Apr. 1834; *Bombay Gazette*, 23 Apr. 1834.

19. Bengal convict transportation lists for 1834 do not survive, but convicts were only transported to Burma during that year. The (surviving) Alipur murder convicts in all probability travelled on the ship *Eamont* to Amherst Town (OIOC P.140.62 [BJC 3 Dec. 1834], nos 84-5).

20. OIOC P.142.38 (BJC 17 Oct. 1845): Return of Bengal convicts who have escaped from the Moulmein Jail from 1836 to this date, 28 Aug. 1845; OIOC P.142.45 (BJC 11 Mar. 1846): H.M. Durand, Commissioner Tenasserim Provinces, to F.J. Halliday, Secretary to Government Bengal, 20 Feb. 1846; OIOC P.146.20 (BJC 4 Aug. 1859): Return of Bengal convicts deceased, escaped and released from 1 May 1858 to 30 April 1859.

21. OIOC P.145.32 (BJC 14 Feb. 1856). H. Fergusson, Superintendent Alipur jail, to A.W. Russell, Under Secretary to Government Bengal, 2 Feb. 1856.

22. OIOC P.140.52 (BJC 21 July 1834): Barwell to Macsween, 5 July 1834; OIOC P.140.52 (BJC 11 Aug. 1834): Barwell to Macsween, 4 Aug. 1834.

23. *Report of the Committee on Prison Discipline, 8 Jan. 1838*, Calcutta, Baptist Mission Press, 1838, Appendix IV.

24. OIOC P.131.59 (BJC 18 Apr. 1815): J. Eliot, Magistrate and Superintendent Alipur Jail, to W.B. Bayley, Secretary to Government Bengal, 17 Apr. 1815.

25. OIOC P.132.13 (BJC 7 Nov. 1815): Eliot to M.H. Turnbull, Secretary to Government Bengal, 18 Sept. 1815.

26. NAM RA137: F. Rossi, Head of Convict Department Mauritius, to G.A. Barry, Secretary to Government Mauritius, 5 June 1820.

27. OIOC P.132.13 (BJC 7 Nov. 1815): Eliot to Turnbull, 16 Oct. 1815.

28. OIOC P.132.28 (BJC 28 June 1816): Eliot to Bayley, 25 June 1816.

29. OIOC P.132.13 (BJC 7 Nov. 1815): Eliot to Turnbull, 18 Sept. 1815.

30. OIOC P 140.31 (BJC 6 Apr. 1833): R. Barlow, Superintendent Alipur Jail, to Macsween, 4 Apr. 1833.

31. OIOC P.143.47 (BJC 8 May 1850): Eliot to J.P. Grant, Secretary to Government Bengal, 24 Apr. 1850; Grant to Eliot, 29 Apr. 1850.

32. It is difficult to calculate the number of Bengal Presidency convicts then in the penal settlements, for during 1836–8 returns were only printed for Penang, where there were 602 Bengal convicts in 1836: OIOC P.140.82 (BJC 19 July 1836): Extract Return Bengal Convicts Penang, 1 June 1836. There were 100 Bengal convicts in Malacca in 1835 (OIOC P.140.69 [BJC 7 July 1835], no. 33). In 1839, there were 190 Bengal convicts in Singapore (OIOC P.141.44 (BJC 7 Apr. 1840): J. Church, Resident Councillor Singapore, to Halliday, 18 Feb. 1840). There were 1200 convicts from the Bengal and Madras presidencies in the Tenasserim Provinces during the same year (OIOC P.140.81 [BJC 5 July 1836]: E.A. Blundell, Commissioner Tenasserim and Martaban Provinces, to Mangles, 6 May 1836. In 1837 the penal settlement in Mauritius also held 730 convicts from Bengal and Bombay. As a crown colony it was not investigated by the committee. Anderson, *Convicts in the Indian Ocean*, Appendix C4.

33. *Report of the Committee on Prison Discipline*, 9.

34. *Report of the Committee on Prison Discipline (quote para. 268). See also Yang, 'Disciplining "Natives"*.

35. Singha, *A Despotism of Law*, 256.

36. OIOC P.141.39 (BJC 5 Sept. 1839): Grant to Halliday, 1 Apr. 1838.

37. OIOC P.141.44 (BJC 14 Apr. 1840): Legislative Department, 6 Feb. 1840.

38. Mouat's report, 1855–6, 13.

39. OIOC F98/31 (Temple Papers): F.J. Mouat, *The Prison System of India*, London, National Association for the Promotion of Social Science, 1872, 13.

40. OIOC P.145.33 (BJC 21 Feb. 1856): Mouat's Memorandum on Patna (Mithapur) Jail, 18 Jan. 1856; OIOC P.145.66 (27 July 1857): Mouat's Memorandum on Bhagalpur Jail, 27 Jan. 1857.

41. 'Prison Discipline in India', 469.

42. *Report of the Inspector of Prisons on the Management of the Jails, from 1845 to 1851, and on the present state of prison discipline in the North West Provinces*, Agra, Secundra Orphan Press, 1852, 3-10 (henceforth *NWP prison report 1845–51*).

43. *Report of the Inspector General of Prisons, North Western Provinces, for the year 1852*, Agra, Secundra Orphan Press, 1853, 7.

44. *Report of the Inspector General of Prisons, North Western Provinces, for the year 1853*, Agra, Secundra Orphan Press, 1854, 10 (henceforth *NWP prison report 1853*).

45. OIOC P.206.62 (IJP 13 July 1860): Memorandum of J.P. Walker, Superintendent Port Blair (formerly Superintendent Agra Jail), 3 July 1860.

46. C.G. Wiehe, *Journal of a Tour of Inspection of the Principal Jails in India made by the Inspector General of Prisons, Bombay Presidency, in December 1862 and January and February 1863*, Byculla, Education Society Press, 1865, 63-4 (quote 64).

47. *Ibid.*, 63.

48. *Report of the Inspector General of Prisons, North Western Provinces, for the year 1854*, Roorkee, Thomason C.E. College Press, 1855 (henceforth *NWP prison report 1854*), 8-9.

49. OIOC P.145.61 (BJC 30 Apr. 1857): Mouat to C.J. Buckland, Junior Secretary to Government Bengal, 21 Mar. 1857.

50. F.J. Mouat, 'On Prison Statistics and Discipline in Lower Bengal', *Journal of the Statistical Society of London*, 25, 2 (1862), 210-11.

51. F.J. Mouat, *Report on the Jails of the Lower Provinces of the Bengal Presidency for 1856–7*, Calcutta, John Gray Calcutta Gazette Office/P.M. Cranenburgh, Military Orphan Press, 1857 (henceforth Mouat's report, 1856–7), 25.

52. Mouat's report, 1856–7, 7, 23-5 (quote 7).

53. Mouat's report, 1855–6, 19.

54. OIOC P.146.12G (BJC 18 Feb. 1858): Statement of cases tried under Act XVI of 1857 in the district of Bhagulpur during the month of January 1858 (1, 2, 7, 8 Jan. 1858).

55. OIOC P.141.24 (BJC 5 June 1838): S. Davies, Civil Surgeon Patna, to F. Skipworth, Magistrate Patna, 22 Jan 1838.

56. Singha, *A Despotism of Law*, 265.

57. Arnold, 'The Contested Prison'.

58. OIOC P.142.45 (BJC 25 Mar. 1846): R.H. Mytton, Superintendent Alipur Jail, to Halliday, 21 Mar. 1846.

59. *Report of the Committee on Prison Discipline*, 30-1. See also Mouat, 'On Prison Statistics', 186.

60. *Report of the Committee on Prison Discipline*, 34.

61. OIOC P.141.39 (BJC 5 Sept. 1839): Grant to Halliday, 1 Apr. 1838.

62. OIOC P.141.37 (BJC 11 July 1839): Halliday to H. Hawkins, Register *Nizamat Adalat*, 11 July 1839.

63. OIOC P.141.23 (BJC 3 Apr. 1838): Patton to Halliday, 30 Mar. 1838.

64. *Ibid.*: F.P. Strong, Surgeon 24 Parganas, to Patton, 29 Mar. 1838; A. Dyson, Alipur Jail Hospital, to Patton, 1 Apr. 1838.

65. OIOC P.141.37 (BJC 15 June 1839): Strong to Patton, 17 Feb. 1839; Halliday to Hawkins, 28 May 1839.
66. OIOC P.141.39 (BJC 3 Oct. 1839): Patton to Halliday, 23 Sept. 1839.
67. OIOC P.141.44 (BJC 31 Mar. 1840): Strong to Hawkins, 15 Oct. 1839.
68. OIOC P.141.45 (BJC 28 Apr. 1840): Halliday to Patton, 6 Feb. 1840; Patton to Halliday, 6 Apr. 1840 (quotes); Halliday to Patton, 28 Apr. 1840.
69. OIOC P.141.55 (BJC 22 June 1841): G.H. Battye, Officiating Superintendent Alipur Jail, to the Court of *Nizamat Adalat*, 31 Oct. 1840.
70. Mouat, 'On Prison Statistics', 187-8.
71. OIOC P.144.6 (BJC 20 Aug. 1851): Petition of Hughli prisoners, n.d. (Aug. 1851). 'Bread' presumably means '*chapatti*' here.
72. OIOC P.128.27 (BJC 29 Apr. 1796): Extract Circular Letter *Nizamat Adalat*, 23 Apr. 1796; J. Fendall, Magistrate Midnapur, to H. Tucker, Sub-Secretary to Government, 20 May 1796; F. Parr, Magistrate Jessore, to Tucker, 19 May 1796; R. Rocke, Magistrate Nadia, to Tucker, 21 May 1796; H. Lodge, Magistrate Sylhet, to Tucker, 26 May 1796.
73. *Ibid.*: W. Hunter, Magistrate Ramghur, to Tucker, 26 May 1796; A. Seton, Magistrate Behar, to Tucker, 16 June 1796.
74. *Ibid.*: Seton to Tucker, 18 June 1796.
75. *Ibid.*: Magistrate Dhaka to Tucker, 7 June 1796.
76. *Ibid.*: Resolution of Government, 18 June 1796.
77. OIOC P.141.54 (BJC 27 May 1841): Halliday to Hawkins, 7 July 1840; A.R. Young, Deputy Secretary to Government Bengal, to Hawkins, 27 Apr. 1841.
78. *Friend of India*, 4 Aug. 1842; 'Prison Discipline in India', 492-4; Yang, 'Disciplining "Natives"', 33.
79. Yang, 'Disciplining "Natives"', 31.
80. *Bengal Hurkaru*, 30 Jan. 1846.
81. J.E.S. Leslie, Officiating Magistrate Shahabad, to J.C. Scott, Sessions Judge Patna, 24 Mar. 1846, cited in K.K. Datta, *Selections from Unpublished Correspondence of the Judge-Magistrate and the Judge of Patna, 1790–1857*, Patna, Superintendent Government Printing Bihar, 1954 ('jails').
82. Sinha, *Veer Kuer Singh*, 25-9.
83. Yang, 'Disciplining "Natives"', 40.
84. Extract letter Superintendent Police Lower Provinces, to Halliday, 16 Mar. 1846, cited in Datta, *Selections* ('jails').
85. Young to Scott, cited in Datta, *Selections* ('jails').
86. Extract letter Superintendent Police Lower Provinces to Halliday, 16 Mar. 1846, cited in Datta, *Selections* ('jails').
87. Cited in Yang, 'Disciplining "Natives"', 37-8 (quote 38). See also Sinha, *Veer Kuer Singh*, 26.
88. OIOC P.141.52 (BJC 26 Jan. 1841): Resolution of Government, 11 Sept. 1840.
89. Arnold, 'The Contested Prison'.
90. Arnold, 'The Colonial Prison', 151-2.
91. *NWP prison report 1845–51*, Appendix H (2).
92. *NWP prison report 1854*, 10.
93. OIOC P.145.33 (BJC 21 Feb. 1856): Mouat's Memorandum on Behar Jail, 12 Jan. 1856.
94. 'Prison Discipline in India', 494, 496.
95. OIOC P.145.12 (BJC 7 June 1855): Inspector of Prisons T. Loch's Circular, 26 Apr. 1855; Loch to Grey, 22 May 1855 (quote). *Lotas* were banned from Alipur in 1834:

OIOC P.145.2 (BJC 21 Dec. 1854): Fergusson to Grey, 18 Sept. 1854. Printed proceedings on the *lota* riots can be found in OIOC P.188.45 (IJP 5 June 1857). See also Yang, 'The Lotah Emeutes'.

96. OIOC P.145.12 (BJC 7 June 1855): H.C. Raikes, Joint Magistrate Champaran, to W. Tayler, Commissioner Patna, 18 Apr. 1856.

97. *Ibid.*: A.E. Russell, Magistrate Tirhut, to R. Forbes, Sessions Judge Tirhut, 10 May 1855.

98. *Ibid.*: Forbes to Grey, 11 May 1855.

99. *Ibid.*: J.B. Drummond, Magistrate Shahabad, to Grey, 16 May 1855.

100. *Ibid.*: Drummond to Grey, 13, 15, 16, 17, 18, 21 May 1855; Dr Harrison's statement of the occurrences connected with the disturbance in the Arrah jail on the 12th, 13th and 14th May 1855, 14 May 1855.

101. *Ibid.*: Minute of F.J. Halliday, Lieutenant-Governor of Bengal, 18 May 1855.

102. *Ibid.*: Grey to Loch, 19 May 1855.

103. *Ibid.*: Drummond to Grey, 21 May 1855.

104. OIOC P.145.59 (BJC 12 Feb. 1857): Mouat to Buckland, 12 May 1856.

105. *Ibid.*: Tayler to Young, 14 May 1856.

106. Alexander Duff, *The Indian Rebellion: Its Causes and Results*, London, James Nisbet and Co., 1858, 355-6. See also Arnold, 'The Colonial Prison', 172-3.

107. *Bengal Hurkaru*, 26 July 1842. The *Friend of India* was in contrast largely supportive of the government's retraction (4 Aug. 1842).

108. Arnold, 'The Colonial Prison'; Yang, 'The Lotah Emeutes'; Yang, 'Disciplining "Natives"'.

109. OIOC P.145.59 (BJC 12 Feb. 1857): R.J. Wigram, Officiating Magistrate Suri, to Young, 19 Apr. 1856; G. Bright, Magistrate Midnapur, to Young, 8 May 1856; W.F. MacDonnell, Magistrate Saran, to Tayler, 9 May 1856; C. Jenkins, Officiating Magistrate Dhaka, to C.J. Davidson, Commissioner Dhaka, 14 May 1856; J.H. Young, Commisioner Burdwan, to Young, 15 May 1856.

110. OIOC P.145.49 (BJC 9 Oct. 1856): Mouat's Memorandum on Mymensingh Jail, 14 Aug. 1856; OIOC P.145.33 (BJC 21 Feb. 1856): Mouat's Memorandum on Champaran Jail, 29 Jan. 1856.

111. OIOC P.145.59 (BJC 12 Feb. 1857): Mouat to Buckland, 12 May 1856.

112. OIOC P.145.22 (BJC 26 June 1856): Mouat to Buckland, 13 June 1856.

113. OIOC P.145.59 (BJC 12 Feb. 1857): A. Grote, Officiating Magistrate Nadia, to Buckland, enc. opinion of Baboo Rajindralal Mitter (on purification of vessels), 23 May 1856.

114. Yang, 'Disciplining "Natives"', 35-7.

115. OIOC P.145.12 (BJC 7 June 1855): Grote to Grey, 23 May 1856.

116. OIOC P.145.59 (BJC 12 Feb. 1857): U. Brodhurst, Officiating Magistrate Gaya, to Tayler, 2 May 1856.

117. OIOC P.145.13 (BJC 7 June 1856): Drummond to Grey, 15, 16, 21 May 1855; Russell to Grey, 26 May 1855.

118. *Ibid.*: Mouat's Memorandum on Champaran Jail, 29 Jan. 1856.

119. OIOC P.145.22 (BJC 26 June 1856): Mouat to Buckland, 13 June 1856.

120. Yang, 'Disciplining "Natives"', 36.

121. OIOC P.145.25 (BJC 13 Dec. 1855): Forbes to Grey, 28 Nov. 1855, enc. Russell to Forbes, 14 Nov. 1855.

122. *Ibid.*: Russell to Principal Assistant to Commissioner Chota Nagpur, Magistrate of Munger, Magistrate Champaran, 29 Nov. 1855; OIOC P.145.33 (BJC 21 Feb. 1856): Mouat's Memorandum on Champaran Jail, 29 Jan. 1856.

123. OIOC P.145.12 (BJC 7 June 1855): Forbes to Grey, 11 May 1855.
124. It is worth noting that in the early nineteenth-century penal settlements of colonial Australia, transported British convicts also called themselves 'government servants' or 'government men', finding the appellation 'convict' offensive.
125. OIOC P.145.33 (BJC 21 Feb. 1856): Mouat's Memorandum on Purnia Jail, 12 Feb. 1856.
126. *Ibid.*: Mouat's Memorandum on Champaran Jail, 29 Jan. 1856.
127. OIOC P.188.45 (IJC 5 June 1857): H.M. Cannon, Inspector of Prisons Panjab, to R. Montgomery, Judicial Commissioner Panjab, 29 Apr. 1856.
128. OIOC P.145.59 (BJC 12 Feb. 1857): E.A. Samuells, Commissioner Cuttack, to Young, 23 Apr. 1856; OIOC P.145.22 (BJC 26 June 1856): Mouat to Buckland, 13 June 1856.
129. There are fascinating parallels here with the practices of other socially fractured and dislocated marginalized Indian communities like transportation convicts or indentured labour migrants. See Anderson, *Convicts in the Indian Ocean*; Marina Carter, *Servants, Sirdars and Settlers: Indians in Mauritius, 1834–1874*, Oxford, Oxford University Press, 1995.

CHAPTER 3
DANCING BY THE LURID LIGHT
OF FLAMES

Introduction

In February 1858 the superintendent of Meerut jail, H.M. Cannon, submitted the usual annual report to the government of the North-West Provinces. There was, however, nothing ordinary about his account. As Superintendent Cannon explained, he was not able to provide a formal report because rebels had either burnt or destroyed all the jail records during the previous year's disturbances. Instead, he presented a narrative of what had happened when mutiny broke out in the town. At the beginning of May, 85 *sowars* of the third regiment of light cavalry were sentenced to imprisonment by a general court martial, 80 for ten years and five for five years. The prisoners arrived at the old jail, which was situated about two miles from the cantonment, on the morning of 9 May.[1] What Cannon did not mention was that these men had been tried over the previous three days for having refused to take the cartridges issued to them for use on parade when ordered to do so by their superior officer, Brevet-Colonel G.M.C. Smyth. These were of course the fated greased cartridges that allegedly were smeared in animal fat and coated with gelatine paper.[2]

J.W. Kaye, who recorded an account of the events at Meerut that day in his classic account *History of the Sepoy War in India*, described what happened next. Guards brought the prisoners before their regiment. They stripped them of their uniforms and accoutrements. Armourers and blacksmiths then came forward with their tools and riveted their fetters, a process that took several hours. In the presence of their old comrades, the 85 prisoners stood with what Kaye described as 'the outward symbols of their dire disgrace fastened on them.' He went on: many of those present were moved with great compassion during this 'piteous spectacle'; in turn many implored the general to have mercy on them. When they saw that this was hopeless, they turned to their comrades and 'reproached them for quietly suffering this disgrace to descend upon them.' According to Kaye, every sepoy present felt a 'rising indignation' in his throat.[3]

In contrast, Superintendent Cannon reported that when the prisoners left for jail there were no signs of 'bad feeling'.[4] Indeed, when they later spoke to the Mughal Emperor, Bahadur Shah, the prisoners themselves said that they had saluted before leaving.[5] However, as Kaye recorded, after the fettering of the *sowars* on parade rumours began to fly around the town, notably that by nightfall the British would put all the regiments in chains.[6] That afternoon firing broke out in the Meerut lines, and a group of armed troopers from the prisoners' regiment rode up to the jail to release their fellow men.[7] Kaye suggested that they had been taunted by the townspeople who had called them cowards for allowing their comrades to wear 'anklets of iron' while they did nothing.[8] The *sowars* too later spoke of the 'great commotion' in Meerut bazaar. The bazaar women mocked and jeered, challenging and emasculating the men with the words 'Give us your arms: we shall fight and liberate the brave officers who have been confined to gaol. You can keep inside the home and can put on bangles.'[9] When the troopers arrived at the jail the guards (who were themselves sepoys of the twentieth native infantry) made no resistance at all, and allowed them to release the men. Blacksmiths were waiting nearby to remove their irons. The 85 prisoners then rode back to the cantonment, leaving the jail intact. It was only when the sepoys of the eleventh and twentieth regiments combined with what Cannon described as the 'bad characters' of the city a few hours later that they broke the jail gates open. They released the 720 prisoners, plundered the jail, and set it on fire.[10] The following day the rebels left for Delhi with the aim of persuading the ageing Emperor Bahadur Shah to support their revolt against British authority. The mutiny-rebellion had begun.

During the night the partially complete new radiating jail in the city was attacked also, not by sepoys, but by men Superintendent Cannon described as Gujar 'banditti' (a well known caste cluster renowned for turbulence) and local villagers. The rebels released all 839 prisoners, and with them set fire to the jail's sleeping quarters, store-rooms, and workshops. They then stripped it of everything of value, stealing doors, door frames, iron bars, timber, brass and iron cooking pots, fetters, prison clothing and bedding, hand-carts, bullocks, and door plates. Further, they robbed the weapon store, removing 162 flint muskets, 50 cap rifles, and dozens of boxes of ammunition. According to Cannon, the rebels destroyed and burnt anything that they could not remove. Most of the permanent guard, the men responsible for guarding the exterior jail, deserted and joined the rebels; just a third remained in the jail the next day. It being a Sunday, the contingent guard, responsible for the internal discipline of the prison, was not on duty. Only about half turned up for work the following morning. Cannon calculated the losses due to the jail's destruction at the considerable sum of 23,000 *rupees*.[11]

The rescue of the imprisoned *sowars* and the breaking open of Meerut's two jails sparked off a pattern of events that spread across the North-West Provinces, western Bihar, and parts of the Panjab during the revolt. Mutinous sepoys and rebels together attacked jails, joining forces with prisoners in arson and plunder. Frequently the newly liberated prisoners then became involved in the general looting and burning of cities, towns, and villages. They targeted particularly government property, stripping offices, district courts, treasuries, railway works, and telegraphs of anything of value and then setting them on fire, often destroying all official records in the process. They also attacked the residences of Europeans and Indian Christians. In total, rebels broke open 41 jails: seven in each of the Bengal Presidency and the Panjab, and 27 in the North-West Provinces. Like the disorder more generally, jail-breaking was confined to northern India. The Bombay and Madras presidencies remained largely unaffected.

The mutinous Meerut *sowars* were outraged by the imprisonment of their fellow troopers, which they saw as a humiliating injustice. In Chapter 2 we discussed the challenge imprisonment posed to Indian cultural values, and we showed the extent to which during the first half of the nineteenth century local communities became engaged in jail controversies over various disciplinary measures including common messing and the substitution of *lotas*. As we will see, jails that were the focus of discontent in the decades before the mutiny-rebellion were also affected during 1857–8. Once again, outside sympathisers challenged the colonial notion of the jail as a closed penal space. The trajectory of the Meerut jail-breaks would come to share a number of features with those that followed, even where prisons had remained relatively tranquil during previous years. Jails were mainly opened from the outside, often by sepoys looking to release locally influential prisoners. Frequently, they were assisted by either the complicity or the desertion of prison guards.

The commissioner of Patna, E.A. Samuells, claimed that the rebels' object was to increase 'to the utmost extent the confusion created by their own proceedings'. This in itself was highly dangerous to local stability.[12] The secretary to the government of Bengal, A.R. Young, also wrote that mutineer-rebels opened prisons in order to intensify unrest: 'The first object of all rebels and mutineers appears to be to inflict the greatest possible amount of mischief to society generally, and to associate with themselves in their work of massacre and destruction the ready instruments that exist in all jails.'[13] Clearly though, there was more to jail-breaking than these comments suggest. To some extent it served various practical purposes, providing an opportunity to plunder valuable hardware, weaponry or stores. It was also a means through which mutineer-rebels could acquire prisoners with whom they felt little social affinity to use as forced labour. Yet for many Indian communities jail-breaking was also a highly symbolic act, because prisons were an imposing representation and embodiment of culturally intrusive forms of colonial governance. As anti-British hostilities spread across north India, perhaps the destruction of jails was inevitable because, as we have seen, by 1857 in the north Indian public imagination incarceration represented the colonial assault on cultures of religion and caste.[14]

The prisoners all gain freedom

Including Meerut, 41 jails across north India were broken open during 1857–8. In the North-West Provinces, rebels broke open 27 of the province's 40 jails: Meerut, Muzzaffarnagar, Bulandshahr, Alighar, Bijnor, Moradabad, Bareilly, Budaun, Shahjehanpur, Mutra, Agra, Etawah, Mainpuri, Etah, Fatehgarh, Kanpur, Fatehpur, Allahabad, Banda, Hamirpur, Azimgurh, Gorakhpur, Jaunpur, Jalaun, Jhansi, Lalitpur, and Damoh. They also opened a number of jails in Bengal: Behar (in Gaya), Shahabad (Arrah), Chittagong, Hazaribagh, Lohardaga, Puruliya (in Manbhum), and Singbhum (Chaibasa). In the Panjab, the affected jails were Delhi, Gurgaon, Hissar, Rohtak, Sirsa, Ludhiana, and Sialkot. In total, just over 23,000 prisoners escaped from jail, the overwhelming majority from the North-West Provinces. Known losses from the destruction and plunder of buildings, stores, and intramural manufactures in the North-West Provinces alone amounted to a massive 220,350 *rupees* (£23,595).[15]

In 1859 the secretary of state for India asked the governments of Bengal and the North-West Provinces to forward statements on the progress they were making in the recapture of these prisoners.[16] Though the destruction of most jail records made the returns subject to some uncertainty, from them we learn the scale of jail-breaking, especially in the North-West Provinces where rebels broke open the largest prisons in India: Agra, Allahabad, and Bareilly.

Table 1. Statement showing the number of prisoners who escaped from the jails of the North-West Provinces during the mutiny of 1857, and are still at large, 14 April 1860

Jail	No. of prisoners who escaped	No. of prisoners recaptured	No. of prisoners still at large
Muzzaffarnagar	329	162	167
Meerut	1541	346	1195
Bulandshahr	c. 70	21	49
Allyghur	227	77	150
Bijnor	349	187	162
Moradabad	707	426	281
Bareilly	2348	648	1700
Budaon	245	60	185
Shahjehanpur	843	436	407
Muttra	138*	150	unknown
Agra	3300	628	2672
Etawah	77	45	32
Mainpuri	490	126	364
Etah	c. 400	128	272
Fatehgarh	c. 1000	392	608
Kanpur	c. 138	23	115
Fatehpur	385	166	219
Allahabad	2650	276	2374
Banda	654	249	405
Hamirpur	153*	10	143
Azimghur	c. 800	62	738
Gorakhpur	1098	127	971
Jaunpur	451	85	366
Jaloun	175*	9	166
Jhansi	c. 110	34	76
Lalitpur	295*	38	257
Dumoh	244	51	193
Total	19217	4962	14267

* No figure available; 1856 average.
Source: OIOC P.206.62 (IJP 27 Aug. 1860).

Table 2. Statement showing the number of prisoners who escaped from the Bengal jails during the mutiny of 1857, and are still at large, 5 June 1860

Jail	No. of prisoners who escaped	No. of prisoners recaptured	No. of prisoners still at large
Gaya	1547	506	1041
Shahabad	143	51	92
Hazaribagh	830	271	559
Lohardaga	271	175	96
Singbhum	145	89	56
Manbhum	260	242	18
Total	3196	1334	1862

Note. The table does not include Chittagong, for which there were no returns.
Source: OIOC P.206.62 (IJP 27 Aug. 1860): R. Thompson, Junior Secretary to Government Bengal, to R. Simson, Under Secretary to Government of India Foreign Department, 18 June 1860.

Table 3. Statement showing the number of prisoners who escaped from Panjab jails during the mutiny of 1857, 15 March 1860

Jail	No. of prisoners still uncaptured
Delhi	273
Gurgaon	c. 37
Hissar	43
Rohtak	24
Sirsa	62
Ludhiana	65
Sialkot	135
Total	639

Source: OIOC P.206.62 (IJP 27 Aug. 1860): E. Thornton, Judicial Commissioner Panjab, to R.H. Davies, Secretary to Government Panjab, 15 Mar. 1860.

To put these tables in perspective, the daily average of prisoners in the North-West Provinces during 1856 was 21,505.[17] In the Panjab in 1853 it was 10,242.[18] Mouat's annual Bengal return for 1855-6 recorded an average prison population of 19,356.[19] We know little about the fate of female prisoners during 1857–8, for in the middle of the nineteenth century they made up a tiny proportion of the jail population.[20] However, there are suggestions that when local uprisings broke out prison superintendents released the women under their charge before mutineer-rebels had the opportunity to break open jails.[21]

As in Meerut, it was usually mutinous *sowars* or sepoys who attacked the jails.[22] Indeed, in an articulation of the extent to which news spread between the districts and jails during the revolt, the arrival of mutineers in towns and cities often heralded prison unrest. Thornhill reported that the prisoners in Agra jail only started to show signs of insubordination when mutineers came to the city.[23] Prisoners elsewhere also eagerly awaited the arrival of rebels.[24] They sometimes even mounted escape bids in anticipation of rebel assistance. Those of Mymensingh jail, for instance, broke out in July 1857, looting the jailer's money and carrying off the guards' swords and muskets. The prisoners believed that the sepoys stationed nearby would assist them.[25] Jail superintendents tried with increasing desperation to quell prisoners' growing rebellion. One tactic was confinement in solitary cells for inmates who spoke openly about the revolt.[26] Another was the release of those imprisoned for minor offences only.[27]

After jails were broken open, frequently prisoners joined mutineers and rebels in stripping them of everything of value. As in Meerut, they took wood, iron bars, doors, locks, and windows, together with intramural manufactures, tools, and stores. Jail buildings and contents were of enormous value to poverty-stricken inmates, as well as a good source of rebel supplies. In a symbolic subversion of the disciplinary regime, mutineer-rebels transformed fetters taken from Gorakhpur jail into weapons.[28] Many escaped prisoners went on to join the revolt outside the jails. In Kanpur rebels and prisoners together robbed the treasury.[29] In Hazaribagh they looted the bazaar.[30] Rebels and prisoners also attacked government institutions and European property, acts that went beyond those provoked by the material needs of revolt or the opportunities disorder presented for personal gain more generally. Such destruction was an important expression of hostility to Company rule and its Indian associates. Rebels destroyed all the records of the inspector-general of prisons in the North-West Provinces.[31] In Kanpur they set European residences on fire. In Puruliya, Arrah, and Lohardaga they plundered and destroyed government offices and official records.[32] In Ludhiana they attacked church and mission premises.[33] After rebels freed the Gaya prisoners, they looted the town and then pursued its fleeing European residents to the grand trunk road. Five prisoners were killed in the conflict with British forces.[34] The prisoners then joined locals in dacoity.[35] Bareilly prisoners proclaimed rebel leader Khan Bahadur Khan King, and then attacked British loyalists including local *zemindars*.[36] Meanwhile, Kanpur and Allahabad prisoners made their way to Fatehpur and helped break open the jail there.[37] What marked escaped prisoners out as different from ordinary rebels was their potential appeal as popular symbols of the possibility of a more general freedom from the colonial yoke. They played out that role with what Rag has described as the 'glee, vitality and … sense of legitimacy' that characterized subaltern rebellion more broadly.[38] As Inspector-General of Prisons Thornhill put it later, with regard to prison discipline 1857 was a year of 'loss and disaster'.[39]

An account of events in Hazaribagh provides further insights into the nature and meaning of mutiny jail-breaks. Two companies of the native infantry on duty in the town at the time (some of whom formed the penitentiary guard) mutinied on 30 July 1857. Later that day the jailer, James Mooney, found sepoys removing the prisoners' fetters and encouraging them to escape and join them.[40] The prisoners left the jail with the rebels, taking a supply of medicine and the two jail doctors with them.[41] They headed for Ranchi under the leadership of a prisoner named Surendra Sahi. He and his brother, Udanta Sahi, had been in jail for the political offence of having formerly proclaimed a Raj in Sambalpur.[42] The Hazaribagh rebels made their way into Chota Nagpur where the commissioner of the district reported that they had acquired a number of followers.[43] Like imprisoned men of rank in jails elsewhere, the Sahi brothers were released in order to head the rebel camp. Most famously, rebels also released *Maulvi* Ahmadullah Shah from Faizabad jail. He went on to play a major part in the revolt in Lakhnao.[44] An influential *zemindar* who had been imprisoned in Agra also provided leadership after the liberation of the jail.[45] Such alliances terrified the British. Many of the prisoners in Hazaribagh were Santals who had been convicted after the *hul* in 1855. To the British, the prospect of their crossing into the far from pacified neighbouring districts and combining with their fellow Santals was extremely worrying.[46] Indeed, it seems that by October released convicts, 'bad characters of all castes', and Santals had formed 'gangs of serious combinations' in the district.[47] This was perhaps the best known tribal revolt of the mutiny-rebellion, the Chero-Bogtah alliance in Palamu. The government offered large rewards for the rebels' arrest.[48] Not all of the Hazaribagh prisoners were involved, however. In the aftermath of the liberation of the jail, as elsewhere in north India some released prisoners chose to seek refuge in the jungles rather than to join the rebels.[49]

The Hazaribagh rebels allowed European jailer Mooney to escape with his life. He reported later the following exchange with one of the mutinous sepoys in the prison: '[O]ne Sepoy, who had his firelock at the ready, called out to me saying "go, go, Sir, or calamity will come on you," another, a little in his rear, called out more noisily "go, Sir, be off, be off"'. Mooney had, he said, taken his advice and left.[50] European jail officials elsewhere were not so lucky. In Bareilly the jail guards shot Superintendent Hansbrow dead. According to one of the escaped prisoners, the superintendent had fired at several of the guards in self-defence and they had shot him back. The *Bengal Hurkaru* remembered his 'cool courage and calm determination', Hansbrow's fate having mirrored that of almost a third of the European residents of the town.[51] Like Indian Christians and British loyalists, Indians complicit in the jail regime were also threatened. When the Gaya jail guards mutinied in June 1858, they killed their native officer, let all the prisoners go, and joined the rebels then passing through the district.[52]

Perhaps unsurprisingly, after the conviction of hundreds of mutineer-rebels a 'second wave' of jail-breaking broke out from the end of 1857. In mid-1858 for example a large body of rebels attacked Gaya jail in order to free a number of *zemindars* imprisoned by the special mutiny commissioners during the previous year, mainly for offences related to plundering.[53] The release of imprisoned sepoys was to the British an even more alarming prospect. Sympathetic regiments were often stationed outside prisons, as in the case of the militia camped just a few yards from Alipur prison. The superintendent of the jail, H. Fergusson, claimed that he had been told of the sepoys 'openly boasting' that even without arms their regiment was more than a match for the European force stationed there.[54] In areas of traditional military recruitment, the British feared that populations were at one with rebel sepoys. The commissioner of Patna wrote that his district was 'essentially military'. If sepoy deserters or mutineers were imprisoned or executed in large numbers, an attack on the jail was likely.[55] After all, as Mukherjee has argued, sepoys were 'peasants in uniform'.[56]

Though Benares jail had remained intact during 1857, in February 1858 24 convicted mutineers escaped. They had been sentenced to transportation by court martial and were mostly kept in the jail's solitary cells. However, with prison labour in high demand for the construction of barracks for European troops, the magistrate of the jail, H.P. Fane, sent almost all the ordinary prisoners to work for the executive engineer and employed most of the sepoys in grinding wheat in one of the wards. While at work the sepoys took a sword hanging in a storeroom, stole the sentry's musket, forced the jail's inner gate, and escaped. Eleven of them were recaptured the same day. They were tried by a drumhead court-martial and ordered to be shot. In a carefully orchestrated social warning, the sentence was carried out in the outer yard of the jail in view of the other prisoners. The remaining escapees were brought in during the night and the following day they were tried by W. Edwards, the special commissioner. He sentenced them all to be hanged; once again the sentence was carried out immediately. The magistrate was reprimanded for the relative freedom he had granted the sepoys, especially when it was revealed that he had removed their handcuffs.[57]

As we have seen, the joining of prisoners with mutinous sepoys and rebels often proved a powerful force. In one of the first mutiny histories, Charles Ball described the scene in Meerut using what Ranajit Guha has famously described as 'the prose of counter-insurgency', a linguistic representation that masked the political motivation for revolt.[58] When the liberated sepoys were taken back to the lines, he wrote, they were followed 'by a tumultuous rabble from the gaol, yelling and shouting, and vociferating savage denunciations of vengeance upon all Europeans.' He went on: 'The prisoners and rabble of the town continued their ravages almost without check.'[59] Derivative nineteenth-century accounts followed the same linguistic pattern, as in T.R.E. Rice's later 1885 account. 'The thirst of the mutineers for the blood of Christians was only stimulated by the slaughter of Finnis,' he wrote. 'The convicts, let loose from the gaols, and fraternising with the native police and the increasing swarm of budmashes, joined in the bloody work. Gangs of these marauders, armed with swords and clubs, roamed about the station, hurled showers of bricks upon every stray European who crossed their path, burst into peaceful dwellings, murdered the inmates, and poured forth again laden with plunder.'[60] Contemporary officials described 'marauding' liberated prisoners and 'bad characters' in the same way.[61] Typically, nineteenth-century British accounts stressed the unity forged between sepoys, rebels, and escaped prisoners. In his description of the 'Siege of Arrah', John Halls put it like this: '[T]hese were not alone the offscourings of the bazaar and the refuse of the jail, but the war-like population of the Rajpoot villages, headed up by perhaps the bravest chieftain who has appeared on the side of the rebellion [Kuer Singh].'[62]

Mark Thornhill, magistrate of Mathura (Mutra), produced the most famous contemporary British narrative account of jail-breaking, some thirty years later describing his encounter with several groups of escaped prisoners from neighbouring Agra. In rather fanciful prose, he claimed that the sound of their clanking fetters both heralded their arrival and portended British disaster. 'They made no attempt to molest us,' he recalled, 'they did not appear to see us; they neither turned their heads nor quickened their pace. They moved on with the same slow, silent steps and vanished in the darkness ... at each step their chains rattled.' For Thornhill, the escaped prisoners were a ghostly apparition like 'phantoms from another world'.[63] Alex Padamsee has interpreted these 'uncanny figures' as a literary metaphor for British dispossession in the revolt.[64] But there were religious connotations in play too, which took on particular significance in the context of 1857–8. Indeed, Thornhill wrote that as fatigue washed over him he thought of himself as having gone to hell, with the escaped prisoners the 'condemned souls' of 'the infernal regions'.[65]

In contrast to the accounts of Ball, Rice, and Halls, Thornhill offered a more nuanced consideration of the relationship between sepoys, rebels, and escaped prisoners, suggesting that far from constituting a united force violent disorder broke out between them over the sharing out of looted treasury money. Many were killed, wounded or badly burnt.[66] This renders more complex the way in which we perceive the relationship between mutineers and rebels who were often in competition rather than in collusion, and brings us to a further dimension to the opening of jails that challenges the notion that there was always natural sympathy or unity between them. Prisoners, especially ordinary labourers, were a useful source of labour for sepoys and rebels, and in this sense jail-breaks were driven by practical needs. According to the *Bengal Hurkaru*, some of the Hazaribagh prisoners were made to carry looted chattels from the treasury for the rebels on their march to Chota Nagpur.[67] This also happened in Barrackpur.[68] In Chittagong, prisoners were released especially for the purpose of carrying mutinous sepoys' loads. Inspector-General of Prisons Mouat described later how the sepoys of the treasury guard had mutinied and plundered their charge. They then broke open the jail gate with muskets and bayonets, and demanded the keys from the *daroga*. The *jemadar* (overseer of the guard) and *burkundazes* (guards) were ordered by threat to bring out the prisoners, while the sepoys guarded the jail and nearby roads in order to prevent them from escaping. They then loaded the prisoners with money from the government treasury together with goods taken from the jail. These included bedding and blankets, tools, cloth, clothing, and jewellery.[69] The judge of Tripura believed that the sepoys had made a prior arrangement with the prisoners, with the latter agreeing to act as guides in exchange for their release. Otherwise, he wrote, the sepoys would not have been able to find their way through uncharted hill country.[70] However, many prisoners escaped from the party because the rebels gave them inadequate rations, leaving them 'half starved'. In a couple of cases, sepoys even bayoneted prisoners for lingering with their loads. A number of prisoners surrendered voluntarily to the British, so distancing themselves from the sepoys' actions. The district judge took them to the jail and in a bid to deter others from following their example made them tell the remaining prisoners what had happened.[71] In Allahabad too sepoys used prisoners to push wheelbarrows full of loot. The *Bengal Hurkaru* reported that the sepoys allowed prisoners and others to divide anything they did not want amongst themselves, though 'more powerful parties' later robbed them.[72]

Predictably, the British condemned such rebel acts. The *Bengal Hurkaru*, for instance, reported the 'diabolical deeds' of the 'demons incarnate'. The Roman Catholic bishop of Agra put it like this: the city's jail blazed while its escaped prisoners danced by the lurid light of the flames.[73] And yet Indians were sometimes just as critical. For instance, rebel leader Fazl-i-Haq wrote scathingly in his 1857–8 memoir of the pleasure, extravagance, luxury, and mischief pursued by 'men of the street'.[74] Escaped prisoners met with considerable hostility from some communities. Indians of rank resented the 'distress and trouble' caused by their 'evil practices'.[75] Local men assisted the British in rounding them up, for instance in the areas around Hazaribagh.[76] They included the *Rajah* of Jhaldah, who had been imprisoned in Hazaribagh jail since the 1840s and was released when it was broken open in August 1857. The special commissioners later remitted the unexpired part of his sentence.[77] One *zemindar* who remained loyal to the British reported that his men had surrounded Singbhum jail (in Chaibasa) to prevent local sepoys from breaking it open. The prisoners refused to take their meal the following day and threw missiles at their guards, but the jail remained safe, he claimed, because he had counselled the latter against allowing the prisoners to escape. He wrote in a petition for some reward: '[B]y my authority I have protected the jail and treasury.'[78] Two days after he sent the petition, however, the Ramghur battalion succeeded in breaking the jail. Two messengers arrived with the news that British rule had ended, and that with the exception of a few men at Allahabad there was barely a white face left in India. According to the assistant commissioner of the district, this was the signal for the release of the prisoners from the jail. The battalion then used them to carry their loads on their march to nearby Ranchi.[79] Prisoners too sometimes saw the promise of a pardon in distancing themselves from the outbreaks. One Puruliya prisoner went to the police as soon as he had been released, and assisted them in driving away a group of rebels who were about to plunder the town bazaar. He was rewarded with his early release.[80] Another Agra prisoner escaped to join loyal Company troops, and was later pardoned for his efforts.[81] Thus jail-breaking reveals something of the social complexities of the revolt, a theme that we will return to in our discussion of the fate of mutineer-rebels (Chapter 5).

Escaped prisoners were important sources of information about the progress of the rebellion, to the British as well as to Indians,[82] and their arrival in the districts even heralded its spread. Indeed, they were involved in the transmission of the rumours that assumed such a central place in the revolt.[83] The conduit of information was all the more pronounced because long-term prisoners were often imprisoned in jails some distance from their districts, and after their release they made for home. Central jails were peculiarly important in this respect. Because so many Allahabad prisoners were from neighbouring districts, once they escaped they became an important source of intelligence. When they arrived back home, they were a sort of signal to revolt, for instance in the villages around Banda.[84] Local rebellion was sparked off when prisoners carried news suggesting that the British were vulnerable. Escaped prisoners from Hazaribagh spread rumours about the imminent end of British rule. British spies in the villages in Sambalpur stated that these rumours were widely believed, and so villagers aided them.[85] Escaped prisoners from Moradabad also told stories of a general massacre of government officials at the time of the jail-break.[86] The British partly ascribed revolt in the Panjab to the widespread belief, spread by liberated prisoners from Agra, that Company rule had come to an end. The secretary to the chief commissioner wrote: 'These men told their kindred of our emptied treasuries and our vacant gaols; our deserted cantonments and our slaughtered countrymen.'[87] Or, as another British official put it, the prisoners carried news of 'the Englishman's disgrace'.[88]

As the extent and impact of jail-breaking became clear during 1857, panic began to spread among British district officers and prison officials. In part this was related to the transfer of troops away from jail duty. In November 1857 the superintendent of Alipur jail complained of his numerically inadequate guard. Calling for at least a hundred European soldiers, he feared for the worse.[89] The archives are full of descriptions of brewing unrest and fears about the consequences of jail-breaks. Magistrates arranged to visit prisons daily, withdrew prisoners from road labour, and where possible increased and further armed their guard.[90] Officials also ordered the confinement of newly convicted local prisoners in distant jails.[91] As news of the outbreak at Meerut spread, in order to strengthen his reinforcements the magistrate of nearby Muzzaffarnagar himself released all the prisoners in the town and ordered the jail guard to join him.[92] When rebels advanced on Agra, the superintendent of the jail released some prisoners.[93] In other places in the Panjab, superintendents removed prisoners to secure buildings out of town and banned prison visits. They took up drawbridges and acquired supplies of blue lights and rockets to serve as signals of attack.[94]

With rebels on the march, district commissioners began to make plans about what to do with large jail populations who they feared would otherwise be released and join the revolt. In what would come to provoke a major change in the punishment of offenders, the commissioner of Patna drew up contingency plans for the prisons under his jurisdiction. He made a clear distinction between misdemeanants and serious offenders. Given that the latter would be likely to resort to acts of violence if released, he recommended that all prisoners convicted of dacoity, highway robbery, serious affrays, burglary, murder or manslaughter should be transferred to Alipur. In the meantime, he suggested that legislative authority be sought for the transfer of some prisoners sentenced to more than three years' imprisonment to the penal settlements in Pinang, Melaka, and Singapore. All those whose retention in India either from 'political reasons' or from the insecurity of the jails was inadvisable should, he suggested, be transported overseas.[95] His request was the catalyst for a major shift in government policy. Under the 'urgent circumstances', the government approved the Alipur transfer. At the same time, it ordered the governor of the Straits Settlements to prepare for the arrival of convicts. Term prisoners would be sent to Melaka and lifers to Pinang or Singapore.[96] A few days later, the government extended the Alipur transfer order to all 'dangerous prisoners' in the presidency.[97]

Sites of Provocation and Coalescence

Beyond the desire to create disorder, acquire property, release sepoys and men of rank or harness labour to assist the rebel caravan, there was a further dimension to jail-breaking. This related to popular feeling about the prison, for jails were places in which cultural interference was pronounced and around which resistance to the Company regime coalesced. Historians have explained the 1857–8 uprising at least in part as a local response to British infringements against 'native tradition', more particularly caste and religion. Various legislative interventions including the widow remarriage and inheritance acts now feature in most historiographies of the revolt. To nineteenth-century writer Kaye, the British were in fact cautious with respect to Indian cultural practices, but *Brahmin pandits* waited for an appropriate moment to convince the general population of a government plot to defile the entire Hindu community. That moment came with the introduction of common messing in prisons in the 1840s for, as he put it, prisoners' 'bodies and souls were in the immediate keeping of the State'. Jail inmates and the inhabitants of the towns came to believe that because the government had made no provision for the appointment of *Brahmin* cooks, it intended to destroy prisoners' caste and to convert them forcibly to Christianity. This was, he said, the beginning of a belief in a more widespread assault on Indian religions that continued with the removal of prisoners' *lotas* in 1855, and culminated in the controversy over the use of greased cartridges in the army.[98]

As we have seen, with the introduction of common messing from the 1840s jails spurred wider social protests in several north Indian towns and cities. Indian communities, including sepoys, sympathized with prison populations subjected to various cultural infringements, notably kin of 'respectable' status. This support was evident during the 1857–8 uprising too. Moreover, the instabilities and opportunities jail-breaking created in many towns and cities became central to Indian experiences of the revolt more broadly. Jail-breaking involved all social classes and cultures, from *rajahs*, sepoys, and *zemindars* to the ordinary labouring poor. As such it was one of the most populist elements of the revolt, and in areas with rich oral traditions of popular history, jail-breaking has become deeply ingrained in memory and folklore. Extracted here are a few lines from the Ballad of Kunwar [Kuer] Singh, perhaps the most famous mutiny song of all, in which rebels liberate Patna jail:

> They are up now at Masaurhi, and Masaurhi *thana* smashed
> The sipahees all gain freedom, and now Punpun too they raid
> And Punpun *thana* smashed
> now a siege in Patna laid
> The prisoners all gain freedom
> And they are up now at Maner.[99]

During 1857 British officials recalled with some anxiety the ties forged between prisoners and disaffected communities after the introduction of common messing in the 1840s.[100] Yet contemporary and later nineteenth-century British writers did not in general taken up Kaye's representation of the significance of jail messing as a cause of the mutiny-rebellion.[101] One notable exception is Frederick Roberts, who in 1858 received the Victoria Cross for his part in suppressing the revolt. At the end of the nineteenth century, with the benefit of hindsight, he claimed that it was when news of jail interventions spread from town to town that popular beliefs about forcible conversions to Christianity began to gain ground.[102]

The impact of jail messing was more central to contemporary Indian accounts of events.[103] In an important indication of the extent of cultural fusion and syncretic practice, Indians wrote that common messing and the religious threat it represented more generally affected both Hindus and Muslims. In his account of the revolt, Fazl-i-Haq described the Company's motives for propagating Christianity, writing that the British 'laboured under the conviction that the persistence of religious differences between the conquer[o]r and the conquered, would prove to be a stumbling stone, in their way of the consolidation of the empire and would ultimately breed revolution'.[104] Letters written by rebel leaders in Patna two years before revolt erupted revealed specifically Muslim concerns about common messing, which they described as 'regulations injurious to the Mahomedan religion'.[105] Indeed, in 1845 when the magistrate of Saran decided to introduce common messing among Muslim prisoners first, believing that they would have no caste objections to it, he was sorely mistaken for the prisoners refused to comply.[106] British loyalist Sayyid Ahmed Khan noted later on that all communities perceived common messing as a general signal that the British wished to do away with religion.[107] The proclamation of Khan Bahadur Khan, an important rebel leader in Rohilkhand who the British executed after the revolt, also described the British as 'people who overthrow all religions'. '[T]hey resolved on compelling prisoners, with the forcible exercise of their authority, to eat their bread,' he wrote. 'Numbers died of starvation, but did not eat it; others ate it, and sacrificed their faith'. The cultural fate of prisoners became bound up with fears about Indian society more generally. Khan Bahadur Khan went on to repeat rumours about the general adulteration of flour, rice, and sugar current at the time: '[The British] now perceived that this expedient did not succeed well, and accordingly determined on having bones ground and mixed with flour and sugar, so that people might unsuspectingly eat them in this way. They had, moreover, bones and flesh broken small and mixed with rice, which they caused to be placed in the markets for sale'.[108] It is interesting that Bahadur Khan's plea for Hindu-Muslim solidarity against the British was framed partly around the issue of consumption. He promised that Muslims would no longer slaughter cows or eat beef if the Hindus would join them.[109] A couple of months after the revolt began Bahadur Shah issued what would become a famous order banning cow slaughter at the approaching festival of Eid.[110]

In February 1858 the commandant of the Bengal police battalion, Thomas Rattray, forwarded a pamphlet to Secretary to Government A.R. Young. It had been written by Shaik Hidayat Ali, an officer in the Sikh Police Battalion (otherwise known as Rattray's Sikhs), on the subject of the Indian revolt. He requested that if Rattray found it of sufficient interest he should translate and publish it. *A few words relative to the late Mutiny of the Bengal Army, and the Rebellion in the Bengal Presidency* provides a fascinating insight into the perspective of an officer allied to the British. At least in part he put the mutiny-rebellion part down to public outrage at the treatment of prisoners in jail, though unlike his contemporaries he argued that Muslims were unaffected by common messing. Rattray's translation of his officer's communications with 'influential people' is worth quoting at length. He claimed that they had told him:

> [I]f any of our brothers commit any offence against the state, according to the nature of the offence and by the laws of the land they get punished; this is all very right and proper; and we have nothing to say against it, that law must be bad which by its infliction ruins our religion, - for instance, when any one is sentenced to imprisonment, immediately on his reaching the prison, his beard and moustache are cut; this to us is a great insult. In jail it is ordered that the prisoners should eat in messes, the Mahomedans by themselves and the Hindoos by themselves; this is no outrage to a Mahomedan, but it is a great one to the feelings and religion of a Hindoo. One Hindoo won't eat from the hand of another unless they happen to be brothers or cousins ... On account of these prison arrangements; it was the general opinion that the Government wished to do away with all caste. When any Hindoo is released from prison, he is always tabooed by his family and looked upon as having lost caste: on this account both the prisoner and his relative[s] become disaffected towards the Government. The above strictness was carried out in many jails, in consequence of which, disturbances broke out in the Gyah, Arrah, Benares and many other jails.[111]

Hidayat Ali was not sympathetic to the rebels; his pamphlet was an attempt to understand the causes of the revolt in order to court favour with the British, for he ended with the offer of his services to government in England. Indeed, in a perspective springing from his elite status he went on to describe the 'bigotry' of the uneducated masses, who thought that if they wore European style clothing they would be converted into Christians: '[T]hey think anything new or anything they don't understand must be meant in some way or other to affect their religion. From this foolishness on their part, all the late anarchy and ruin has come to pass.'[112]

Chapter 2 showed how important issues of religion and caste were in the complex interplays between power, resistance, and identity formation in north Indian jails during the first half of the nineteenth century. It is clear that these struggles continued into 1857–8. As we have seen, despite their efforts prison administrators never instituted common messing fully. In every prison, prisoners could plead for a special exemption on the basis of high caste or status. If successful, jail officials supplied them with rations with which they could cook their own food, rather than issuing them with cooked food from a communal pot. Though there are no figures for the North-West Provinces, it is notable that all the Bengal jails affected by the rebellion had exempted prisoners, some of them in significant numbers, which is strongly suggestive of the extent of continued resistance to common messing. In the Patna division of Bihar, a month before the mutiny began just over ten per cent of Gaya prisoners were exempted (111 out of 858). The Shahabad (Arrah) figure was about the same (59/427). As we have seen, both jails had been the scene of bitter resistance against various measures relating to prison discipline over the preceding few years. The proportion of exemptions was even more striking in Chota Nagpur. Only one prison remained intact during 1857–8: Sambalpur, where all prisoners were arranged in messes. A year earlier in Puruliya and Hazaribagh jails, both of which were broken open during the revolt, the extraordinarily high figure of about one-third of prisoners (39/128 and 94/310) were exempted from common messing. Almost half of prisoners in another liberated jail – Chaibasa - had exemptions (62/142). The comparative figure for Alipur was about a quarter (394/1721).[113]

The unrest that had characterized many attempts to implement new disciplinary measures in prisons during the first half of the nineteenth century, particularly from the 1840s, continued in the months leading up to the outbreak of the revolt. Newly appointed inspector of prisons F.J. Mouat made two tours of Bengal presidency jails, the first during 1855. With his arrival in and movement between so many jails, prisoners' fears about the purpose of his visits and the potentially new forms of intervention that they might herald were surely rife, particularly as the tour coincided with a series of innovative disciplinary measures and the drawing up of new jail rules. In November 1855, for instance, Hughli prisoners petitioned against a series of measures, including the jailer's destruction of old clothing, the withdrawal of pillows, restrictions in receiving visitors, and the removal of walls around the cooking sheds.[114] A year later prisoners in Dhaka claimed that their 'holy books' were removed, and that they were no longer allowed fruits or *tulsee* (basil) with which to perform *puja* (prayer) rituals. This meant that they were unable to satisfy 'all the requirements of the pure Hindoo Religion'. Further, they were concerned about rumours of the imminent introduction of earthen vessels into the jail.[115] At the end of 1856, there was an outbreak in Lakhnao jail in the newly annexed district of Awadh. Though the prisoners were not subject to messing, their firewood ration was so inadequate that they were unable to cook their food. Ominously, the sepoy guard did nothing to prevent the escape of 150 prisoners.[116]

As we have seen, Hidayat Ali's pamphlet noted the 'great insult' prison regulations on shaving provoked. This was a reference to new rules put in place first in the North-West Provinces and then in Bengal. The government ordered that as soon as the appeal process was over, all male prisoners sentenced to imprisonment with labour would have their hair shaved and their beard trimmed every two weeks, unless it caused 'personal disgrace'. Muslims' beards would be trimmed to the length of a closed fist only. It gave magistrates the discretion to exempt any prisoner from this rule where it might prove 'offensive or degrading'. Sikhs would not be subject to the measure at all.[117] Nevertheless, the order caused uproar in many prisons and prisoners refused to submit to it on religious or other grounds. Some Dhaka prisoners, for instance, claimed that long hair prevented headaches.[118] As during riots over common messing and the substitution of *lotas*, local communities became involved in the controversy. Muslims in Allahabad were said to be 'exasperated' by the order.[119] In Bengal the Muslim Association of Calcutta contacted Mouat to express its concerns. His response was that they had misinterpreted rules that ordered the *trimming* rather than the *shaving* of beards. Matters were not helped when in one jail – Munger - officials mistranslated the order to the shaving of all beards to the length of one inch, which had not been the government's intention at all.[120] While he claimed to be sympathetic to prisoners' religious practices, Mouat saw objections to the measure as 'prejudices which I know to be unconnected with religion ... in bar of the rigid discipline which I am resolved to maintain.'[121] Prisoners in two of the Patna division jails much affected by earlier unrest, Arrah and Gaya, were strongly disaffected by the circular, and as during the *lota* riots a couple of years previously seemed to command support from outside. In December 1856, the magistrate of Behar transferred six Gaya prisoners to Alipur after they refused to work and tried to persuade others to follow their example. They were followed by 14 Rajwars, a low-caste group that the magistrate viewed as particularly refractory and hard to control.[122] At the beginning of 1857 prisoners in Arrah made an organized attempt to prevent their heads being shaved, though they were eventually made to submit to the disciplinary procedure.[123]

In Bengal, during the first half of 1857 Mouat made the first moves to establish an exclusively female penitentiary,[124] to introduce new uniforms, and to force prisoners to wash their own clothes. Hindu prisoners petitioned against the proposed clothing on the grounds that wearing trousers and a shirt, or clothes that were 'old, torn, sewed, colored, dirty or with loose threads lengthways at each end' affected caste. The government consulted a *pandit* who rejected the prisoners' claims. By this time revolt had broken out, and in July 1858 the lieutenant-governor ordered that Hindu prisoners did not have to wear trousers.[125] In 1857 Mouat also proposed to end the system whereby prisoners could avoid sentences of hard labour, and also therefore common messing, through the payment of a fine. As Mouat put it, penal labour was an essential part of jail discipline and prisoners did not repay their debts to the state if they simply opened their wallets. This was a particular problem in the peculiarly Indian context where apparently mischievous natives were unwilling to work for an honest wage. Mouat wrote:

> If idleness be at any time and in any place the parent of vice, it is especially so in a jail, where the evil communications that corrupt good manners are abundant ... The absence of all ordinary motives and incentives to exertion, the utter dearth of intellectual resources, and the proneness to plot and scheme mischief, are all developed in the highest degree in Asiatics. My belief is that more Dacoities, false charges, and crimes of every sort are plotted in prisons than any where else and that this arises in a great measure from the imperfect separation of convicts, and the idleness which permits the non-labouring prisoner to sleep away his days, and pass his nights in scheming, if not practicing evil when he is entirely removed from observation ... It is the crime and not the criminal which should be regarded in the award of punishment. The rich man should never be able to purchase immunity from what is deemed disagreeable, which the poor man is compelled to suffer in silence from his want of the means to secure similar indulgence.[126]

Finally, because there was a shortage of low-caste prisoners who could be employed as *mehtars* (sweepers) Mouat called for their more equal distribution between jails. He proposed that they should work only in the removal of sewage, that most polluting of labour. All other prisoners would be responsible for the general cleaning of yards, wards, cook-rooms, and drains. This was a measure designed to save on the expense of hiring free men, but was almost certain to excite the ire of prisoners. The Bengal government was well aware of this and so referred the proposal to the government of India for orders.[127] As the revolt broke out just a few weeks later, each of the proposed measures was put aside.

The same cultural uneasiness gripped prisons in the North-West Provinces during the same period. In one ominous incident just a few days before the Meerut sepoys mutinied, a jail *burkundaze* named Brindabun

Tewaree was arrested in the Midnapur lines trying to incite the sepoys to break open the jail. Three sepoys and a *havildar* (sergeant) said that the man had told them that the district magistrate and other officers had been to the jail, fed the Hindu and Muslim prisoners with beef and pork, flogged them, and 'filled their mouths with forbidden food.' Magistrate E.H. Lushington quickly denied the allegation. Rather he explained that he had ordered *Brahmins* to cook and distribute food to prisoners in their wards rather than the jail yard. Forty-seven prisoners refused to eat, and because of their dogged resistance he flogged 'three or four', including two undertrial sepoys. The prisoners all agreed to take their meals and so he left the jail. The district magistrate found Brindabun Tewaree guilty of inciting sedition and mutiny, and he was hanged on 8 June. The magistrate claimed that he had been the leader of several hundred 'desperate adherents' who planned to break open the prison. The government warned Lushington to be cautious in any changes to jail management that might be misinterpreted and cause alarm.[128] As during earlier unrest, the incident reveals both the centrality of common messing to public imaginings of the jails, especially the sympathy prisoners of rank aroused, as also the speed with which rumours about changes to the disciplinary regime spread outside their walls. It is perhaps significant in this respect that according to the *Bengal Hurkaru*, as sepoys broke open Allahabad jail during 1857 they cried '*Ram Chundra ki joy*' ('victory to Lord Ram'), clearly a Hindu inspired slogan.[129]

In the context of so much prison instability surrounding issues of caste and religion, both in the years leading up to and during the revolt, it seems unbelievable that in September 1857, with the penal infrastructure in almost total disarray, Mouat defended aggressively the practice of conducting post-mortems on prisoners. The lieutenant-governor of Bengal had rather nervously drawn his attention to the fact that in practice prisoners' families could not always object, as they were allowed to do, because they lived some distance from jails. He asked Mouat to modify the rules to take account of this. In particular, he recommended that prisoners themselves could indicate their desire not to be made subject to the civil surgeon's scalpel if they were to die in jail.[130] This was not the first time the two had clashed over issues of prison discipline. The lieutenant-governor had counselled Mouat a few months before the mutiny broke out that he was not to ignore prisoners' 'religious prejudices' merely because he believed that they were mistaken.[131] Mouat's response on the issue of post-mortems was that the suggested change would in effect put an end to the practice. 'Were it known in jails', he wrote, 'that a wish on the subject would in all cases be attended to, every convict capable of uttering such a wish would undoubtedly do so.' He advised the government neither to draw attention to the issue nor to legislate on it too closely. Rather, discreet professionals would ensure that 'respectable' prisoners were not made subject to it. In the meantime, the prospect of a post-mortem was a deterrent against crime.[132] Notwithstanding Mouat's objections, as the medical board controlled the medical supervision of jails the new rule was adopted.[133] Mouat's simultaneous attempt to discontinue opium allowances for addicts was more successful. His belief that withdrawal symptoms had been greatly exaggerated, and after a brief period of 'great mental prostration and misery' addicts improved in health, was circulated to district magistrates and civil surgeons for advice.[134]

Despite the undoubted significance of the north Indian prison as a place of provocation and coalescence during the revolt, solidarity between rebels and prisoners was always potentially fragile. We noted earlier that although rebels sometimes released specific prisoners, usually mutinous sepoys or local elites, and formed alliances with them, they used others as forced labour. It would be a mistake to assume that underlying the rebellion were widely shared grievances about innovations in jail discipline, however important they were to some communities in some places. As we saw in Chapter 2, during the first half of the nineteenth century free communities and sepoys were concerned largely with the fate of imprisoned kin of 'respectable' status, whether Muslim or Hindu, rather than the entire jail community. The same pattern is evident during the mutiny-rebellion. Prisons were sites of cultural provocation and coalescence, not because differing communities had identical interests and concerns but because prison struggles were also metaphors for broader social fears about the compromising of the faithful.

'Nothing more than their duty': prison guards

Before the rebellion jail guards were organized in two sets, the permanent and the contingent guard. The permanent guard was in charge of surveying the exterior of the prison; supposedly effort was made to prevent it from associating with the prisoners. It was drilled in military fashion and armed with muskets. Such guards were often referred to as *burkundazes*, the generic term for armed employees in civil departments. The contingent guard, on the other hand, watched the prisoners while at work and superintended the internal discipline of the jail. It was armed simply with bamboo *lathis*.[135] In the North-West Provinces and the Panjab jail guards were soldiers enlisted especially for jail duties, under the sole control of the magistrate. The magistrate and local military officers controlled the guards used in Bengal.[136]

British administrators complained about the quality of their jail guards throughout the first half of the nineteenth century. Indeed, Mouat wrote after his first tour of inspection that nothing had struck him more forcibly than their 'manifest inefficiency generally, the indifferent manner in which they are armed, [and] their free and easy communication with the prisoners'.[137] According to the session judge in Benares, they were often only half-drilled. Many supposed guards were in fact substitutes for friends or relations on leave. Most had never handled a musket before. In any case, he wrote, guards were unwilling to shoot prisoners or stab them with bayonets because of the inevitable enquiry that would follow, leading to suspension or punishment. The prisoners both knew and took advantage of this.[138]

Prison authorities faced enormous difficulties in recruiting and retaining prison guards. The problem in part related to the reluctance of guards to sleep inside the jails. As Thornhill put it in 1858, their duties involved 'irksome confinement and distasteful association with criminals.' The relatively low pay on offer presented little by way of compensation. Therefore, it was hard to find reliable men for the job. Thornhill wrote that it was not unknown for guards to fall asleep while watching prisoners at work on the roads, and then be killed with their own weapons by their fleeing charge.[139] If Mouat's annual reports are to be believed, jail guards were not infrequently in the pay of rich convicts, both to exempt them from labour and procure luxuries like tobacco and marijuana.[140] As long as Indian jailers were used, he wrote, 'penal and profitable industry, reformation, efficacy of punishment, and strict discipline are well nigh impossible.'[141] For this reason, on the eve of revolt Mouat was advocating the replacement of jail guards with soldiers.

During 1857–8 British administrators were nervous about the apparently uncertain position of jail guards, for they shared the perspectives of both prisoners and the local community. The permeability of the jails during this period made guards important carriers of news. They were also able to impart information which aided rebels in formulating the best tactics for opening a jail. Guards were after all from the same communities as the mutineer-rebels. Moreover, many were themselves military men and so they often shared their goals. The sentries in Lohardaga, Puruliya, and Chaibasa were for example sepoys in the Ramghur battalion. Mouat complained that too many of them had local ties and connections and so could not be trusted. He doubted that they could be relied upon in an emergency, as it was to prove.[142] The guards in Chaibasa prison, broken open in September 1857, did nothing to prevent it.[143] Neither did the supposedly loyal guard in Ludhiana.[144] The magistrate of Bijnor wrote in May 1857 that he had 'strong reason' to believe that the prison guards had connived in the escape of 349 prisoners. The jail had been razed to the ground.[145] A month later, the guards also sealed the fate of Bareilly prison.[146] This was part of a general pattern of what Thornhill later described as the 'faithlessness and pusillanimity of the jail guards as a body' in the North-West Provinces.[147] The guards accompanying a group of prisoners being transferred out of Gaya even combined with them, shooting the *jemadar* and escaping.[148] Like their prisoner charges, guards sometimes then joined mutineer-rebels in revolt.[149] Thornhill reported that the Gorakhpur jail guard constituted 'the most formidable part of the rebel army' in the region.[150] In at least one case, the special commissioners sentenced a prison guard for his part in rebellion.[151] Guards even tried to incite outbreaks outside the jails. The *burkundaze* of Burdwan jail, for instance, was hanged after he tried to persuade a local battalion to mutiny.[152]

As the number of deserters and mutineers in jail rose, the question of the loyalty of prison guards became paramount. The magistrate of Allahabad wrote that the few guards who had returned to the jail after it was broken open were relatives and friends of the mutineers. Their sympathies lay with sepoys sentenced to life imprisonment for mutiny or sedition, which would lead to further problems with jail security.[153] The superintendent of Alipur expressed similar fears about his militia guard, sepoys with 'many friends and relations among the Military Convicts'. If a disturbance broke out among the prisoners and the military guard assisted them, as would be expected, 'two thousand desperate Criminals, scummed from every District in Hindoostan, would be let loose upon Calcutta.'[154] In at least one case, a man was tried for having tried to instigate two jail guards to join the rebellion directly.[155] The Hamirpur jail guards made up part of the rebel force against the British in Banda.[156]

Less direct but of no less consequence in assuring the escape of prisoners was the fact that sometimes jail guards simply fled. Mouat wrote that *darogas* and their subordinates were a 'pack of cowards'.[157] The Agra jail guard deserted their posts because they thought they were about to be disarmed by a detachment of Europeans, an act that would have left them highly vulnerable to assault by prisoners. Despite the setting of the workshops on fire two days later the prison then remained secure for over a month until it was attacked by what was described as 'an overwhelming force' of mutinous sepoys.[158] It is sometimes difficult to draw a line between abetment and inactivity among guards. According to Thornhill, most of the guards of Benares jail did not assist their sepoy charge in escaping, though some of them allowed their muskets to be taken. He explained that the *émeute* differed from other recent jail-breaks because the guard was not generally sympathetic to the prisoners. Rather, there had been a confrontation between 'desperate men' (prisoners) and the 'habitually indolent' (guards). Indolence, of course, exercised 'a more powerful influence than apprehension of personal danger.'[159] Given its belief that the guard had not assisted the outbreak, the government issued it with a shared reward of several hundred *rupees*.[160] A few months later, however, the commissioner of the district, F.B. Gubbins, described the prison guard as 'a source of uneasiness and distrust to us'.[161] He called for European troops to replace them.[162]

And yet not all guards or jailers went over to the rebel cause. In Tirhut for instance, despite the best efforts of mutinous *sowars* the guard loaded their weapons against them, forcing their retreat from the prison gates.[163] Walker's assistant in Agra, Lalla Muthoora [Muttra] Doss, showed such loyalty that Walker requested later that he accompany him to his new posting in the Andamans. Thanks to its Indian jailer, initially Delhi jail remained intact during the revolt. Munshi Jiwan Lall, a British spy who lived within the walls during the rebellion, later described what had happened. The prisoners had received news of the arrival of the Meerut sepoys in Delhi with 'loud cries', he wrote, 'and a scene of great excitement ensued.' The jailer Tokur Lal managed to prevent an outbreak, however. When a trooper rode up to the jail and tried to entice the guard to open the gates, he shot him dead. 'Throughout the day,' Jiwan Lall recalled, 'he restrained all by his presence.'[164] According to Mouat, the deputy *daroga* and all the *burkundazes* in Arrah also 'behaved well'.[165] Given the lack of a feasible alternative force in guarding the jails, when Indian prison guards defended jails or prevented escapes during the revolt they were well rewarded. Although it was asserted that they did 'nothing more than their duty', such loyalty to the British was by no means assured.[166] Ironically, however, the involvement of jail guards in releasing prisoners reassured the colonial authorities. They could put outbreaks down to their faults or the 'mischief' of local 'bad characters', rather than the more threatening spectre of a rebellious army or population at large.[167]

In the North-West Provinces, the military police took over the guarding of jails in the aftermath of the rebellion. By 1859, all jails were guarded by detachments from the police battalion.[168] By the end of 1858, the Bengal authorities had in place a set of rules for military guards in jails. Replacing previously piecemeal arrangements, the rules stated explicitly that their duty was to prevent escapes, to resist by force any such attempt, and to facilitate at all times the maintenance of 'order and discipline'. Sentries would carry loaded arms, and if any disturbance broke out all guards would be placed under arms. Keys would be closely watched during the night. If prisoners attempted to break out of jail, they would be warned three times 'in a loud tone of voice' that if they did not surrender they would be fired on. The rules strictly prohibited guards from communicating with prisoners, either by words or signs. Finally, they were neither to engage in contraband trading in goods like tobacco or liquor with prisoners nor to receive letters on their behalf.[169]

Recapturing convicts

With the destruction of so many jails, by the autumn of 1857 the number of prisoners who remained at large, over twenty thousand, had become a potential source of extreme political embarrassment, especially to the government of the North-West Provinces. There is no question that the British pursued escaped prisoners aggressively. Contemporary *Narratives* are full of descriptions of the recovery of plundered property, the arrest of rebels, and the capture of escaped prisoners.[170] One contemporary observer wrote of a district magistrate's search for an escaped Meerut prisoner in a village close to the cantonment. The villagers denied any knowledge of him and so the magistrate set the village on fire. Thirteen people died.[171] This type of violence typified the British response to jail-breaks. British officers sometimes summarily hanged or shot escaped prisoners, especially those who were sepoys. Otherwise, they were somewhat troubled what to do with absconders, for putting them in secure jails ran the risk of spreading unrest into tranquil prisons.[172]

The attacks on jails and the desertion of guards were also huge obstacles to the imprisonment of offenders convicted either before or during the revolt. As we have seen, the Bengal government issued orders for the removal of some prisoners to Alipur and others to the Straits Settlements in order to free up jail space. The government of the North-West Provinces also called for proposals on the best course of action to take. The commissioner of Meerut proposed that all prisoners returning within a specified period and who had not been guilty of 'actual violence or rebellion' should not be made liable to extra imprisonment on account of having escaped from a jail when it had been broken open from the outside. Additionally, those prisoners who surrendered and then gave information about the whereabouts of other escapees should earn some remission of sentence.[173] Given that most prisoners were jailed for simple misdemeanours, the government went even further, proposing as a 'measure of wise policy' the remission of the sentences of all escaped prisoners who had been jailed for minor offences. The government acknowledged that because most prison records had been destroyed prisoners might well downplay the seriousness of their initial offence to take advantage of the amnesty. However, with no secure jail buildings let alone jail guards to speak of, and the prospect of large numbers of rebels and mutineers to deal with, it saw the proposal as a measure through which escaped prisoners might become 'peaceable members of the community' rather than a hostile anti-British force.[174]

The government then asked for the opinion of the *nizamat adalat* on the Meerut proposal, as was usual practice in framing proclamations. Two of the judges, C. Raikes and R.B. Morgan, feared that offering prisoners a general amnesty might be ascribed to weakness on the part of the government. They proposed that instead magistrates should be empowered to release recaptured convicts originally sentenced for misdemeanours. The third judge, H. Unwin, thought that given the more pressing needs of bringing in mutineers and rebels and of rebuilding the jails, magistrates should be directed to recapture prisoners convicted of offences 'positively dangerous to the community', like murder, highway robbery, dacoity, theft or offences against the person only.[175] The government agreed to adopt Unwin's proposals with a few modifications. In lieu of a general proclamation, local officers would be given the discretionary power to release all misdemeanants who surrendered within a given period, and the government would issue free or conditional pardons in all other cases. In effect, this was an attempt to direct police attention towards the recapture of escaped convicts who had been sentenced for serious crimes. This would, the government said, overcome the differences in circumstances in the districts. Moreover, in an allusion to the increasing criminalization of particular communities, those 'predatory classes' that had not committed serious crimes but were a 'danger to the community' could also be brought in.[176]

At the end of the year, the governor-general approved the measure.[177] It passed into law as Act V – 'an act for the punishment of certain offenders who have escaped from jail and of persons who shall knowingly harbour such offenders' – in January 1858. The details of the act were as follows. Certain prisoners who had escaped since 1 May and who did not surrender themselves to a magistrate or police officer within a month of the passing and proclamation of the act (by 18 February), and certain prisoners who escaped subsequent to the passing of the act, would be sentenced to life transportation. The same provision was extended to particular undertrial prisoners. Petty offenders were not included. Only those involved in the following crimes were subject to the act: mutiny; desertion; murder; attempted murder; thagi, believed at the time to be a form of ritual murder; dacoity; robbery; belonging or having belonged to a gang of thags, a gang of dacoits or a 'wandering gang associated for the purposes of theft or robbery'; and all crimes against persons or property attended with great personal violence. Additionally, anybody harbouring such prisoners would be liable to a fine and imprisonment for up to seven years. Landowners or their managers were made responsible for giving district magistrates and the police intelligence of escaped prisoners who entered land under their control. Otherwise they too were liable to a 200 *rupee* fine and six months' imprisonment. The act also gave district magistrates the power to pardon escaped prisoners not detained for the specified crimes on the condition that they give information that might lead to the arrest of prisoners who were, and the right to pardon 'in respect of the crime or offence', in other words to pardon all misdemeanants. Finally, the act ordered that those escaped prisoners guilty of the specified offences were to be tried by sessions judges or special commissioners. The judgments were not subject to appeal unless the defendants were Europeans.[178] While there were clear practical benefits to the act, its aim was at least partly to relieve hostility against the government, which otherwise would result from 'a sense of impending recapture and punishment.'[179]

Almost inevitably, however, there were problems in the operation of the act. Some of these related to its general provisions and others to particular circumstances. We will return to the first point in a moment. In relation to the latter, in August 1857 for instance, the authorities empowered a committee of *rajahs* then in charge of the district of Gorakhpur to throw open the prison gates. Given the widespread public sympathy with the prisoners, the idea was to avoid a riot. Yet even these prisoners were made subject to Act V. The commissioner argued that the release was as much the consequence of the instability then characterizing the district as if it had been the direct act of mutineers, rebels or the prisoners themselves.[180] The governor-general agreed.[181]

The debate about the merits of the act more generally aroused the same sort of controversy as that which had taken place a few months earlier about other official measures. The officiating session judge of Benares, F.B. Pearson, for instance, was very hostile to the act's provisions. 'I am averse from any measure', he wrote, 'which will have the effect of making any class of the community, especially a portion of the criminal population, a gainer by the mutiny and rebellion and the crimes which have attended them.' He agreed that it would in theory alleviate the practical problem of what to do with recaptured prisoners, but argued that the police would in all likelihood concentrate on the arrest of petty offenders, an easier task than tracking down mutineers and rebels. Therefore, the measure would lead to the accumulation of large numbers of minor criminals in the jails, precisely the opposite to what was intended. Pearson also drew attention to the inconsistency of differentiating between past and present offenders so that the latter would remain in prison and the former at large.[182] The judge of Fatehpur raised another objection, arguing that the provisions on minor offenders should be clarified to declare pardons to all those sentenced to less than six months. Otherwise, the leniency embodied in the act would be counteracted by the severity of other emergency laws, notably the transportation of 'heinous' offenders. Rather, he said, they should simply serve out their remaining terms.[183]

A further difficulty, as the sessions judge of Ghazipur pointed out, was that escaped prisoners might believe the government 'unable or afraid' to punish.[184] The commissioner of Gorakhpur, C. Wingfield, noted also that as heinous offences were usually punished with life transportation very few such prisoners would have escaped. In any case, there was then no inducement for men and women awaiting their shipment overseas to surrender as their position could not be made worse by recapture. Rather, he said, life prisoners failing to surrender within a specified period should be made subject to death.[185] Despite these reservations, however, in March 1858 government implemented and extended the provisions of the North-West Provinces orders.[186] Given that British rule had not been restored entirely, it was difficult to frame a general proclamation that would suit all districts across the provinces. Therefore, commissioners would simply be instructed to confine their efforts to the recapture of heinous offenders.[187] A further amendment was passed through Act XXII. This authorized the infliction of corporal punishment on prisoners in place of simple imprisonment. Its purpose was to limit the jail population.[188]

The issue was less pressing in Bengal, because a much smaller number of the presidency's prisoners had escaped. Nevertheless, the government had to make some decision about what to do with recaptured or surrendered inmates. It resolved to transfer them to Alipur, the most secure prison in the presidency, and made no distinction between their offences.[189] Recaptured prisoners were in the meantime interrogated about their experiences and became an important source of information about the movements of rebel caravans. As they were gradually brought in, the Chittagong prisoners were especially useful in this respect. Rebels had pressed them into forced labour and they had undergone what officials described as a harsh ordeal.[190]

As we have seen through the returns furnished three years later, the recapture and retrial of escaped prisoners was of ongoing concern to government. A year after Act V was passed district commissioners were already reporting difficulties in its implementation. The main problem was that transportation for life was the only sentence that could be awarded for certain recaptured prisoners, and magistrates and special commissioners had no discretion in this respect. Second, it was doubtful that the provisions of the act had become generally known within the month allowed to prisoners to surrender. The special commissioner of Banda, F.O. Mayne, wrote that it was unjust to transport all such offenders for life, especially when their original sentences varied so greatly. Moreover, during the time allowed for surrender (up to 18 February), the British had fled from many districts. Mayne suggested that as long as they had not joined in the rebellion prisoners should serve their remaining sentence. The commissioner of Allahabad suggested also that the act be amended.[191] The governor-general agreed that the measure was harsh, writing of the injustice of a man originally sentenced to a few years' imprisonment transported overseas 'merely because, when the prison doors were opened by the mutineers, he accepted the freedom given to him, and went peaceably to his home'. Moreover, knowledge of the act may not have reached those who were affected by it, especially in parts of the country completely out of British control. He recommended that the magistrates be given more discretion and ordered that the subject be brought before the legislative council.[192]

As it came under increasing criticism, the government of the North-West Provinces reiterated the pressure it had been under at the beginning of 1858, when most jails had been either badly damaged or destroyed and the districts were in revolt. In this context, it argued, it had been important to remove rebels and dangerous offenders 'from the scene of their successful exploits', even if this meant term prisoners being transported overseas for life. When the threat of all out rebellion had receded, the government amended its legislation. Act XVII (1860) promised all escaped prisoners who surrendered themselves, except those convicted of murder or *thagi*, the remission of between a quarter and half of their sentence.[193] As Secretary to Government G.E.W. Couper put it, by this time there had been no enduring embarrassment arising from the mass escapes and only a handful of serious crimes committed by such individuals had come to light.[194]

Conclusion

Despite the huge amount of energy deployed in framing appropriate legislation, most escaped prisoners were never recaptured. Almost three quarters of North-West Provinces escapees remained at large (74 per cent) two or three years later. The figure in Bengal was slightly lower – 58 per cent – but still substantial. In the Panjab, government issued proclamations offering escaped prisoners either release on payment of a fine (prisoners under sentence for minor crimes) or the remission of half their remaining term (heinous offenders). District magistrates were also allowed to use their discretion and could release prisoners, reduce terms of imprisonment or commute sentences altogether on payment of a fine or subjection to corporal punishment. However, just 13 prisoners surrendered themselves. Six hundred and eight remained unaccounted for. The judicial commissioner presumed that most had died in the disturbances.[195] Mouat too thought that given the widespread distress across north India most Bengal prisoners had probably been too scared to return home and so had died.[196] Certainly, during the unrest there were reports of liberated prisoners being found starving. According to the *Bengal Hurkaru* some even asked to be readmitted to jail where they might receive rations.[197]

There remain other possibilities. Mouat claimed that in 1858 the British discovered a 'large and prosperous' colony of escaped convicts in the jungles bordering the Himalayas. The colony apparently predated the revolt, with escaped prisoners engaged in clearing and cultivating land. Though Mouat maintained that the existence of the colony was widely known by prisoners, there are no other traces of it in the colonial archives.[198] After the revolt some Muslim leaders undertook *hijrat* (migration on religious grounds) to the Arabian Peninsula.[199] Might some of the Muslim subaltern classes have followed them to such an apparently safe location? Additionally, coinciding with the mutiny was a massive boom in world sugar prices and Indian indentured labourers were recruited for work on overseas plantations in unprecedented numbers. Mauritius alone received 38,735 Indian labourers in 1858 and 33,927 the following year. This was more than double and nearly treble the number received in any one of the preceding ten years.[200] In 1875 a major royal commission exploring conditions among indentured labourers on the island was published. The commission claimed to have uncovered a couple of instances in which escaped mutineers had taken service on the island. In the first case, it reported that a man called Parushram told the commissioners that the immigration office had changed his name when his photograph was taken. On enquiry, the commissioners found that his name had not been changed when he arrived shortly after the mutiny. He was from Ghazipur, which was suggestive to them of his mutinous past. In the second case, they asked a man named Mahadoo about his former means of livelihood. After some hesitation he admitted that he had been a sepoy but said that he could not remember the number of his regiment. The commissioners concluded that as he had originally told them that he was from Kolhapur (where the native infantry had mutinied), but had then changed his story, it was probable that he had belonged to a mutinous regiment. The point is not the truth or otherwise of the claims of the royal commission or their witnesses, but rather the fact that in the aftermath of revolt Indians were given an unprecedented opportunity to migrate and, just a few years later, indenture was seen as a possible escape valve for wanted men.[201]

At this time British Guiana also received indentured labourers. As George K. Alapatt shows, there is little evidence that recruiting agents examined the antecedents of labourers before they signed contracts of indenture. Moreover, the main areas of recruitment for Guiana at the time were the main areas of rebel activity. Fifteen years later, indentured labourers rioted at two sugar estates in British Guiana, Anna Regina and Devonshire Castle. The police opened fire and killed five men. During the ensuing inquest several eye witnesses testified that ex-sepoys had been implicated in the riots. One Indian police constable said that he heard the men saying that they would "'make a great war, they were going to kill some.'" The press with a certain paranoia declared that their object had been to murder the white community and play 'on a small scale in British Guiana the part their country men played in the terrible drama at Cawnpore, sixteen years ago.' However, neither the inquest nor the supreme court that tried 15 of the rioters came to any conclusions on the issue of sepoy leadership.[202]

The almost wholesale destruction of so many jails across north India, especially in the North-West Provinces, caused massive problems for the maintenance of political authority in the aftermath of the revolt. The following chapter will explore how the government attempted to cope with only limited jail accommodation for recaptured or surrendered prisoners, mutinous sepoys, and offenders sentenced under the special commissions set up to deal with 'mutiny' offences. Further, it will examine rebel experiences of incarceration. It will suggest that 1857–8 was an important moment in the formation of colonial penal policy, for although there were few innovations on the mainland, it assured the abandonment of penal settlements in the Straits Settlements and Burma, and Britain's consequent resettlement of the Andaman Islands as a penal colony. And so it is to jails and penal settlements in the aftermath of revolt that we now turn.

Notes

1. OIOC P.234.37 (NWPJC Apr. 1858): H.M. Cannon, Superintendent Meerut Jail, to Thornhill, 23 Feb. 1858. See also OIOC W5824: Narrative of events attending the outbreak of disturbances and the restoration of authority in the district of Meerut, in 1857–8.
2. Rebel leader Fazl-i-Haq also mentioned the significance of the greased cartridges: Haq, 'The Story', 30.
3. Kaye and Malleson, *vol. II*, 36, 38.
4. OIOC P.234.37 (NWPJC Apr. 1858): Cannon to Thornhill, 23 Feb. 1858.
5. 'Speech of the sepoys before Bahadur Shah', n.d. (May 1857), cited in *FSUP I*, 405-7.
6. Kaye and Malleson, *vol. II*, 41.
7. OIOC P.234.37 (NWPJC, Apr. 1858): Cannon to Thornhill, 23 Feb. 1858.
8. Kaye and Malleson, *vol. II*, 42.
9. 'Speech of the sepoys before Bahadur Shah', n.d. (May 1857), cited in *FSUP I*, 406.
10. OIOC P.234.37 (NWPJC, Apr. 1858): Cannon to Thornhill, 23 Feb. 1858.
11. *Ibid.*: Cannon to Thornhill, enc. an abstract of property plundered from the Meerut Jail during the outbreak on the night of the 10th May 1857.
12. OIOC P.188.46 (IPC 28 Aug. 1857): E.A. Samuells, Commissioner Patna, to A.R. Young, Secretary to Government Bengal, 12 Aug. 1857.
13. Bengal narrative of events, 12 Sept. 1857, cited in PP 1857–8 (2295): Papers relative to mutinies in East Indies: Appendix.
14. Rebels viewed other forms of institutional confinement in much the same way. One Allahabad magistrate perhaps missed the point about Indian perceptions of the difference between 'charitable' and 'government' institutions when he reported the asylums 'demolished with as much ill-will as our public offices'. (M.H. Court, Magistrate Allahabad, to C. Chester, Commissioner Allahabad Division, 21 July 1857, cited in *FSUP I*, 476).
15. OIOC P.235.7 (NWPJP 1 – 18 Oct. 1859): Thornhill to G.E.W. Couper, Secretary to Government North-West Provinces, 8 July 1859. Conversion calculated with reference to A. Piatt Andrew, 'Indian Currency Problems of the Last Decade', *Quarterly Journal of Economics* (1901), 515.
16. OIOC P.206.61 (IJP 17 June 1859): Mouat to Grey, 12 May 1859; Couper to Grey, 25 May 1859.
17. *Prison Returns of the North West Provinces for the Year 1856*, Roorkee, Thomason College Press, 1859, Table II.
18. This is the nearest pre-revolt figure available. *Report of the Inspector-General of Prisons in the Punjab, for the year 1853*, Agra, Secundra Orphan Press, 1854, 1. In 1859 the daily average was 11,416, with the total admissions numbering 34,522. *Report of the Inspector-General of Prisons in the Punjab for the year 1859*, Lahore, Chronicle Press, 1860: Appendices I, XVII.
19. Mouat's report, 1855-6, 4. By 1859-60 52,068 prisoners passed through the jail in a year: Mouat's report, 1859-60.
20. Satadru Sen, 'The female jails of colonial India', *Indian Economic and Social History Review*, 39, 4 (2002), 417-38.
21. OIOC P.234.46 (NWPJC 21 Oct. – 22 Nov. 1858): J.H. Batten, Sessions Judge Kanpur, to Muir, 13 Oct. 1858.

22. Kaye and Malleson, *vol. II*, 160-1, 178-9, 193, 233; OIOC P.235.7 (NWPJC 1 – 18 Oct. 1859): Thornhill to Couper, 8 July 1859. On Kanpur see also 'Narrative of the mutiny at Cawnpore', n.d., cited in PP 1857-58 (2363): Papers relative to mutinies in East Indies: Appendix B.
23. OIOC P.234.35 (NWPJC 1 - 15 Mar. 1858): Thornhill to E.C. Bayley, Officiating Deputy Secretary to Government North-West Provinces, 4 Mar. 1858.
24. Private daily report of H.C. Metcalfe, 20 Nov. 1857, cited in PP 1857-58 (2449): Papers relative to mutinies in East Indies.
25. Mouat's report, 1858-9, 55.
26. J.M. Lowis, Magistrate Patna, to Young, 13 June 1857, cited in PP 1857-58 (2302): Papers relative to mutinies in East Indies: Appendix A.
27. OIOC P.234.46 (NWPJC 21 Oct. – 22 Nov. 1858): Batten to Muir, 13 Oct. 1858.
28. Abstract translation of a petition from Khodabuksh Khan, 29 Sept. 1857, cited in PP 1857-58 (2363): Papers relative to mutinies in East Indies: Appendix B.
29. 'Translation of the diary of the Nunna Nawab, a native gentleman residing in Cawnpore, containing an account of the occurrences there from June 5 to July 2 1857', cited in PP 1857-58 (2363): Papers relative to mutinies in East Indies: Appendix B.
30. J.M. Graham, Commanding officer Hazaribagh, to Military Secretary to Commander-in-Chief, 3 Aug. 1857, cited in PP 1857-58 (2294): Papers relative to mutinies in East Indies: Appendix.
31. OIOC P.235.7 (NWPJP 1 – 18 Oct. 1859): Thornhill to Couper, 8 July 1859.
32. Bengal narratives of events, 25, 31 Aug. 1857, 5, 19 Sept. 1857, cited in PP 1857–8 (2295): Papers relative to mutinies in East Indies: Appendix; W. Tucker, Magistrate Munger, to Young, 11 Aug. 1857; J.S. Davies, Senior Assistant Commissioner Lohardaga, to E.T. Dalton, Officiating Commissioner Chota Nagpur, 7 Aug. 1857, cited in PP 1857-58 (2316): Papers relative to mutinies in East Indies: Appendix B.
33. R. Temple, Secretary to Chief Commissioner Panjab, to G.F. Edmonstone, Secretary to Government of India, 25 May 1858, cited in PP 1859 Session I (238): Papers relating to mutiny in Punjab, 1857.
34. *Bengal Hurkaru*, 10, 26 Aug. 1857.
35. OIOC P.145.72 (BJP 10 Sept. 1857): Tucker to Young, 22 Aug. 1857.
36. OIOC P.234.46 (NWPJC 21 Oct – 22 Nov. 1858): Report of cases tried by the magistrate of Bareilly invested with the power of special commissioner under Acts IX, XIV of 1857; *Bengal Hurkaru*, 13 July 1857.
37. Kaye and Malleson, *vol. II*, 275.
38. Rag, '1858', 124-5.
39. OIOC P.235.7 (NWPJP 1 – 18 Oct. 1859): Thornhill to Couper, 8 July 1859; Littledale, Officiating Judge Arrah, to Young, 7 Aug. 1857, cited in PP 1857-58 (2316): Papers relative to mutinies in East Indies: Appendix B..
40. OIOC P.188.46 (IPC 14 Aug. 1857): Mouat to Young, 4 Aug. 1857, enc. James Mooney, Jailer Hazaribagh Penitentiary, to Mouat, 4 Aug. 1857.
41. Choudhury, *1857 in Bihar*, 38.
42. OIOC P.145.72 (BJC 10 Sept. 1857): G.F. Cockburn, Superintendent Tributary Mehals, to Young, 26 Aug. 1857. On the Sahi brothers, see Ratanlal Joshi, *The Martyrs*, Bombay, Udbodhak Granthmala, 1994, 66-9. On rebellion in Chota Nagpur more broadly, see Roy Choudhury, *1857 in Bihar*.
43. OIOC P.146.1 (BJC 15 Oct. 1857): R.J. Leigh, Senior Assistant Commissioner Sambalpur, to Dalton, 2 Oct. 1857.

44. Mukherjee, *Awadh in Revolt*, 140-2.
45. Commissioner Allahabad to R. Strachey, Secretary to Government Central Provinces, 31 Oct. 1857, cited in PP 1857-58 (2449): Papers relative to mutinies in East Indies. See also OIOC P.235.3 (NWPJP 18 – 31 Aug. 1859): F.O. Mayne, Magistrate Banda, to Thornhill, 26 July 1859.
46. *Ibid.*: E. Grey, Assistant Magistrate Govindpur, to Young, 8 Aug. 1857. Also cited in PP 1857-58 (2316): Papers relative to mutinies in East Indies: Appendix B.
47. OIOC P.146.3 (BJC 12 Nov. 1857): Dalton to Young, 25 Oct. 1857; OIOC P.146.4 (BJC 26 Nov. 1857): J.S. Davies, Senior Assistant Commissioner Manbhum, to Buckland, 14 Nov. 1857.
48. OIOC P.146.3 (BJC 12 Nov. 1857): Young to Dalton, 10 Sept. 1857. See also Singh, 'The Tribals', 77-81.
49. OIOC P.145.72 (BJC 10 Sept. 1857): Dalton to Young, 1 Aug. 1857; J. Simpson, Principal Assistant Commissioner Hazaribagh, to Young, 3 Aug. 1857.
50. OIOC P.188.46 (IPC 14 Aug. 1857): Mouat to Young, 4 Aug. 1857; Mooney to Mouat, 4 Aug. 1857 (quote). Also cited in PP 1857-58 (2316): Papers relative to mutinies in East Indies: Appendix B.
51. *Bengal Hurkaru*, 31 Aug., 9 Sept. 1857.
52. OIOC P.188.55 (IPC 16 July 1858): Young, for information, 30 June 1858; Mouat's report 1858-9, 9.
53. OIOC P.188.55 (IPC 30 July 1858): A. Money, Magistrate Behar, to Young, 17 June 1858.
54. OIOC P.188.47 (IPC 13 Nov. 1857): Fergusson to Young, 5 Nov. 1857.
55. H.C. Wake, Commissioner Patna, to Young, 8 July 1857, cited in PP 1857-58 (2302): Papers relative to mutinies in East Indies: Appendix A.
56. Mukherjee, *Awadh in Revolt*, 167.
57. OIOC P.234.34 (NWPJC Jan. – Feb. 1858): H.P. Fane, Magistrate Benares, to W. Edwards, Session Judge Benares, 10 Feb. 1858; Muir to Edwards, 20 Feb. 1858.
58. Ranajit Guha, 'The Prose of Counter-Insurgency', in Ranajit Guha (ed.), *Subaltern Studies II: Writings on South Asian History and Society*, New Delhi, Oxford University Press, 1983, 1-42.
59. Charles Ball, *A History of the Indian Mutiny: giving a detailed account of the Sepoy insurrection in India; and a concise history of the great military events which have tended to consolidate British empire in Hindostan, vol. I*, London, London Printing and Publishing Co., 1858, 57, 60.
60. T.R.E. Rice, *A History of the Indian Mutiny*, London, W.H. Allen, 1885, 99.
61. Bengal narrative of events, 19 Sept. 1857, cited in PP 1857-8 (2295): Papers relative to mutinies in East Indies: Appendix.
62. John James Halls, *Two Months in Arrah in 1857*, London, Longman, Green, Longman, and Roberts, 1860, 80.
63. Mark Thornhill, *The Personal Adventures and Experiences of a Magistrate during the Rise, Progress and Suppression of the Indian Mutiny*, London, John Murray, 1884, 144-57, 195-6 (quotes 146, 147).
64. Padamsee, *Representations*, 131.
65. Thornhill, *The Personal Adventures*, 148.
66. *Ibid.*, 86.
67. *Bengal Hurkaru*, 8 Sept. 1857.
68. P.H.K. Dewool, Commanding Thirty-Fourth Regiment Native Infantry, to Assistant Adjutant-General, Barrackpore, 24 Nov. 1857, cited in PP 1857-58 (2330): Papers relative to mutinies East Indies: Appendix B.

69. OIOC P.146.5 (BJC 3 – 10 Dec. 1857): Magistrate Chittagong to Young, 19 Nov. 1857; OIOC P.146.7 (BJC 24 Dec. 1857): Mouat to Buckland, 18 Dec. 1857, enc. list of prisoners released and captured with the value of the property carried off.

70. OIOC P.146.10 (BJC 31 Dec. 1857): H. Metcalfe, Judge Tripura, to Buckland, 23 Nov. 1857.

71. OIOC P.146.6 (BJC 10 – 17 Dec. 1857): Metcalfe to Buckland, 27 Nov. 1857.

72. *Bengal Hurkaru*, 18 Sept. 1857.

73. OIOC P.188.49 (IJC 19 Feb. 1858): Persico to C. Beadon, Secretary to Government of India, 30 Oct. 1857. Also at OIOC P.234.34 (NWPJC Jan. – Feb. 1858).

74. *Bengal Hurkaru*, 28 July 1857; Husain, 'Fazle', 360.

75. Abstract translation of a petition from Saeed Mahomed Buksh, Darogah of the Thannah at Aurrungabad, in Behar, to the Government, 5 Aug. 1857, cited in PP 1857-58 (2316): Papers relative to mutinies in East Indies: Appendix B.

76. G.F. Cockburn, Commisioner Cuttack, to Young, cited in PP 1857-58 (2449): Papers relative to mutinies in East Indies.

77. OIOC P.145.73 (BJC 17 Sept. 1857): E.H. Lushington, Officiating Commissioner Burdwan, 28 Aug. 1847; OIOC P.146.12G (BJC 18 Feb. 1858): Lushington to Young, 23 Nov. 1857; Bengal special narrative of events, 8 Feb. 1858, cited in PP 1857-58 (2449): Papers relative to mutinies in East Indies.

78. OIOC P.145.75 (BJC 1 Oct. 1857): Petition of Moharajah Chucker Ahur Sing Deo Bahadoor, *Zemindar* of Pergunnah Sree Killa, 1 Sept. 1857.

79. OIOC P.146.1 (BJC 15 Oct. 1857): R.C. Birch, Senior Assistant Commissioner Chaibasa, to Mouat, 19 Sept. 1857; OIOC P.146.1 (BJC 22 Oct. 1857): Birch to Young, 3 Oct. 1857.

80. OIOC P.146.4 (BJC 19 Nov. 1857): G.N. Oakes, Principal Assistant Commissioner Manbhum, to Dalton, 31 Oct. 1857.

81. OIOC P.234.43 (NWPJC 6 - 31 Aug. 1858): J.P. Walker, Superintendent Agra Jail, to Thornhill, 17 July 1858.

82. Thornhill, *The Personal Adventures*, 146. See also William Edwards, *Personal Adventures During the Indian Rebellion in Rohilcund, Futtehghur, and Oude*, London, Smith, Elder, and Co., 1858, 41.

83. On the significance of rumours see Guha, *Elementary Aspects*, 251-68.

84. OIOC P.234.47 (NWPJC Dec. 1857): Statement of F.O. Mayne, Special Commissioner Banda. See also Roy, *The Politics of a Popular Uprising*, 218-9, 255, 257.

85. 'Translation of a statement made in Ooryah before the Tehseeldar of Boad on September 22 1857, by Ram Mahanty, and two other persons', cited in PP 1857-58 (2363): Papers relative to mutinies in East Indies: Appendix B.

86. C.B. Saunders, Magistrate and Collector Moradabad, to Thornhill, n.d. (June 1857), cited in PP 1857-58 (2294): Papers relative to mutinies in East Indies: Appendix.

87. Temple to Edmonstone, 25 May 1858, cited in PP 1859 Session I (238): Papers relating to mutiny in Punjab, 1857.

88. Charles Raikes, *Notes on the Revolt in the North-Western Provinces of India*, London, Longman, Brown, Green, Longmans and Roberts, 1858, 149.

89. OIOC P.188.47 (IPC 13 Nov. 1857): Fergusson to Young, 5 Nov. 1857.

90. Macdonnell to Young, 13 June 1857; Rajshahye Memorandum, 2 July 1857, cited in PP 1857-58 (2302): Papers relative to mutinies in East Indies: Appendix A.

91. Strachey to Magistrates Jaunpur and Azamghar, 28 Nov. 1857, cited in PP 1857-58 (2363): Papers relative to mutinies in East Indies: Appendix B.

92. Stokes, *The Peasant Armed*, 179.

93. J.R. Colvin, Lieutenant-Governor North-West Provinces, to Brigadier-General Havelock, 22 July 1857, cited in PP 1857-58 (2294): Papers relative to mutinies in East Indies: Appendix.

94. Temple to Edmonstone, 25 May 1858, cited in PP 1859 Session I (238): Papers relating to mutiny in Punjab, 1857.

95. OIOC P.145.73 (BJC 17 Sept. 1857): Samuells to Young, 12 Aug. 1857.

96. *Ibid.*: Beadon to Young, 28 Aug. 1857.

97. *Ibid.*: Buckland to Mouat, 1 Sept. 1857.

98. Kaye and Malleson, *vol. I*, 141-5 (quote 142).

99. Extract from 'The Ballad of Kunwar Singh', in Joshi, '1857 in Folk Songs', 271-87. *Thana* = police station.

100. S.H.C. Tayler, Officiating Magistrate Behar, to Young, 11 June 1857, cited in PP 1857-58 (2302): Papers relative to mutinies in East Indies: Appendix A.

101. Though it is briefly referred to in some nineteenth-century accounts, including Robert Montgomery Martin, *The Indian Empire: history, topography, geology, ... government, finance, and commerce. With a full account of the Mutiny of the Bengal Army, vol. III*, London, London Printing and Publishing Co., 1858-61, 180; Frederick Roberts, *An Eye Witness Account of the Indian Mutiny*, New Delhi, Mittal Publications, 1983 (first published 1896), 232-3.

102. Roberts, *An Eye Witness Account*, 232-3.

103. This is perhaps reflected in the inclusion of jail administration as a cause of the revolt in *FSUP I*, 257-64.

104. Fazl-i-Haq Khairabadi, *Saurat-ul-Hindya*, cited in *FSUP I*, 489. See also Haq, 'The Story', 28-9; Husain, 'Fazle Haq', 358-9.

105. Postscript of a letter from Musseh-oos-Zuman to Peer Ali Khan, n.d. (prob. 1856), cited in PP 1857-58 (2316): Papers relative to mutinies in East Indies: Appendix B.

106. Yang, 'Disciplining "Natives"', 36.

107. Khan, *The Causes of the Indian Revolt*, I.12.

108. Proclamation of Khan Bahadur Khan, n.d. (forwarded in correspondence dated Mar. 1858), cited in *FSUP I*, 442-4 (quotes 442-3, 443). On bone dust rumours, see *FSUP I*, 395-7.

109. It is perhaps a matter of some irony that in order to prevent the rumoured construction of a shrine over his body, the officer overseeing Khan Bahadur Khan's trial decided that after he was hanged he would be buried in Bareilly jail. H.R. Clarke, Joint Magistrate Bareilly, to W. Roberts, President of Special Commission for the trial of Khan Bahadur, 26 Mar. 1860, cited in *FSUP V*, 614-5.

110. Prohibition of Cow Sacrifice by Bahadur Shah, 28 July 1857, cited in *FSUP I*, 421-2.

111. 'A few words relative to the late Mutiny'.

112. *Ibid.*

113. Mouat's report, 1856-7, 7, 10, 52, 71, 72, 79.

114. OIOC P.145.27 (BJC 27 Dec. 1855): Sessions Judge Hughli to Russell, 28 Nov. 1855.

115. OIOC P.145.42 (BJC 26 June 1856): Petition of certain prisoners to Grey, 25 Apr. 1856; C. Jenkins, Officiating Magistrate Dhaka, to Mouat, 20 May 1856; Buckland to certain prisoners, 20 June 1856.

116. *FSUP I*, 259-64.

117. OIOC P.145.50 (BJC 30 Oct. 1856): Mouat's circular, 2 Oct. 1856.

118. OIOC P.145.48 (BJC 16 Oct. 1856): Jenkins to Mouat, 4 Sept. 1856. See also

OIOC P.145.19 (20 Sept. 1855): Petition of certain Prisoners in the Burdwan Jail, 17 July 1855.

119. *Bengal Hurkaru*, 8 Aug. 1857.

120. OIOC P.145.46 (BJC 9 July 1857): Mouat to Buckland, 4 Apr. 1857.

121. Anderson, *Legible Bodies*, 122-3.

122. OIOC P.145.52 (BJC 18 Dec. 1856): W. Brodhurst, Officiating Magistrate Behar, to Buckland, 4 Dec. 1856; Buckland to Brodhurst, 13 Dec. 1856.

123. Mouat's report, 1856-7, 10; OIOC P.145.52 (18 Dec. 1856): Brodhurst to Buckland, 4 Dec. 1856.

124. OIOC P.145.65 (BJC 2 July 1857): Mouat to Buckland, 2 Apr. 1857.

125. OIOC P.146.42 (BJP Aug. 1861): N. Chevers, Officiating Inspector-General of Jails, to J.D. Gordon, Junior Secretary to Government Bengal, 24 July 1861.

126. OIOC P.145.64 (BJC 25 June 1857): Mouat to Buckland, 3 Apr. 1857; Buckland to Mouat, 22 Apr. 1857.

127. OIOC P.145.65 (BJC 2 July 1857): Mouat to Buckland, 24 Mar. 1857; Buckland to Mouat, 2 May 1857.

128. E.H. Lushington, Officiating Magistrate Midnapur, to Beadon, 4, 8 June 1857; Beadon to Lushington, 6 June 1857; Young to Lushington, 11 June 1857, cited in PP 1857-58 (2302): Papers relative to mutinies in East Indies: Appendix A.

129. *Bengal Hurkaru*, 18 Sept. 1857. The breaking of Allahabad jail was reported in the *Illustrated London News*. See Peters, "'Double-dyed Traitors'", 127.

130. OIOC P.146.1 (BJC 22 Oct. 1857): E.H. Lushington, Officiating Assistant Secretary to Government Bengal, to Mouat, 4 Aug. 1857; Buckland to Mouat, 22 Sept. 1857.

131. OIOC P.145.64 (BJC 25 June 1857): Buckland to Mouat, 31 Jan. 1857.

132. OIOC P.146.1 (BJC 22 Oct. 1857): Mouat to Buckland, 30 Sept. 1857.

133. *Ibid.*: Buckland to Mouat, 19 Oct. 1857. On post-mortems in jails, see also David Arnold, *Colonizing the Body: State Medicine and Epidemic Disease in Nineteenth-Century India*, Berkeley, University of California Press, 1993, 5-6.

134. OIOC P.145.75 (BJC 8 Oct. 1857): Mouat to R.N. Shore, Magistrate Cuttack, 15 Sept. 1857.

135. OIOC P.234.37 (NWPJC Apr. 1858): Thornhill to Muir, 22 Mar. 1858.

136. OIOC P.145.74 (BJC 24 Sept. 1857): Mouat to Buckland, 8 Sept. 1857.

137. Mouat's report, 1855-6, Appendix I, ix-xi (circular no. 32, 31 Dec. 1855).

138. OIOC P.234.36 (NWPJC 15 - 31 Mar. 1858): Edwards to Muir, 26 Feb. 1858.

139. OIOC P.234.37 (NWPJC Apr. 1858): Thornhill to Muir, 22 Mar. 1858.

140. Mouat's report, 1855-6, 17.

141. Mouat's report, 1856-7, 7.

142. OIOC P.145.64 (BJC 25 June 1857): Mouat to Buckland, 27 Mar. 1857.

143. OIOC P.146.1 (BJC 15 Oct. 1857): Birch to Mouat, 19 Sept. 1857.

144. G.H.M. Ricketts, Late Deputy Commissioner Ludhiana, to G.C. Barnes, Commissioner and Superintendent Cis-Sutlej States, 22 Feb. 1858, cited in PP 1859 Session I (238): Papers relating to mutiny in Punjab, 1857.

145. OIOC P.234.41 (NWPJC 1 – 26 July 1858): A. Shakespear, Magistrate Bijnor, to Thornhill, 3 July 1858.

146. *Bengal Hurkaru*, 13 July 1857; OIOC P.188.55 (IPC 2 July 1858): Young to Money, 25 June 1858.

147. OIOC P.235.7 (NWPJP 1 – 18 Oct. 1859): Thornhill to Couper, 8 July 1859.

148. North-West Provinces Narrative of Events, 25 June 1858, cited in cited in PP 1857-58 (2448): Papers relative to mutinies in East Indies.

149. F.M. Bird, Joint Magistrate Azamgarh, to Strachey, 18 Nov. 1857, cited in PP
     1857-58 (2449): Papers relative to mutinies in East Indies.

150. OIOC P.235.7 (NWPJP 1 – 18 Oct. 1859): Thornhill to Couper, 8 July 1859.

151. OIOC P.235.6 (NWPJP 17 – 30 Sept. 1859): Register of trials held during the
     month of October 1858.

152. Bengal Narrative of Events, 15 Aug. 1857, cited in PP 1857–8 (2295): Papers
     relative to mutinies in East Indies: Appendix.

153. OIOC P.206.61 (IJP 18 Feb. 1859): Court to Chester, 20 Oct. 1857.

154. OIOC P.188.48 (IPC 8 Jan. 1858): Fergusson to Young, 28 Nov. 1857.

155. OIOC P.146.12K (BJC 18 Mar. 1858): Memorandum of E. Latour,
     Commissioner Baraset, n.d.

156. Roy, *The Politics of a Popular Uprising*, 49.

157. Mouat's report, 1858-9, 55.

158. OIOC P.234.35 (NWPJC 1 - 15 Mar. 1858): Thornhill to Bayley, 4 Mar. 1858;
     OIOC P.206.62 (IJP 13 July 1860): Walker's Memorandum, 3 July 1860; Colvin,
     30 June 1857, cited in PP 1857-58 (2294): Papers relative to mutinies in East
     Indies: Appendix.

159. OIOC P.234.37 (NWPJC Apr. 1858): Thornhill to Muir, 22 Mar. 1858.

160. OIOC P.234.34 (NWPJC Jan – Feb. 1858): Fane to Edward, 20 Feb. 1858.

161. OIOC P.234.41 (NWPJC 14 June 1858): F.B. Gubbins, Commissioner Benares, to
     Muir, 2 June 1858.

162. OIOC P.234.41 (NWPJC 1 - 6 July 1858): Bayley to Gubbins, 10 July 1858.

163. Forbes to Samuells, 9 Nov. 1857, cited in PP 1857-58 (2449): Papers relative to
     mutinies in East Indies.

164. 'Narrative of Munshi Jeewan Lál', in Charles Theophilus Metcalfe, *Two Native
     Narratives of the Mutiny in Delhi, translated from the originals*, Westminster, Archibald
     Constable and Co., 1898, 84.

165. Mouat's report, 1858-9, 12.

166. OIOC P.234.43 (NWPJC 6 - 31 Aug. 1858): W. Nembhard, Deputy
     Commissioner Jubbulpur, to Thornhill, 17 July 1858.

167. OIOC P.188.55 (IPC 2 July 1858): Young to Money, 25 June 1858.

168. OIOC P.235.7 (NWPJP 1 – 18 Oct. 1859): Thornhill to Couper, 8 July 1859.

169. OIOC P.206.60 (IJC 19 Nov. 1858): Rules for the military guards in the jails of the
     Lower Provinces, 26 Oct. 1858. See also Mouat's report, 1858-9, Circular Orders,
     26 Oct. 1858.

170. For instance, Bengal narrative of events, 25 Aug. 1857, cited in PP 1857–8 (2295):
     Papers relative to mutinies in East Indies: Appendix; Bengal narrative of events, 10
     Oct. 1857, cited in PP 1857-58 (2363): Papers relative to mutinies in East Indies:
     Appendix B.

171. John Lang, *Wanderings in India* (1859), cited in *FSUP I*, 410.

172. Macdonnell to Young, 13 June 1857, cited in PP 1857-58 (2302): Papers relative to
     mutinies in East Indies: Appendix A.

173. OIOC P.188.49 (IJC 8 Jan 1858): F. Williams, Commissioner Meerut, to
     Thornhill, 12 Oct. 1857.

174. *Ibid.*: Thornhill to H. Dashwood, Register *Nizamut Adalat*, 29 Oct. 1857.

175. *Ibid.*: Dashwood to Thornhill, 6 Nov. 1857.

176. *Ibid.*: Thornhill to Dashwood, 18 Nov. 1857.

177. *Ibid.*: J.W. Dalrymple, Under Secretary to Government of India, to Thornhill, 31
     Dec. 1857.

178. OIOC P.146.12G (BJC 18 Feb. 1858): Act V (An act for the punishment of certain

offenders who have escaped from jail and of persons who shall knowingly harbour such offenders), 29 Jan. 1858.

179. OIOC P.234.36 (NWPJC 15 - 31 Mar. 1858): F.B. Pearson, Officiating Session Judge Benares, to Strachey, 26 Jan. 1858.

180. OIOC P.234.35 (NWPJC 1 - 15 Mar. 1858): C. Wingfield, Commissioner Gorakhpur, to Muir, 12 Feb. 1858.

181. *Ibid.:* Memorandum of Bayley, 3 Mar. 1858.

182. *Ibid.*

183. OIOC P.234.36 (NWPJC 15 - 31 Mar. 1858): R. Money, Officiating Session Judge Fatehpur, to Strachey, 26 Jan. 1858.

184. *Ibid.:* A. Ross, Officiating Session Judge Ghazipur, to Strachey, 9 Feb. 1858.

185. *Ibid.:* Wingfield to Strachey, 27 Jan. 1858.

186. *Ibid.:* Muir to Dashwood, 16 Mar. 1858.

187. OIOC P.234.37 (NWPJC Apr. 1858): Thornhill to Dashwood, 18 Mar. 1858.

188. *Ibid.:* H.G. Astell, Judge Jaunpur, to Strachey, 26 Jan. 1858.

189. OIOC P.145.73 (BJC 17 Sept. 1857): Samuells to Young, 12 Aug. 1857; Mouat to Buckland, 31 Aug; 1857.

190. OIOC P.146.6 (BJC 10 – 17 Dec. 1857): Metcalfe to P. Chapman, Officiating Commissioner Sixteenth Division, n.d.; Metcalfe to Buckland, 27 Nov. 1857.

191. OIOC P.206.62 (NWPJP 18 Nov. 1859): Mayne to Thornhill, 11 Aug. 1859; Bayley, Officiating Commissioner Allahabad, to Muir, 17 Aug. 1859.

192. OIOC P.206.60 (IJC 20 Sept. 1858): Edmonstone to Beadon, 20 Sept. 1858.

193. OIOC P.206.62 (IJP 27 Aug. 1860): Grey to Couper and Thompson, 27 Aug. 1860.

194. *Ibid.*: Couper to Beadon, 27 Apr. 1860.

195. *Ibid.*: Thornton to Davies, 9 Nov. 1860.

196. OIOC P.146.28 (BJP [jails] June 1860): Mouat to Thompson, 1 June 1859, enc. Statement shewing the number of prisoners who escaped during the Mutiny of 1857, and are still at large.

197. *Bengal Hurkaru*, 27 Aug. 1857.

198. Mouat, 'On Prison Discipline', 44.

199. Powell, *Muslims and Missionaries*, 291-2.

200. Carter, *Servants, Sirdars and Settlers*, 27.

201. PP 1875 (24): Mauritius (Treatment of Immigrants), Report of the Royal Commissioners appointed to inquire into the Treatment of Immigrants in Mauritius, 1875 (visits to Mon Choix and L'Union estates, 9 and 26 Sept. 1872). (I thank Marina Carter for this reference).

202. George K. Alapatt, 'The Sepoy Mutiny of 1857: Indian Indentured Labour and Plantation Politics in British Guiana', *Journal of Indian History*, 59, 1-3 (1981), 309-12 (quotes 311, 312).

CHAPTER 4
PENAL CRISIS IN THE AFTERMATH OF REVOLT

Introduction

The revolt in the North-West Provinces, Bengal, and the Panjab left the government with a serious problem: where to put recaptured and surrendered prisoners, and the increasing number of new offenders convicted by the special commissioners for crimes associated with the revolt. As we have seen, rebels damaged or destroyed many jails. In addition, government often converted those that remained intact into military barracks, necessitating structural changes such as the pulling down of outbuildings and walls.[1] As well as the difficulties caused by the lack of accommodation for prisoners, the mass desertion of prison guards in some areas meant that their security could not be guaranteed. There were few if any European soldiers to spare to ease the shortage. Further, hundreds of prisoners had been sentenced to transportation overseas, but there was no means of forwarding them from the districts to the holding jail at Alipur. The river steamers usually employed for the purpose were busy carrying European officers, civilians, and wounded soldiers.[2]

This chapter will explore the development of a penal crisis in the aftermath of the revolt. District magistrates made a series of pleas for a solution to the many problems they faced, but in the short term there were only limited options. Especially in the North-West Provinces, jails needed major repairs, complete rebuilding or new sets of prison guards. An uneasy attempt to deal with the lack of jail accommodation came with the transfer of large numbers of prisoners to more secure jails, notably Alipur in the Bengal Presidency. As we will see in the pages that follow, this policy sometimes had devastating consequences for prison death-rates, and almost certainly contributed to the extraordinarily high levels evident during 1857-9. It also hastened the spread of news, and often instability, between the districts. The movement of prisoners between jails was therefore not a solution to the issue of jail accommodation, either in the short or in the long term.

Provoked by plans drawn up by the commissioner of Patna to ease jail overcrowding, in August 1857 the Bengal government decided to transfer all prisoners sentenced to more than three years' imprisonment to its penal settlements in the Straits. Those sentenced to a term of years would go to Melaka and those sentenced to life to either Pinang or Singapore. The decision caused an outcry in the Straits, and with only an Indian garrison to rely on the government there refused to accept what it saw as the most dangerous class of prisoners in all India. The authorities in the Tenasserim Provinces in Burma, another destination for India's transportation convicts, also approached the issue of receiving prisoners from India with some trepidation. Though eventually the Tenasserim Provinces agreed to accept convicts, the Straits did not, and its penal settlements were eventually closed off altogether. Given the relatively large number of prisoners sentenced to terms of imprisonment or transportation in the aftermath of 1857–8, this decision had a profound impact on jail overcrowding, especially in the holding prison at Alipur.

Two years before the mutiny-rebellion broke out, the East India Company's court of directors instructed the governor-general to consider the resettlement of the Andaman Islands. An earlier attempt to establish a penal settlement there in 1793 had failed, for it was devastated by disease (even the surgeon succumbed). The British withdrew in 1796 and transferred the surviving convicts to Pinang.[3] In 1855, the government of India expressed interest in resettling the Andamans, though the policy decision to do so was not taken until 1858. Their location and exceptional harbour made them the perfect choice as a place for the repair of Company ships. Moreover, and for the same reasons, they were safe resorts during naval conflicts. However, their indigenous inhabitants were hostile and in previous years had killed a number of sailors seeking refuge. The British hoped that settlement would ease relations and deter Malay pirates who were active in nearby waters. We will explore British settlement of the Islands as a legacy of the 1857–8 revolt in Chapter 5. In the meantime readers might like to note that continuing uncertainty about the prospects for the transportation system underlay many of the anxieties expressed by penal administrators in north India during 1857–8.

Jail overcrowding and the problem of prisoner transfers

Within a few weeks of the outbreak at Meerut, news of the revolt began to filter back to Britain. At the beginning of 1858, Queen Victoria sent the Swedish artist Egron Lundgren to India, his brief to produce a pictorial record of the mutiny-rebellion. The Queen herself commissioned a number of watercolours, including scenes of temples, bathing *ghats* (riverside steps), elephants, and a *nautch* (dance) in which Lundgren himself appeared.[4] During his trip, Lundgren visited Benares jail. Later, he wrote of the dreadful conditions in the jail hospital, and painted two watercolours of rebel prisoners:

> There were no beds, and these pathetic souls lay almost naked, each on his pile of rags and tatters; all had heavy shackles on their arms and legs, linked together with chains. Most of them were quite emaciated and almost skeleton-like; they suffered from dysentery and many of them, as it seemed to me, were dying. White-haired old men with wrinkled, brown bodies, lay cheek by jowl with youths who seemed quite debilitated, all with these dreadful shining fetters about their wasted limbs.[5]

Lundgren's description differed little from official reports of the day. There is no question that during 1857–8 many north Indian jails, and temporary prison buildings, were overcrowded and full of sick prisoners.

As the number of inmates across north India swelled in the aftermath of mutiny-rebellion, jail administrators looked to prisoner transfers as a means to solve the problem of overcrowding. Between April 1858 and April 1859, almost 12,000 prisoners were transferred to or between jails in Bengal alone, an extraordinarily high number given that the average daily number of prisoners in the presidency that year was just 20,282.[6] The issue of transfer was particularly acute in Alipur, for it was both the holding jail for transportation convicts and the only really secure jail in the Bengal Presidency. As such, and with no counterpart in the North-West Provinces, it received a constant stream of serious offenders from across north India, either for safe custody or transportation overseas. Allahabad central jail had been badly damaged and had no reliable guards. Most had left with the rebels, and officials described those who came back as 'relatives and friends' of the mutineers. The commissioner of the city wrote that to imprison dangerous offenders there would almost certainly lead to another outbreak. Therefore he had no choice but to send them to Alipur.[7] There were real difficulties in recruiting new jail guards. Inspector-General Thornhill reported that in the aftermath of the revolt, the quasi-military associations of jail guarding made it unattractive to potential recruits.[8]

Alipur jail had 71 wards and was capable of holding 2,335 prisoners according to a calculation of 24 superficial square feet per inmate.[9] On the eve of the revolt, the jail held well below this number, 1,721 prisoners.[10] During 1857–8 the capacity of the jail was recalculated to allow for the accommodation of a maximum of 1,307 prisoners. In the aftermath of the rebellion it averaged a population of 1,895, the most prisoners it had ever received during a single year.[11] Invariably, a general lack of organization characterized the running of the prisons at this administratively chaotic time. Alipur seems to have suffered particularly in this respect. Often it received prisoners for transportation without prior warning or accompanying warrants, and paperwork that was full of errors.[12] Given the widespread destruction of jail records, this was hardly surprising.

In September 1857, in a bid to reduce numbers, the Bengal authorities authorized the transfer of 250 Alipur prisoners to Hughli, Baraset, and Burdwan jails. As we will see in a moment, though the Straits government had by this time refused to receive further transportation convicts, the Indian authorities shipped a hundred more to the Company settlement at Arakan. This eased overcrowding to some extent, though Mouat suggested also that old infirm prisoners in the jail be set free. They were no doubt heinous offenders, he wrote, but they occupied space required for new prisoners, and were too feeble to commit further crimes. The lieutenant-governor refused to sanction Mouat's request, instead ordering the transfer of aged and infirm prisoners to Howrah.[13] Within just two months, once again Alipur jail was full to the brim, and fears of an outbreak were foremost in the superintendent's mind.[14] The situation worsened as the jail's upper storey underwent repairs and seven of the wards had to be emptied.[15] Although by mid-1858 the Andaman Islands had been opened up as a penal settlement, so easing the situation in Alipur to some extent, prison overcrowding more generally continued in the immediate aftermath of the revolt, particularly in regions that remained unstable. As disturbances continued in the Chota Nagpur district through 1858-9, for instance, prisons became especially full. Mouat's 1859 inspection report of Manbhum noted that it was 'disastrously overcrowded'.[16]

Although rebels attacked prisons in the North-West Provinces most, because so many prisoners escaped from custody the problem of jail accommodation was far less acute than in Bengal, at least in the short term. It was only when the special commissioners began to try mutineers and rebels as the rebellion subsided that the issue of what to do with prisoners arose. In February 1858, for example, the authorities decided to transfer all life prisoners in Kanpur to Benares, which was then secure.[17] Later that year, under Act XI of 1858, they flogged and then released unconditionally misdemeanant prisoners in Sagar jail.[18] Indeed, the very basis of Act XI was to prevent the jails being crowded with petty offenders.[19] By this time, the authorities in the North-West Provinces were so desperate for jail accommodation that they placed prisoners in tombs, *serais* (temporary buildings for travellers and livestock), and an old lunatic asylum.[20] A *hammam* (bathhouse) near Allahabad was even adapted as a prison.[21]

Prisoners sentenced to transportation often spent months in jail awaiting shipment, often in appalling conditions. Prisoners of high social standing, who made up a higher than usual proportion of prisoners in the aftermath of revolt, felt the deprivations incarceration implied especially acutely. Transported rebel Fazl-i-Haq recorded his 'grief and pain' at substituting his life of plenty and ease for a life of shame, embarrassment, and loss of honour. He recorded his horror at being made to wear prison clothes and sleep on bedding as coarse as 'thorn-bush or a burning ember'. His jailers did not give him a *lota*, the food rations were paltry, and the drinking water warm. 'In spite of old age and weakness every moment I was subjected to humiliation and insults,' he wrote.[22] Munir Shikohabadi described in great detail the physical suffering, mental anguish, and cultural transgressions suffered by men of rank:

The story of my prison term
Will cause my lips to drip with blood.

So many hardships I endured
Through fate's decree in Banda jail.

My cell was dark and like a grave
Still tighter than a fetter's link.

For urine and for excrement
I had a pigsty by my bed ...

... I lacked all means to cleanse myself
So how could I perform my prayers?

My pain from lack of opium
Surpass all my powers to tell.

The harshness of my fate was worse
Than even a non-Muslim's death.

We lived on curses or on wounds[23]
For that was all fate's kitchen stocked.

The bread resembled cakes of dung
Wheat-bread was rare as elixir.

For vegetables we fed on grass
As dry as rust upon a sword.

Far worse than feed for buffaloes
The *dhal* was hard as beads on chains,

Bad-smelling, gritty, tasteless, foul
And colder than an old man's heart.

I slept on sackcloth, while my rug
Was warmer than a Kashmir shawl.

The cell was hotter still than hell
And made my limbs burn up like fire.

We shivered in the winter's cold
Just like Kashmiris with no clothes.

The toil, suffering and pain
Were greater than can be described.[24]

These verses confirm other contemporary accounts of jail conditions. They also raise the interesting issue of the effect of opium withdrawal endured by many prisoners of high status in jail. Given contemporary statistics from the Andamans penal colony (Table 7), Munir's habitual use of the drug seems to have been typical.

Here we will dwell for a moment on the differential effect of punishment on prisoners of high status. Munir's verses raise the spectre of the effects of the social inversion such prisoners faced in jail. Prison guards, he claimed, were deliberately cruel to high-born or educated men. His perspective mirrored that of colonial administrators at the time who complained unrelentingly about the problems of managing unreliable and corrupt jail guards. The poem continued:

No fault was needed to arouse
The hostile guards who staffed that hell

The learned and the nobly born
Were picked for special cruelty.

Sadistic, shameless, false they were
Abusing all within their power.

Their lips had learnt the cruel art
Of wounding from the blades of swords.

Unmatched in trickery and thuggery
They left us nothing, even life.[25]

Munir next documented his transfer from Banda to Allahabad central jail, followed by his chain gang (*challan*) march to Calcutta. He found this public spectacle a humiliating experience. Inverting the usual metaphors for penal transportation, Munir saw his voyage to the Andaman Islands not as a penalty but as a chance to escape the indignities of imprisonment. Indeed, he dated his poem using the chronogram (*tarikh*)[26] 'safe rescue from the house of chains':

My hardships in Allahabad
Surpass all my descriptive powers.

To Calcutta then I marched on foot
Stumbling with the chains I wore.

With handcuffed wrists and fettered legs
I looked as weak as fabled Qais.[27]

I suffered much upon the way
From those whom fate put in my path.

Unconscious, naked, with no home
I found myself in fate's harsh grip.

So from the west I was brought east
Paraded as a criminal.

An image taken of me showed
My face grown pale in black and white.[28]

My time in jail was ended when
To *Kala Pani* I was sent.[29]

This last verse is extremely significant in the aftermath of a revolt which some believed was a war of religion, for '*kala pani*' – literally translated as 'black water' – was a metaphor for the apparent religious or caste transgressions experienced by convicts of high caste or status when they travelled across the sea. Commonly, colonial officials believed that it was this which made transportation so terrifying for Indians, a theme we will explore further in the chapter that follows.

During the crisis that spread across north India during 1857–8, death-rates rocketed. It is difficult to estimate precisely how the devastation and displacement, not to mention the British military response to mutiny and rebel activity, affected local demography. Nevertheless, as we have seen in correspondence about the fate of escaped prisoners in the districts, it was accepted generally that given the precarious social and economic conditions, many if not most had died. There had been famine in the same regions during 1856, and a cholera epidemic was only just subsiding. The events of 1857–8 therefore hit some communities particularly hard. Mouat later wrote that though there were no reliable statistics on health and mortality among the north Indian population, fatal epidemics of cholera and fever 'traversed the length and breadth of the land in that year'.[30] Figures available for the British army are a useful indicator of the extent of the problem. Of the 9,467 deaths of British soldiers, only 586 men died in combat or from their wounds. The rest died from disease.[31]

From the beginning of the century to the 1860s, prison mortality in specific jails not infrequently reached 25 per cent per annum. Famines and food shortages affected death-rates, for rural crime went up with the rise in grain prices and unemployment, jails became overcrowded, and disease broke out among prison communities already on the verge of starvation. The main causes of death were cholera, malaria, dysentery, and diarrhoea. In a couple of exceptional cases, more than half of all prisoners died during a single year. The situation did not really improve until the end of the nineteenth century.[32]

Prisons experienced appalling death-rates in the aftermath of revolt. The death-rate in Delhi jail during 1858 was a phenomenal 26.23 per cent, three times the previous average. Inspector-General of Prisons in the Panjab C. Hathaway put the figures down to prisoners' 'previous confinement, exposure, or hardships, or possibly fear of capital punishment'.[33] Another prison administrator wrote of 'the re-action that generally supervenes on long-continued excitement'.[34] A series of epidemics swept across the North-West Provinces during the first half of 1860. Agra jail was so badly affected by cholera that 654 prisoners out of a total jail population of 5723 died. Inspector-General of Prisons Stewart Clark put the outbreak down to the admission of sick prisoners from the jungles of Nepal, to which numbers of mutineer-rebels had fled, the 'wretched condition' of many others, and poor quality and badly ventilated temporary prison accommodation.[35] In 1861, death-rates across the North-West Provinces hit 10.73 per cent, the highest figure ever. An unprecedented 50 per cent of the prisoners admitted to Meerut jail during 1861 died. Clark reported that outside Agra, Meerut, and Allahabad central prisons jail discipline had almost completely broken down. Prisoners were no longer classified, and most were working and sleeping some distance from the jails. A further factor was the 'superior class' of mutineer-rebel prisoners who had been accustomed to comfortable living and plentiful food. In Allahabad central jail, mortality was the highest among such men sentenced to transportation: in 1861 six per cent during an average stay of just 67.7 days.[36]

A key factor in prisoner mortality was employment, for prisoners working outdoors suffered from much higher death-rates than those working indoors.[37] In 1856, for instance, rates among Bengal prisoners working on the roads were 17.4 per cent, in indoor manufactures 10.25 per cent, and as jail servants 7.06 per cent. Rates among women were much lower, 4.62 per cent.[38] The civil assistant surgeon of Alipur jail hospital explained this gender differential through reference to the apparent ease with which they bore restraint: 'their life being one of bondage, they do not feel the deprivation of liberty as men are wont to do'.[39] More substantively, of course, women were not put to work at outdoor labour. The length of time a prisoner had spent in jail was also a factor in mortality statistics. Mouat reported that more than a quarter of deaths occurred among prisoners who had been in jail for less than three months. He reasoned that this was either because they were sickly on admission or because they succumbed to epidemics more quickly than prisoners who had been in jail for some time. A further factor in the opinion of some prison medical officers was religion, with Hindus said to be more likely to die in jail than Muslims. Finally, *adivasi* communities like Santals suffered the worst rates.[40] In the aftermath of the 1855 Santal *hul*, for instance, numbers of prisoners perished. Prison officials crammed them into inadequate facilities, did not give them warm clothing or blankets, and banned them from lighting fires. Later in 1860 Mouat even suggested that because a sentence of imprisonment was a near death sentence for tribal communities, the 'jungly races' generally should be sent to the new penal settlement in the Andaman Islands rather than be kept in mainland jails.[41]

Though death-rates in Bengal jails varied in the aftermath of the revolt, they were generally elevated. Mouat later wrote that 1858 had been the sickliest of the previous 25 years in Bengal. Between 1849 and 1859, prisoner mortality from cholera and 'ordinary diseases' was on average 8.38 per cent. The rate in 1857 was 12.09 per cent, and in 1858 it was 13.52 per cent.[42] These averages masked some much higher figures. Eighteen per cent of prisoners who were imprisoned in Jubbulpur jail died during 1856, for instance. During the first ten months of 1857 20 per cent suffered the same fate. Administrators put sickness down to the 1856 famine, the cholera epidemic, and overcrowding.[43] The government was keen to transfer inmates to other jails in order to ease problems but, as Mouat wrote in 1859, jail transfers always 'ended unhappily'. When prisoners were moved during the monsoon they tended to fall ill during the journey, and then died soon after their arrival. They also affected the health of other prisoners in their new jail. Although it was not altogether clear that prison sickness was caused by the change in climate, 'extreme depression' often resulted among prisoners who saw removal from their home district as a considerable aggravation of their original sentence. They could not be persuaded to view the transfer as an act of kindness. 'I seldom enter a jail where they do not implore me to send them back again', Mouat wrote, 'declaring that they prefer death in their own Zillahs [districts], to a miserable existence elsewhere.' According to Mouat, the only solution was a system of central imprisonment like that in the North-West Provinces.[44]

The Bengal jail most affected by high mortality during and after the rebellion was Alipur. Indeed, such unprecedented death-rates afflicted that prison during 1858-9 that the government rescinded its August 1858 circular ordering magistrates to transfer there all dangerous characters sentenced to more than three years' imprisonment.[45] Mouat put the appalling conditions down to the influx of up-country prisoners *en route* to the Andamans, many of whom he claimed were unfit to travel. During 1858-9 440 of the 2,011 prisoners passing through the jail died: a massive 21.88 per cent. Hospital gangrene and cholera broke out; Mouat described the prison as little more than a 'pest house'. The prisoners had, he said, affected the health of both Alipur prisoners and convicts by then in the Andamans.[46] Civil Assistant Surgeon H. Baillie expressed the view that many of them would have died in the district jails had they not been sent to Alipur.[47] Although Mouat reported that he hoped that he would never again have to record 'so disastrous a history' as that of 1858 at Alipur,[48] a year later rebel prisoners were still being shipped to the jail for transportation, and they often suffered considerable hardship on the way. The officiating superintendent wrote in April 1859 of a group of 236 convicts from Allahabad: '[T]hey were unwashed apparently for weeks, and it was almost impossible to approach them from the stench that prevailed over the whole mass'.[49] The government of the North-West Provinces promised to tighten up the rules for the transfer of Allahabad convicts to Calcutta for transportation.[50] On closer inspection it is clear that the vast bulk of deaths in Alipur occurred among such transferred men. During 1859 some 10.23 per cent of transfer prisoners died, compared to two per cent of local prisoners. The Bengal government condemned the often 'disgraceful and inhuman' way in which convicts were dispatched for Calcutta.[51]

There was another potential factor concerning jail mortality after 1858, though it is rather more difficult to quantify. Indeed, it takes us beyond raw statistics, and beliefs about propensity to disease, towards a study of the *mentalité* of prisoners, particularly those sentenced during the disturbances of 1857–8. Colonial officials reported that some transportation prisoners were unable to bear the prospect of shipment overseas, and so committed suicide before they were embarked.[52] In 1859, one capitally condemned prisoner had his sentence commuted to transportation, but appealed against the sentence on the grounds that he would rather be hanged.[53] The superintendent of Meerut jail reported the same year how old men 'courted death as a relief from their potential fate.'[54] In part, such anxieties related to cultural fears over sea voyages and the potential ritual transgressions they invoked. However, to be sure, terror of exile to an unknown land was also significant.

The 1858 annual report of the civil assistant surgeon of Alipur jail hospital is also worth quoting at length:

[I]n addition to the physical causes which undermined the constitutions of a large number who were admitted into Hospital, a principal (mental) one ought not to be overlooked, *viz.* the unusual *depression of mind* which was apparent among many, especially those, who had been duped into taking part in the late mutinies, and who, consequently, suffered from all the effects of *remorse*. These men mostly sunk into a listless, torpid state of despondency, become bloated, dropsical, and emaciated to the last degree, refusing food except such as was calculated to increase their maladies. Under such a combination of circumstances, remedies frequently exerted scarcely more than a temporary effect, and in some produced no impression whatever on their diseases.[55]

He noted that *dacoits* too, from their formerly 'irregular life', suffered disproportionately during imprisonment. Baillie's interpretation of the state of mind of mutineers and rebels, notably his belief that many of them were suffering from great remorse, when it might have been frustration, disappointment, anger or what we would today call depression, is somewhat problematic, especially because the prisoners themselves do not speak of their feelings through the archives. However, his report is significant because it provides a first hint towards understanding at least part of the reason for the high death-rates experienced in Alipur, unmentioned by Mouat or any other official. This was prisoners' refusal to eat their rations. It is difficult to say whether their motives were grounded in the protection of caste or status, or whether their actions were a type of co-ordinated hunger strike as seen during the first half of the nineteenth century. Whatever the case, it is difficult to avoid the conclusion that such resistance, whether cultural, coincidental, and/or organized informed high death-rates in the jail, for despite evidence of culturally syncretic practices in other respects, high-caste Hindu prisoners died in greater numbers than other Hindus or Muslims.[56] As we will see in our analysis of the transportation of mutineers and rebels to the penal settlement in Arakan during the same period, the Alipur prisoners were not alone in refusing food. And of course hunger-striking remained an important strategy for political prisoners into the twentieth century.[57]

As well as affecting health and mortality, the transfer of prisoners between districts also had an effect on the trajectory of the revolt itself. Like escaped prisoners, transferred inmates were important carriers of news, and took with them information about the progress of the rebels. With 12,000 on the move between the towns, not to mention the 20,000 on the loose, prisoners were a key element of the information network that both accompanied and fanned the flames of the mutiny-rebellion. Moreover, transferred rebel prisoners carried information into secured jails. In 1858, for instance, two prisoners - Puriag Doobey and Buldeo Doobey (uncle and nephew) - were sent from Arrah to Munger after an escape attempt. They were peasant followers of rebel leader Kuer Sing and contemporary officials described them as 'turbulent characters'. The district magistrate wrote that they and other transferred prisoners had since their arrival 'created an uneasy insubordinate spirit in the jail', and that he had been forced to take measures to separate them from the local prisoners. When British troops left the town in December 1857, they tried to instigate a second outbreak.[58] The two men were tried before the special commissioner for treason. Witnesses recalled how on 22 December, just before the prisoners were being locked up for the night, the two men shouted the war-cry 'muhabeer!', and tried unsuccessfully to encourage the prisoners to break jail and plunder the treasury. The defendants claimed that the other prisoners had asked them to stand up for them against the magistrate and wanted to escape. In a frustratingly limited glimpse into jail life, they used the expression *suwal juwab* (question/answer) and *oozul* (principle) to explain the nature and meaning of their role as intermediaries. The men were found guilty, and sentenced to life transportation.[59]

'A most shameful outrage on public safety':
convicts in the penal settlements

The population of Singapore grew from 16,000 in 1827 to 81,000 in 1860, a fivefold increase. The largest single community was the Chinese, making up some 67 per cent of the total. Although the European population expanded from 94 souls in 1827 to around 500 in 1860 it remained a tiny minority. However, working with Chinese middlemen, Europeans provided most of the trading capital vital to the success of the port. In 1846, half of the merchant houses were British. Singapore served as an *entrepôt* in East India Company trade, but its position was what C.M. Turnbull has described as 'delicate', for trade was subject to extreme boom and slump. Nevertheless, between 1842 and 1857 its value doubled.[60] At this time, the Straits Settlements (as Singapore, Melaka and Pinang were known collectively after 1826) was a residency of the Bengal Presidency, and tensions between Singapore and India − not to mention those between local merchants and government - were often fraught. One of the main problems faced by the Straits, especially Singapore, was the shortage of labour. This explains Singapore's initial enthusiasm about receiving Indian convict workers, the first batch of whom arrived in 1825.

Stephen Nicholas and Peter R. Shergold have estimated that the Straits Settlements together received on average 200 arrivals per year from the three Indian presidencies, making a grand total of 15,000 convicts during its penal era.[61] Probably, this is an underestimate: one contemporary report stated that Singapore alone had received 16,000 convicts by 1858.[62] Convicts were put to work on a variety of public works projects like clearing land, quarrying, road and bridge building, and brick making, with a view to their reformation through industrial training. The convict system was based on the code of rules devised by Governor Butterworth in 1845. The code divided convicts into six classes, and each had varying privileges with regard to money gratuities, fettering, labour, and rations. Convicts could rise or fall through the classes, providing both positive and negative incentives for good behaviour. Women and invalids fell in the sixth class. Fifth-class convicts were those transported for serious offences, and those who had committed further crimes in the settlement. The fourth class consisted of newly arrived convicts, those promoted from the fifth class and those degraded from higher classes. Convicts in the third class were promoted from the fourth class. Second-class convicts worked as peons or convict overseers *(tindals)*. First-class convicts had served 16 years of their sentence and were allowed to live out of the convict lines on a ticket-of-leave.[63] The achievements of transported convicts in the Straits Settlements were certainly impressive.

Indeed, writing of a visit in 1861 Mouat declared that the convict system was superior to that of India or elsewhere. Of St Andrew's cathedral he wrote: '[T]here exists in no other country a more remarkable example of the successful industrial training of convicts.'[64]

As Singapore became more prosperous, however, European merchants began to question the wisdom of continuing convict transportation. In 1851, the *Singapore Free Press* wrote of the Straits as a 'common sewer'. Three years later, it lamented that Singapore held 'the very dregs of the population'.[65] Such concerns were informed partly by worries about the influence on convicts of the so-called Chinese 'secret societies'. They also reflected fears about the type of convicts then being received, notably *thags* who in the view of many officials were a cult of hereditary ritual murderers: the scourges of India.[66] As Turnbull argues, weak government, financial restrictions, 'secret societies', and a large transitory population combined to make Singapore a violent place during the first part of the nineteenth century.[67] At this time, relations between the merchant and governing class were not good, so much so that the former nicknamed Governor W. Butterworth (1843-55) Butterpot the Great. In 1851, the government of India separated the Straits territories from Bengal and put them under the direct charge of the governor-general. The merchant community hoped that this would improve their administration, particularly with relation to much needed improvements to the port. It did not, and by the mid-1850s regular public meetings were called to challenge official policy.

In May 1857, news of the Indian revolt reached the Straits. Earlier that year there had been strikes and riots by Chinese and Indian communities over municipal and police reforms. By August rumours were circulating that the 3,000 Indian convicts then in Singapore were planning an uprising. This coincided with the government of India's request for the Straits to receive an unspecified number of dangerous Alipur prisoners. A few months later, the Singapore merchant community sent a petition to parliament, asking for their separation from India and future direct rule from London. This set in train the transfer of the Straits Settlements to the colonial office, which was completed in 1867.[68]

The 1857 panic in Singapore was composed of two interrelated elements. In a petition to Governor E.A. Blundell, the merchant community questioned the loyalty of the Indian garrison. With many of the convicts in the settlement 'political offenders', with influence over others and possibly means of communication with India, it argued that Indian sepoys could not be relied on and urged that Europeans troops be sent as soon as possible. Otherwise, any sign of unrest could prove 'desperate and humiliating'.[69] The governor assured the merchants that as the garrison was composed of men from the Madras army it was likely to remain loyal.[70] Second, merchants and the Anglo-Indian community protested against a recent decision on the part of the governor to allow the convicts to carry their *tabut* (model of the tomb of Hussain) through the town during the annual *Muharrum* procession, which marked the end of a period of mourning by *Shiah* Muslims for the death of the Prophet's grandson. The year before, Blundell had banned convicts from going outside their lines, but they had broken out, gone to the resident councillor's house, insulted him, and thrown their *tabut* into the court-house compound.[71] Despite these events, Blundell thought that to ban the procession altogether so soon after the Indian revolt might be misinterpreted as a religious restriction. This, he wrote, would have the effect of 'needlessly exasperating the convict body, and driving them to Acts of desperation'. Rather, he ordered that convicts should be restricted to processing just outside the walls of the lines and down the most direct road to the seashore. He assured local residents that any disturbance would be met with a strong hand.[72]

Most local inhabitants remained unimpressed and published a further petition in the press. They argued that the convicts would interpret this permission as an admission of weakness on the part of government.[73] Despite the governor's reassurances, and given the trajectory of jail-breaks in north India, it is hardly surprising that the idea that the convicts would break jail and Indian troops would not fire on them became widespread. Several families were apparently sent aboard ships in the harbour for safety. The press reported the existence of a 'feverish anxiety' which had led to women fainting in church at the slightest unexpected noise. Blundell then reported that the convicts themselves decided not to celebrate *Muharrum* in the usual way, though we do not know whether this was a voluntary act on the part of Muslim convict or community leaders, or the result of some carrot and stick disciplinary measure. Whatever the case, the governor claimed that the more he tried to alleviate the community's fears, the more he was distrusted.[74]

The local press represented the permission granted to the convicts to leave their lines as 'injudicious in the extreme … a most shameful outrage upon public safety'. Convict rebels might be joined by ticket-of-leave men and the Malay and Chinese communities, leading to general chaos. Moreover, in a revelation of what was at the bottom of much of the panic surrounding 1857 it lamented that the whole convict system was 'rotten to the core'. The Straits housed 'the most desperate wretches in existence' in a relatively lax regime:

[T]he time has now come when they have become an incubus on the Settlement. We are no longer an infant colony – that stage has been passed when convict labour is either desirable or necessary. But the treatment of the convicts reflects strongly upon a system which holds out greater privileges than are conferred on nearly all the lower classes of natives. Either let the flow of convicts cease, or place them under a proper System, with a large body of European Troops to keep them down. We would rather dispense with their services altogether, and return to the various Presidencies their offscourings.[75]

It is clear that what made the Straits system so successful, the rehabilitation of convicts through forms of labour directly linked to a penal class system, was becoming increasingly incompatible with Singapore's status as a commercial port.

We mentioned above that in September 1857 Governor Blundell responded negatively to the government of India's request that the Straits Settlements receive all prisoners sentenced to more than three years' imprisonment. This was an attempt on the part of the Indian authorities to alleviate the problem of prison overcrowding in the presidencies. Blundell's response, however, clearly reflected the growing feeling expressed in the local press that the existence of penal settlements was incompatible with economic success. In his reply to the government of India, Blundell wrote that prison accommodation was very limited. Singapore only had room for about 300 men, and Pinang about 60. Second, the system of discipline in operation in the Straits was not designed for the safe custody of 'desperate men'. There were no free guards; rather, the petty officers were themselves convicts. Moreover, convicts were dispersed across the town and island on various public works projects. Third, the European community in Singapore was both apprehensive of and annoyed by its selection as the destination for large numbers of dangerous convicts. It apparently felt them to be a danger to life, property, and mercantile affairs. At Melaka, where there was only a small garrison and a limited number of Europeans, he wrote, the presence of such convicts would be 'positively dangerous'.[76]

After making enquiries from Mouat, in what was in effect a dismissal of most of Blundell's reservations and a request that he reconsider his response, the government simply replied that no more than 400 prisoners would be sent.[77] It added that in future convicts would not be allowed to have *tabut* processions.[78] No response was made to Mouat's apprehension that a large number of 'turbulent and refractory individuals' might arrive from the Panjab and the North-West Provinces at any time, and it would not be desirable to send them to the Straits (or Arakan), even if those settlements would accept them. Mouat urged that they might instead be shipped to the West Indies as compulsory labourers. Removed to an ex-slave population that had no sympathy with them, they would be unable to 'plot mischief' or commit crime.[79] This suggestion came shortly before the West Indies Committee, a powerful lobby of planters, requested that once British authority had been restored, rebel sepoys could be transported to the Caribbean as labourers. One historian has interpreted the enthusiasm for the scheme on the part of planters in British Guiana as an attempt not only to fill a growing labour gap left by the abolition of slavery, but also as a way to create a 'buffer force' to ease tension between white colonists and the predominantly black population. Guiana's court of policy adopted three resolutions calling on the East India Company to send 10,000 ex-sepoys to the colony. Its combined court raised the desired number to 30,000 and, at the end of 1857, forwarded the proposal to the secretary of state for the colonies. In mid-1858, the colony repeated its request, though on this occasion it sought to limit the number of 'grave mutineers' to one thousand.[80] Local planters suggested the French colony of Bourbon (Réunion) as another potential destination for rebel sepoys.[81] The government of India thought that Western Australia, still a convict settlement at the time, was a further possibility.[82] Despite the enthusiasm of some officials, none of the proposals was taken seriously. Charles Raikes, judge of Agra, argued that mutineer sepoys ought to be banished from India for life, not as convicts but as emigrants. 'Either mutiny must be connected in the mind of our subjects with death, either social or physical,' he wrote, 'or we shall have more mutinies.'[83]

At the beginning of 1858, government shipped 94 convicts from Bombay to Pinang, 78 of them for mutiny or sedition. The resident councillor of the island protested in the strongest terms. The convicts, he said, were 'desperate characters' of far superior intelligence than the men he usually received. One man was a discharged *subadar*; a large proportion of the remainder consisted of *havildars* (native non-commissioned officer sergeants), and *naiks* (native non-commissioned officer corporals). The superintendent of convicts spelt out his concerns in the language of contamination, expressing fears that such men still possessed considerable influence over their sepoy compatriots and would poison the minds of the convicts already in Pinang.[84] The government of India's response was to sanction an increase in the military establishment for the purpose of guarding the men.[85] Perhaps to the relief of the local administration, nine of the men (11.53 per cent) were dead by the middle of the year.[86] Subsequently, the government of

India ordered the shipment of over 200 more convicts to the Straits, 189 from Bengal and 39 from Bombay. When the first batch arrived on 18 May, the authorities urged additional precautions for their safeguard. They issued overseers with revolvers, and asked the government of India for additional European troops.[87] Though not convicted directly of mutiny or sedition, these convicts had been concerned in the disturbances more generally, and so the government classified them as political offenders and transferred them to Port Blair once it was established as a penal colony.[88]

By the time Blundell responded to the government of India's initial request, it had decided to ship several hundred prisoners to Arakan. The jails at Akyab, Ramree, and Sandoway were then under the control of the Bengal Presidency, and so the government was able to sanction the transfer (rather than transportation) of prisoners under Act VII of 1850. This avoided legal difficulties with respect to the alteration or aggravation of sentences, and, at least in theory, opposition from local authorities. According to Mouat's calculations on the less generous old scale of measurement (24 superficial square feet per prisoner) there was space for 758 men there. In August 1857, the government of Bengal decided to send two batches of 250, made up of men sentenced to transportation or long-term imprisonment. Additionally, old life prisoners were freed and some short-term prisoners transferred to other jails. The government believed that this would free up space for dangerous offenders in Alipur.[89]

Mouat ordered the superintendent of Alipur to select only fit convicts for removal to Arakan. With an eye on the development of Alipur's manufactures, he added that as they were to be employed on the *bunds* (causeways) and roads, 'intelligent handicraftsmen' would not be sent. Only well-behaved old prisoners would be released, and only healthy prisoners would be selected for transfer. Mouat went to the prison to oversee personally the embarkation of the first batch of convicts. He reported later that he had explained to them that under the ticket-of-leave system by then in force in Arakan, by 'good conduct and industry' they could obtain privileges impossible at Alipur.[90]

Despite his assurances to the contrary, according to Mouat the prisoners selected for transfer to Arakan thought they were being sent as an additional punishment for bad conduct. He added that although the sepoys in the party were 'much cast down', and were upset that no detailed enquiries had been made into their cases, they did not resist embarkation.[91] Mouat had made careful calculations about the capacity of Arakan's jails, but when they arrived the commissioner would not take more than 80 men. He selected those he thought most fit for labour, though in practice most were capable of little more than spinning jute. Three were so ill that they had to be carried from the landing *ghat* to the prison. The commissioner placed the convicts in the dilapidated Akyab jail. It had just one serviceable ward which was used as a hospital. The remaining wards had been burnt down in a fire three years beforehand, and replaced by temporary sheds made of bamboo and mat. Even these were in a terrible state: in one of them the bamboo supports were rotten and the roof had almost fallen in. Given the lack of accommodation, the commissioner put the rest of the convicts on board a steamer on its way to Kyaukpyu.[92]

At the time, according to the local commissioner, the Indian convicts already in Moulmein were extremely agitated about the events taking place in north India. When news of the north Indian outbreaks reached Burma, the European community panicked. Some left their homes and sought refuge on board ships. Others procured arms and ammunition. A couple of months earlier, 50 Indian convicts had been sent to Moulmein.[93] Although none of them were mutineers, Commissioner A. Fytche reported that their arrival heralded 'a most unsteady feeling'. The new convicts, he said, had brought exaggerated stories about events in the North-West Provinces with them, fuelling unease in the town. He feared a combination between the convicts already in Moulmein (250 of who were ticket-of-leave men living and working at large), the jail *peons* (attendants), and the town police, all of whom were from the same regions as the rebels. Fytche claimed to have heard rumours that they might even join with the free Muslim community of the town and break open the jail. With no European infantry and only a small military force from Madras, he put the 50 convicts back on board their ship and ordered their return to Alipur.[94]

When the ship touched at Pegu, the commissioner there decided that as he had a *pukka* (brick) jail at his disposal he would land them. There were no other Indian convicts in the prison, and the commissioner hoped that isolation would curb their 'mischievous influence'. The congratulatory response to his initiative also confirmed the commissioner's conjecture that the Bengal government would rather not have received the convicts back.[95] There is no record of what happened in the meantime, but by the end of September Commissioner Fytche reported that convict excitement had passed. He was therefore ready to receive the convicts housed temporarily at Pegu, together with one hundred more from Alipur.[96] The political economy of the new British settlements in Burma was far removed from that of the Straits. The main difficulty the administration faced was the shortage of local labourers. Indeed, at the beginning of 1857, the commissioner of Arakan reported that if he were to write of the real difficulties he faced in this respect it would be thought an exaggeration.[97] Even Mouat, in principle fiercely opposed to the employment of prisoners on outdoor labour, acknowledged that the practice was necessary there. 'What is in itself undesirable', he reported, 'is in Arakan a necessity'.[98] Therefore, after the mutiny-rebellion, in contrast to Singapore, the authorities did not see Indian convicts as a threat to the stability of the Arakan region but rather as assurances of its further progress and development.

In September 1857, with large numbers of rebel prisoners due to arrive at Alipur at any moment, Mouat again raised the question of the settlement of the Andamans.[99] A steady stream of prisoners had begun to arrive in Alipur from the North-West Provinces, and it was not long before the jail became overcrowded once again. Indeed, by November, there were over two hundred prisoners either sentenced to life imprisonment or awaiting transportation.[100] Despite the Straits Settlements' position on the receipt of Indian convicts, the Bengal government again suggested the transportation of offenders there.[101] At the time, the question of the settlement of the Andamans was still under the consideration of the government of India.[102] At the beginning of 1858, the Alipur life prisoners were sent to Arakan,[103] which by the third quarter of 1859 had also received over three hundred Alipur term prisoners under Act XXII of 1858. The authorities used the same legislation to ship 50 more to Sandoway.[104] But in the aftermath of the Singapore panic, on 1 December 1857 the government suspended the transportation of mutineers, deserters, and rebels.

The petition of a group of Singapore merchants and inhabitants against such transportation must have arrived in India a few days after this decision was reached. Already, the Straits had received a handful of mutineers, and rumours that others were on their way were rife. Once again, petitioners argued that the convict warder system was incompatible with the safe custody of these types of offenders who had, Blundell represented, a 'tie of brotherhood', a common language, and a shared hatred of the British. The presence of such men would endanger the material progress of the settlements, especially if they stimulated a large transient Chinese community to violence. Moreover, the continuation of convict transportation to what were primarily commercial settlements was inappropriate. Convicts had been an invaluable labour force when the British first took control of the Straits, but they were no longer wanted.[105] With the transportation of mutineers, deserters, and rebels already suspended, the governor-general simply replied that the establishment of a new penal settlement in the Andamans was under consideration.[106] Only one exception appears to have been made to the rule suspending transportation. Two convicts, Ghoolam Ghouse and Sheik Munnoo, convicted of instigating rebellion by putting up treasonable placards in the Muslim quarter of Madras, were shipped to Tenasserim at the beginning of 1858. With that place specified in their sentence, the alternative would have been to allow them to escape punishment altogether.[107]

'Clothed in silk and purple': hunger-striking in Arakan

In his annual report of 1857–8, Mouat reported that out of a daily average of 350 prisoners in Akyab jail, 301 had died. The largest proportion (100) had succumbed to dysentery. The other main causes of death were cholera and fever. There was one suicide. The convicts received during the year were mostly gangs from Calcutta.[108] Given the massive upheavals of the mutiny-rebellion, and subsequent problems with jail overcrowding and transfer, it is perhaps unsurprising that some of them arrived in Arakan in a pitiful state. Of the 80 men sent in September 1857, for instance, only 16 were under the age of 50. Just eight were judged able to perform a day's work. Nevertheless, the convicts were split into two groups, and one gang was put to work at the station, and the other clearing jungle in the Noakhali salt water marshes. According to the civil assistant surgeon, J.W. Mountjoy, 'Hindu' and 'Bengali' convicts then refused to eat. Just one man, a *Brahmin* sepoy from the fifty-sixth regiment, 'threw aside the sacred thread and extended his range of food'. In March and April, cholera broke out in both gangs, swiftly followed by bowel disorders, fevers, abscesses, and ulcers.[109]

Mountjoy reasoned that the high death-rates that ensued were caused by 'moral causes acting on the physical frame'. 1857 had been a healthy year, but 1858 a year of great sickness. He concluded that the mutiny-rebellion had brought hopes of freedom, and when these were dashed, despondency and despair followed. Many of the convicts were peculiarly sensitive because they had come from the rebellious district of Puruliya (Manbhum). He went on:

> In very despair I told them, that by refusing food altogether they were poisoning the air of the Hospital, and so hurting the sensible prisoners who wished to recover. I then explained to them that if they were obstinately bent on dying, I should prefer to see them to die in a cleanly way by hanging or drowning, but that their present indolent plan of voluntary starvation so vitiated the air by the stench produced, as to injure the health of the other classes of prisoners.[110]

Moreover, he complained, the convicts had refused to take medicines. He could not pity them, he said, when they followed such a path: '[F]ood is the basis on which health, strength and labour rest.'[111]

It is true that, in previous years, the Indian convicts in Akyab had been relatively healthy. The mean death-rate for 1846-56 was just 5.07 per cent.[112] Officials put higher rates during the decade, for instance the 6.5 per cent seen during the second half of 1853, down to changes in diet or accommodation.[113] Mountjoy was somewhat selective in his memories of 1857, however, for there had been a serious outbreak of scurvy during the year, caused by a lack of fresh vegetables. As a result, the death-rate had risen stubbornly to 15.58 per cent.[114] Nevertheless, the situation in 1858 was unprecedented, and at the close of the following year the Bengal government asked Mouat to go to Arakan to take preventative measures against its recurrence. He came to the conclusion that it had been caused not by the convicts refusing food, but by their working in the salt-marsh. Their camp had been ill-chosen, and no sanitary measures had been put in place. Moreover, unusually hot weather and high rainfall had combined to render the year particularly unhealthy.[115] At the time of Mouat's visit, sickness was still prevalent in the jail. Most of the remaining Indian convicts died during that year.[116]

Mountjoy, however, remained firm in his beliefs. It was not that Arakan itself was unhealthy, but rather that Hindu, Bengali, and in an allusion to the existence of culturally syncretic practices men he described as 'Hinduised' Muslims refused to take their rations when sick. Rather they chose to drink only *conjee* (water in which rice has been boiled). Caste sensibilities remained strong, and were no doubt fortified by rumours about the mutiny-rebellion. Mouat wrote of the convict thus:

> He ever appears to be on the watch, lest the European should manoeuvre away his caste. A week or so ago an Indian asked me to cure his enlarged Spleen, I directed him to take a tea-spoonful of Quinine daily, and purchase a bottle of Vinegar. The Quinine accorded with his ideas, provided he could get it given him, but the Vinegar engendered fearful doubts; he there and then consulted a Brahmin on the subject, who decided that he must not use any Vinegar, unless made with his own hands.[117]

Mountjoy's claim about Indian patients being unwilling to accept western medical treatment was nothing new. During the first half of the nineteenth century, it was not uncommon for Indian convicts to hide physical complaints as their transportation overseas approached. Invariably, medical officials detained sick convicts in jail, away from acquaintances old and new, and with little hope of removal to a more salubrious place. This perhaps explains the almost constant complaints of officials in the penal settlements about the poor health of newly received convicts, and the indignant retorts of Indian jail officials that they only ever sent those fit for transportation.[118] Similar fears may have informed the keeping of illnesses like diarrhoea and dysentery secret.[119]

Yet Mountjoy's claims were not simply about Indian convicts' refusal of medicine. They were also to do with a more general refusal to eat. He compared Indians unfavourably with the Santal convict rebels transported to the settlement after the *hul*, for they ate all their food.[120] 'The remedy', Mountjoy went on, 'is in the hands of the convicts ... There is no reason, but their own whining obstinacy, why they should die.' Rather, like Santals and Mughs, they should eat their jail rations and take advantage of their employment at outdoor labour to procure herbs, leaves, and other consumables.[121]

It is worth mentioning that Mouat's and Mountjoy's positions on the devastating death-rates that afflicted Arakan during 1858 were the culmination of considerable animosity between the two men, particularly over the issue of authority during an outbreak of scurvy in 1857.[122] While it is impossible to pinpoint the exact cause of high death-rates during the year, it seems likely that they were the result of a combination of the climate, working conditions, poor sanitary provision, convict suspicions about medical treatment, and convict attempts to retain strict rules of commensality at mealtimes. The latter of course took on a whole new dimension in the context of the mutiny-rebellion, due to the widespread belief that the British intended to convert forcibly Indians to Christianity. There was, of course, a close relationship between prison and army discipline. Indeed, Mountjoy compared 'the pampered convict' with 'the petted Indian army'. Were convicts clothed in silk and purple, he opined, they would still cry and plot for more, remaining as dissatisfied as the recently mutinous sepoys. Yet, both Mouat and Mountjoy denied the convicts agency with respect to their rations. To Mouat, convict protests were irrelevant. Though Mountjoy understood the cultural principles from which convict resistance stemmed, that resistance was only evidence of the 'gross ignorance and prejudice' through which convicts 'whined, cried, sulked with their food, became skeletons ... and died'.[123]

Prisons in the aftermath of revolt

Despite the destruction of so many jails across north India and the escape of thousands of prisoners, perhaps surprisingly mainland jails did not become a particular priority after 1857–8. Once the immediate crisis had been resolved, at least in part through the opening up of the Andaman Islands as a penal colony, there was no radical programme of jail building or rationalization. Rather, government repaired or rebuilt and reoccupied damaged prisons. In some places like Meerut compensatory fines were levied on local communities involved in attacks on jails, which paid for part of the cost.[124] The government turned down more radical and thus expensive schemes like a central jails programme in Bengal.[125] Other major building works predated the revolt. Post-1858, the government of the North-West Provinces pressed ahead with its programme of constructing radiating central prisons, each consisting of a central watchtower and cellular wings. It had first suggested the building of such jails in 1846, and in the aftermath of the revolt work continued on the construction of new or the alteration of existing jails such as Agra and Allahabad.[126] As a result of the imprisonment of long-term offenders in such institutions, the government did not in general restore to their former strength local jails holding only short-term prisoners. It even abandoned badly damaged prisons such as those in Kanpur and Fatepur, on the grounds that there was easy access to the jail at Allahabad. There were a few exceptions to this general pattern, for instance Bijnor jail which had been built with what Thornhill described as 'perishable matter'. He planned to replace it with a more secure building on the radiating principle.[127] It is important, however, not to overstate the extent of architectural innovations during this period. As Arnold has shown, even where they existed by the 1860s often separate cells and central watchtowers had fallen into disuse.[128] Moreover, there was what Thornhill himself described as a 'perceptible relaxation' in discipline in the North-West Provinces. With the loss of the entire infrastructure of intramural labour, after the revolt most prisoners worked and slept out. There was no classification except in a handful of jails.[129]

There were, however, two important developments in the areas of the North-West Provinces most affected by jail-breaking. First, in common with urban planning more generally, officials cleared land around large prisons to provide a more open view.[130] Second, there was a move towards the relocation of already planned central prisons out of urban areas, especially those with large European populations.[131] Given that the vast majority of prisons were small institutions located in urban districts, it is again important not to overstate the extent of this innovation. There were no further developments in prison discipline for some years, and they had little to do with the revolt. According to Mouat, they came only because of the personal interest of the then viceroy of India, John Lawrence, who had overseen earlier prison reforms in the Panjab. He set up an Indian Jail Committee in 1864.[132]

Perhaps the most important change was in how imprisonment was both imagined and represented in the aftermath of the revolt, for the mutiny-rebellion marked an important shift in how British and Indians alike viewed prisons. They became not so much places of discipline and punishment as spaces of cultural confrontation and struggle. We will return to the longer term meaning of this change in the conclusion. In the meantime, it is worth noting that with scattered unrest continuing into 1859, officials were extremely nervous about public perceptions of the prison. In 1859, Governor-General Canning stated clearly that he did not want Indians to perceive jails as places of religious conversion. Therefore, missionaries should only go into prisons at prisoner request.[133] Invariably, government turned down further demands for missionaries by jail officials, or even missionaries' own attempts to preach in jails.[134] Administrators were critical of Canning's supposedly lenient treatment of rebels, which they believed had failed to crush 'the spirit of rebellion' and fuelled further jail unrest.[135] They dealt swiftly with potential outbreaks. When a plot to break out of Birbhum jail came to light at the beginning of 1859, for example, the guards were seen as so untrustworthy that local officials transferred insurgent prisoners to Alipur.[136]

In keeping with a more general policy of religious non-interference, in the aftermath of the mutiny-rebellion jail administrators approached changes to prison discipline with a certain amount of anxiety. There was a discernable shift in the attitude of penal administrators like Mouat, who was now unwilling to risk unrest in the face of prisoner discontent and so was more likely to concede to their demands. In 1859 he wrote: 'The prejudices and practices of various guilds and sections of the community in different parts of the country, although not strictly sanctioned by Shaster or Ved[a] [sacred texts] have, in many cases, assumed the full force of a religious right, which it is neither safe nor prudent altogether to disregard.'[137] Thus innovations were enforced gradually and through dialogue with prisoners, rather than in consultation with their representatives outside the jail. This of course gave Indian communities enhanced input into general shifts in religious and caste categories.

During the second half of the nineteenth century, rumours about inappropriate colonial interventions continued to circulate around jails. At the beginning of 1859, for instance, reports that the government intended to convert the prisoners of Arrah jail to Christianity through the removal of their *lotas* once again gathered force.[138] More rumours about government interference with caste practices in the prison circulated later that year after the officiating joint magistrate ordered the jail cooks to prepare the meals of prisoners working on the roads. Prisoners saw this as an indication of a more general attempt at forced conversion.[139] At about the same time, in Shahabad jail a *sowar* refused to take food from a *Brahmin* cook. Though he recognized that there was no religious sanction against his aversion, he argued that there was a social one, stating "'our fathers never did it'". In the new spirit of social accommodation that characterized post-mutiny jail practices, Mouat agreed, arguing that 'immemorial custom' was as reasonable a ground for exemption from common messing as religion. 'It is better in such cases to yield a little,' he wrote, 'than to run the risk of exciting general discontent'. In order to prevent suspicions that government sought to interfere in religion and caste, he told the district magistrate that 'in the present temper of the times' he should avoid jail innovations of all kinds.[140] And yet jail unrest continued unabated. In 1860, there was a further riot in Allahabad jail over common messing.[141] In 1861, Arrah jail was the scene of another attempted outbreak when rumours circulated that the new commodes and urinals introduced into the sleeping wards were to be used for preparing food.[142] Subsequently, the government of Bengal ordered Mouat to carefully ascertain prisoners' '*real* feeling on the subject', and if commodes and urinals were likely to cause discontent he should remove them.[143] Government also conceded to the shared sympathies of Hindu and Muslim prisoners. In 1860, for instance, the magistrate of Faridpur (Dhaka division), C.F. Harvey, took away the prisoners' *lotas* and then entered the cook rooms. He claimed that the rice was dirty and badly prepared, and so flogged two of the cooks. This, the prisoners complained, spoiled their food. Subsequently, both Hindus and Muslims went on hunger strike with the support of people outside the prison. The magistrate lamented the daily annoyances of his prisoners' 'imaginary prejudices', but Mouat ordered the immediate restoration of their *lotas* and cautioned him against raising questions of religion and caste in jail.[144]

However, it was not long before prison administrators became impatient with prisoners' seemingly endless social posturing. Less than five years' after the revolt, Bengal's officiating inspector-general of jails, Norman Chevers, complained of the refusal of jail sweepers to sweep up night soil. The government would not countenance such 'trivial objections', he complained, especially if they were unsanctioned by Hindu *pandits*. The acquisition and propagation of caste restrictions by prisoners as a means of elevating social status appears to have been widespread by this time. According to Chevers, increasingly even those formerly employed in menial duties, including hill tribes, claimed exemptions from particular types of labour on the basis of 'caste'. Ignoring the continued opportunities for social mobility imprisonment presented, he remained confident that prison did not violate caste - or at least caste as understood by 'respectable' Hindus.[145]

Conclusion

The government of India was faced with a series of penal difficulties in the aftermath of the 1857–8 revolt, for thousands of prisoners had escaped and dozens of jails were badly damaged or destroyed. There was no space to imprison those who surrendered or were recaptured, let alone those who were convicted of mutiny offences. Moreover, with the closing off of the penal settlements in the Straits and Burma there was a backlog of transportation convicts. Even where prison accommodation was available, there were few reliable jail guards. Many prisons were so overcrowded that the government introduced a policy of transferring prisoners to secure jails, but this had the unintended effects of both spreading instability and elevating the already high prison death-rates. Despite the serious impact of the mutiny-rebellion on north Indian jails, post-1858 financial constraints prevented the government from sanctioning any radical innovations in jail construction. However, at least for a few years it was anxious to avoid accusations that it was interfering in religious practices or caste, and so it was conservative in its approach to changes to the jail regime. The revolt also secured the establishment of a penal colony on the Andaman Islands, which in an invocation of the cultural transgressions implied by sea voyages was known popularly then, as now, as 'kala pani'. The relationship between the Indian uprising and British settlement of the Andamans is the focus of Chapter 5, which discusses the transportation of mutineer-rebels to the Islands in the wake of the events of 1857–8.

Notes

1. OIOC P.235.7 (NWPJP 1 – 18 Oct. 1859): Thornhill to Couper, 8 July 1859.
2. OIOC P.234.34 (NWPJC Jan. – Feb. 1858): M.H. Court, Magistrate Allahabad, to F. Gubbins, Officiating Commissioner Allahabad, 15 Feb. 1858.
3. Mathur, *Kala Pani*, 15-20. For a useful selection of primary source documents, see also M.V. Portman, *A History of our Relations with the Andamanese, vol. I*, Calcutta, Superintendent Government Printing, 1899, ch. 4.
4. Some of these paintings are held in the Windsor Collection. See Delia Millar, *The*

Victorian Watercolours and Drawings in the Collection of Her Majesty the Queen, vol. II, London, Philip Wilson, 1995, cat. nos 3674-707.

5. Sten Nilsson and Narayani Gupta, *The Painter's Eye: Egron Lundgren and India*, Stockholm, National Museum, 1991, 88-9.
6. Mouat's report, 1857–8, 18; Mouat's report, 1858-9, 41.
7. OIOC P.206.61 (IJP 18 Feb. 1859): Chester to Strachey, 7 Nov. 1857; Court to Chester, 20 Oct. 1857.
8. OIOC P.234.37 (NWPJC Apr. 1858): Thornhill to Muir, 22 Mar. 1858.
9. Mouat's report, 1855-6, 46.
10. Mouat's report, 1856-7, 52.
11. Mouat's report, 1858-9, 31: H. Baillie, Civil Assistant Surgeon 24 Parganas, Annual report of the Alipur jail hospital, n.p.
12. OIOC P.146.16 (BJP Apr. 1859): C.F. Montresor, Officiating Superintendent Alipur, to Young, 9 Apr. 1859.
13. OIOC P.146.12D (BJC 28 Jan. 1858): Mouat to Buckland, 30 Sept. 1857, enc. List of infirm and blind life prisoners in Alipur jail, 25 Sept. 1857; Buckland to Mouat, 19 Oct. 1857.
14. OIOC P.146.12D (BJC 28 Jan. 1858): Fergusson to Buckland, 28 Nov. 1857; OIOC P.146.12H (BJC 25 Feb. 1858): Mouat to Buckland, 21 Jan. 1858.
15. Mouat's report, 1858-9, 72.
16. OIOC P.146.17 (BJP 19 May 1859): Mouat's memo on Manbhum jail, 9 Mar. 1859.
17. OIOC P.234.34 (NWPJC Jan. – Feb. 1858): Court to Gubbins, 15 Feb. 1858; Muir to Gubbins, 23 Feb. 1858.
18. OIOC P.234.39 (NWPJC 15 – 31 May 1858): Muir to Thornhill, 22 May 1858.
19. OIOC P.234.41 (NWPJC 1 - 26 July 1858): Thornhill to Muir, 14 June 1858.
20. *Prison Returns of the North West Provinces, 1860*, Allahabad, Government Press, 1861 (henceforth *NWP prison returns 1860*), 1.
21. OIOC P.234.34 (NWPJC Jan – Feb 1858): Walker to Thornhill, 2 Feb. 1858.
22. Haq, 'The Story', 27, 52 (quote 52).
23. 'Eat curses' is Urdu idiom for 'be cursed'.
24. Shackle notes: 'the tension between the formal order of the verse and the chaotic disorientation which it describes is … an important part of the poem', hence the translation reproduces metrical regularity, though not rhyme. Shackle, 'Munir Shikohabadi'.
25. Shackle, 'Munir Shikohabadi'.
26. Chronograms ascribe each letter of the Urdu alphabet a numerical value. *Saf nikle khana-e zanjir se* ('safe rescue from the house of chains') adds up to AD 1860. Shackle, 'Munir Shikohabadi'.
27. In a famous ancient Arabic tale, Qais (also known as Majnun) was rendered weak by his love of Laila.
28. This may be a literary representation of the process of photography which of course at the time imaged full colour as black and white.
29. Shackle, 'Munir Shikohabadi'.
30. Mouat, 'On Prison Statistics', 195, 204.
31. Arnold, *Colonizing the Body*, 65.
32. *Ibid.*, 103-4, 106.
33. *Report of the Inspector-General of Prisons in the Punjab for the year 1858*, Lahore, Punjabee Press, 1859 (henceforth *Punjab prison report 1859*), 54.
34. *Prison Returns of the North Western Provinces, 1861*, Allahabad, Government Press,

1862, (henceforth *NWP prison returns 1861*), 4.

35. *NWP prison returns 1860*, pp. 52, 58, 64; *NWP prison returns 1861*, 4.

36. *NWP prison returns 1861*, 2, 5, 24.

37. T.C. Loch, *Report on the jails of Bengal, Behar and Orissa for the year 1854-5*, Calcutta, Thomas Jones *Calcutta Gazette* Office, 1856, 2.

38. Mouat's report, 1855-6, 13-14.

39. Mouat's report, 1857–8: Annual report of the Alipur Jail hospital, n.p.

40. Mouat's report, 1855-6, 13-14.

41. OIOC P.146.38 (BJP Mar. 1861): Mouat to Rivers Thompson, Junior Secretary to Government Bengal, 26 Dec. 1860.

42. Mouat, 'On Prison Statistics', 195.

43. OIOC P.234.37 (NWPJC Apr. 1858): J. Forsyth, Director General Medical Department, to Strachey, 26 Feb. 1858.

44. OIOC P.146.21 (BJP 20 Oct. 1859): Mouat to Thompson, 18 Aug. 1859.

45. Mouat's report, 1858-9: Mouat's circular, 16 Aug. 1858.

46. OIOC P.146.15 (BJP 24 March 1859): Mouat to Buckland, 27 Dec. 1858; Mouat's report, 1858-9, 28, 74.

47. Mouat's report, 1857–8: Annual report of the Alipur jail hospital, n.p.

48. Mouat's report, 1858-9, 74.

49. OIOC P.146.16 (BJP Apr. 1859): Montresor to Young, 9 Apr. 1859.

50. OIOC P.146.17 (BJP 19 May 1859): Couper to Young, 5 May 1859.

51. OIOC P.206.69 (IJP July 1864): J. Geoghegan, Under Secretary to Government Bengal, to Mouat, 2 June 1864.

52. For instance, Gooroo-Churn Doss, Deputy Magistrate Jessore, to the Commissioner for the Suppression of Dacoity, 2 Aug. 1857, cited in PP 1857-58 (2316): Papers relative to mutinies in East Indies: Appendix B.

53. The government, however, insisted on his transportation: OIOC P.235.6 (NWPJP 17 – 30 Sept. 1859): Mayne to Thornhill, 23 Sept. 1859; Couper to Thornhill, 30 Sept. 1859.

54. OIOC P. 235.7 (NWPJP 1 – 18 Oct. 1859): Cannon to Thornhill, 24 Mar. 1859.

55. Mouat's report, 1857–8: Annual report of the Alipur jail hospital, n.p. (emphasis in original). There are interesting parallels here with the 'nostalgia' – severe depression related to exile and the longing for home - that afflicted communard convicts shipped from France to the penal colony of Nouvelle Caledonie in 1872. See Alice Bullard, *Exile to Paradise: Savagery and Civilization in Paris and the South Pacific, 1790-1900*, Stanford, Stanford University Press, 2000, ch. 7.

56. Mouat, 'On Prison Statistics', 203.

57. Taylor Sherman, 'Political Prisoners and Hunger Strikes in India Jails, 1929-1938', unpublished paper presented at *Convicts Discussion Workshop III*, University of Leicester, Jan. 2006.

58. OIOC P.146.12D (BJC 28 Jan. 1858): Tucker to Young, 16 Jan. 1858; OIOC P.146.12G (BJC 18 Feb. 1858): Statement of cases tried under Act XVI of 1857 in the district of Bhagulpur during the month of January 1858 (1, 2, 7, 8 Jan. 1858).

59. OIOC P.146.12G (BJC 18 Feb. 1858): Statement of cases tried under Act XVI of 1857 in the district of Bhagulpur during the month of January 1858 (1, 2, 7, 8 Jan. 1858).

60. C.M. Turnbull, *A History of Singapore, 1819-1988*, Singapore, Oxford University Press, 1989, 36-9, 42-3.

61. Stephen Nicholas and Peter R. Shergold, 'Transportation as Global Migration', in Stephen Nicholas (ed.), *Convict Workers; Reinterpreting Australia's Past*, Cambridge,

Cambridge University Press, 1988, 30.

62. *Bombay Gazette*, 14 Sept. 1858.

63. OIOC P.142.37 (BJC 17 Sept. 1845): Governor W. Butterworth to Turnbull, 26 Feb. 1845; OIOC P.142.49 (BJC 24 June 1846): Governor W. Butterworth to Turnbull, 23 Apr. 1846. The system was also adopted in the Tenasserim Provinces, though it did not become operational in Arakan for another decade: OIOC P.142.44 (BJC 25 Feb. 1846): H.M. Durand, Commissioner Tenasserim Provinces, to F.J. Halliday, Secretary to Government Bengal, 19 Dec. 1845; OIOC P.145.64 (BJC 25 June 1857): Mouat to Lushington, 13 Apr. 1857.

64. McNair, *Prisoners Their Own* Warders, 10.

65. Turnbull, *A History of Singapore*, 55.

66. Anderson, *Legible Bodies*, 4-6, 25-30.

67. Turnbull, *A History of Singapore*, 56; Turnbull, 'Convicts in the Straits Settlements', 92-6.

68. Turnbull, *A History of Singapore*, 66, 69-70.

69. OIOC P.188.47 (IPC 2 Oct. 1857): Petition of M.F. Davidson, C. Spottiswoode, and 11 others, 4 Aug. 1857,

70. *Ibid.*: E.A. Blundell, Governor Straits Settlements, to Beadon, 28 Aug. 1857.

71. *Ibid.*: Petition of J. Purvis, Spottiswoode, and fifteen others, 18 Aug. 1857.

72. *Ibid.*: Blundell to Messrs Jarvie, Spottiswoode, and others, 19 Aug. 1857.

73. *Ibid.*: Memorial of the Christian Inhabitants of Campong Bencoolen, and the adjoining Campongs (A. Poons, A. Simonides, W. Woodford, and 27 others), 21 Aug. 1857.

74. *Ibid.*: Blundell to Beadon, 28 Aug. 1857; 'The Panic', n.d.

75. *Ibid.*: 'The Panic', n.d.

76. OIOC P.188.48 (IPC 8 Jan. 1858): Blundell to Beadon, 11 Sept. 1857.

77. *Ibid.*: Dalrymple to Blundell, 31 Dec. 1857.

78. OIOC P.188.47 (IPC 2 Oct. 1857): R.B. Chapman, Officiating Under Secretary to Government of India, to Blundell, 30 Sept. 1857.

79. OIOC P.188.48 (IPC 8 Jan. 1858): Mouat to Buckland, 24 Oct. 1857.

80. Alapatt, 'The Sepoy Mutiny of 1857', 303-8.

81. OIOC P.407.7 (BomJCC 27 March 1858): Messrs Vinay Fils, 11 Feb. 1858.

82. NAI Home (Judicial 12 Mar. 1858), no. 14; OIOC L.PJ.296: Bengal judicial despatch no. 8; *The Times*, 19 Nov. 1857.

83. Raikes, *Notes on the Revolt*, 154-5 (quote 155).

84. OIOC P.188.50 (IJP 12 Feb. 1858): Blundell to Beadon, 17 Dec. 1857; W.J. Lewis, Resident Councillor Pinang, to Blundell, 13 Dec. 1857; G.T. Hilliard, Superintendent of Convicts Pinang, to Lewis, 14 Dec. 1857.

85. OIOC P.188.50 (IJC 12 Feb. 1858): Dalrymple to Blundell, 1 Feb. 1858.

86. OIOC P.188.56 (IJC 20 Aug. 1858): Nominal roll of nine convicts of the mutineers received from Bombay, who have died since their arrival, 21 June 1858.

87. OIOC P.188.56 (IJC 27 Aug. 1857): J.F.A. McNair, Executive Engineer and Superintendent of Convicts and Roads, to H. Somerset Mackenzie, Resident Councillor Singapore, 18 May 1858; Blundell to Mackenzie, 12 June 1858.

88. OIOC P.188.56 (IJC 20 Aug. 1858): Blundell to Beadon, 12 June 1858; McNair to Somerset Mackenzie, 18, 27 May 1858.

89. OIOC P.146.12D (BJC 28 Jan. 1858): Mouat to Buckland, 25 Aug. 1857; Buckland to Mouat, 25 Aug. 1857.

90. *Ibid.*: Mouat to Montresor, 26 Aug. 1857.

91. OIOC P.146.12D (BJC 28 Jan. 1858): Mouat to Buckland, 31 Aug. 1857.

92. *Ibid.*: G. Verner, Officiating Commissioner Arakan, to Buckland, 5 Sept. 1857.
93. *Bengal Hurkaru*, 17 Aug. 1857; OIOC P.146.12D (BJC 28 Jan. 1858): List of 50 convicts to Moulmein *per Fire Queen*, 9 July 1857.
94. OIOC P.146.12D (BJC 28 Jan. 1858): A. Fytche, Officiating Commissioner Tenasserim and Martaban Provinces, to Lushington, 22 July 1857.
95. *Ibid.*: H. Hopkinson, Commissioner Arakan, to Lushington, 24 July 1857; Buckland to Lushington, 9 Sept. 1857.
96. *Ibid.*: Fytche to Buckland, 22 Sept. 1857.
97. OIOC P.145.64 (BJC 25 June 1857): Hopkinson to Buckland, 13 Feb. 1857.
98. OIOC P.145.66 (BJC 2 July 1857): Mouat to Young, 13 June 1857. See also Mouat's report, 1856-7, 21-2.
99. OIOC P.146.12D (BJC 28 Jan. 1858): Mouat to Buckland, 30 Sept. 1857.
100. *Ibid.:* Fergusson to Mouat, 28 Nov. 1857.
101. *Ibid.:* Fergusson to Buckland, 28 Nov. 1857; Buckland to Secretary to Government of India Home Department, 3 Dec. 1857.
102. *Ibid.:* Buckland to Mouat, 19 Oct. 1857.
103. OIOC P.146.12H (BJC 25 Feb. 1858): Fergusson to Mouat, 19 Jan. 1858.
104. OIOC P.206.62 (IJP 20 Apr. 1860): Couper to Grey, 8 Nov. 1859; OIOC P.146.21 (BJP 20 Oct. 1859): Numerical list of term convicts transported to the penal settlements from the Alipur Jail, n.d.
105. OIOC P.188.49 (IJP 8 Jan. 1858): Blundell to Beadon, 26 Nov. 1857, enc. Memorial of Merchants F.M. Davidson, A. Logan, R. Bain, C.H.H. Wilson and Other Inhabitants of Singapore, n.d.
106. OIOC P.188.49 (IJC 8 Jan. 1858): Beadon to Blundell, 23 Dec. 1857.
107. OIOC P.188.50 (IJC 26 Feb. 1858): T. Pycroft, Chief Secretary to Government Madras, to Beadon, 6 Feb. 1858; Dalrymple to Pycroft, 20 Feb. 1858.
108. Mouat's report, 1857–8, Appendix I, 111-13; J.W. Mountjoy, Civil Assistant Surgeon Akyab, Annual Report of Akyab Jail hospital, 1858.
109. *Ibid.*: Mountjoy to Shepherd, 11 Sept. 1857.
110. *Ibid.*
111. *Ibid.*
112. Mouat's report, 1855-6, Appendix I, 85
113. OIOC P.144.61 (BJC 1 June 1854): Hopkinson to Grey, 10 March 1854; OIOC P.144.65 (BJC 17 Aug. 1854): Mountjoy to W.J. Law, Second Principal Assistant Commissioner Akyab, 22 Sept. 1853.
114. OIOC P.145.74 (BJC 24 Sept. 1857): Extracts from Mountjoy to Law, n.d. See also Mouat's report, 1856-7, 92, 94.
115. OIOC P.146.28 (BJP June 1860): Grey to Mouat, 29 Dec. 1859; Mouat's memo., 30 Apr. 1860.
116. Mouat's report, 1859-60, 38.
117. Mouat's report, 1859-60, Appendix I, 118.
118. Migratory indentured labourers too were notorious for refusing to take medical treatment. An 1859 medical report on the second largest jail in Mauritius, Powder Mills, wrote of prisoners concealing illness in case they were detained in hospital at the expiration of their sentence: NAM RA1564 (Prison Committees 1860): Annual Report of Sanitary Condition of Powder Mills Prison, 1859.
119. OIOC P.145.61 (BJC 2 Apr. 1857): Koylash Chunder Dutt, Sub-assistant Surgeon Sambalpur, to R.J. Leigh, Senior Assistant Sambalpur, 5 Feb. 1857. As Arnold has shown, in later years Indian communities were in general unwilling to accept

medical interventions like smallpox vaccination, to the point that they held back progress in the eradication of endemic disease. See *Colonizing the Body*, ch. 3.

120. Annual report Akyab Jail hospital: Mountjoy to T. Shepherd, Second Principal Assistant Commissioner, 11 Sept. 1857 (n.p.)

121. Mouat's report, 1858-9, 119.

122. OIOC P.145.74 (BJC 24 Sept. 1857): Extracts from Mountjoy to Law, n.d.; OIOC P.146.2 (BJC 29 Oct. 1857): Mouat to Buckland, 7 Jan. 1857.

123. Mouat's report, 1859-60, Appendix I, 119.

124. *Punjab prison report 1858*, p. 59; OIOC P.206.60 (IJP 16 July 1860): Williams to Couper, 23 Feb. 1860; *NWP Prison Returns 1860*, 50-1.

125. OIOC P.146.14 (BJP Feb. 1859): Buckland to Mouat, 22 Feb. 1859.

126. OIOC P.206.62 (IJP 20 Apr. 1860): Couper to Grey, 8 Nov. 1859.

127. OIOC P.235.7 (NWPJP 1 – 18 Oct. 1859): Thornhill to Couper, 8 July 1859.

128. Arnold, 'The Colonial Prison', 164-5.

129. OIOC P.235.7 (NWPJP 1 – 18 Oct. 1859): Thornhill to Couper, 8 July 1859; *NWP Prison Returns 1861*, 5.

130. OIOC P.234.37 (BJC Apr. 1858): Cannon to Thornhill, 23 Feb. 1858.

131. OIOC P.234.48 (NWPJC 10 - 31 Dec. 1858): Thornhill to Muir, 15 Dec. 1858.

132. F.J. Mouat, 'On Prison Discipline and Statistics in Lower Bengal', *Journal of the Statistical Society of London*, 30, 1 (1867), 22-4.

133. NAI Home (Judicial 20 May 1859), no. 13: Beadon to R.H. Davies, Secretary to Government Panjab, 10 May 1859. See also P.234.58 (NWPJC 21 May – 27 June 1859).

134. OIOC P.146.51 (BJP June – Aug. 1862): G. Plowden, Commissioner Burdwan, to H. Bell, Under Secretary to Government Bengal, 6 June 1862.

135. *Bombay Gazette*, 27 Sept. 1858.

136. OIOC P.146.15 (BJP Mar. 1859): O.W. Malet, Sessions Judge Birbhum, to Mouat, 10 Jan. 1859.

137. OIOC P.146.21 (BJP 8 Sept. 1859): Mouat to Young, 9 Aug. 1859.

138. OIOC P.146.13 (BJP 27 Jan. 1859): A.N. Cole, Deputy Magistrate Sasseram, to Money, 8 Jan. 1859; Samuells to Young, 12 Jan. 1859.

139. OIOC P.146.21 (BJP 8 Sept. 1859): W.J. Herschel, Officiating Magistrate Shahabad, to Mouat, 4 Aug. 1859; H.D.H. Fergusson, Commissioner Patna, to Young, 6, 8 Aug. 1859; R.J. Wigram, Officiating Joint Magistrate Sarun, to Fergusson, 7 Aug. 1859; Mouat to Young, 9 Aug. 1859.

140. OIOC P.146.21 (BJP 8 Sept. 1859): Mouat to Herschel, 9 Aug. 1859.

141. *NWP prison returns 1860*, 8.

142. OIOC P.146.46 (BJP Jan. 1862): N. Chevers, Officiating Inspector-General of Jails Bengal, to J.D. Gordon, Junior Secretary to Government Bengal, 20 Dec. 1861.

143. OIOC P.146.53 (BJP [jails] Oct. – Nov. 1862): Gordon to Mouat, 20 Aug. 1862.

144. OIOC P.146.26 (BJP [jails] Apr. 1860): C.F. Harvey, Magistrate Faridpur, to Thompson, 23, 25 Mar. 1860; Mouat to Thompson, 28 Mar. 1860; Harvey to Mouat, 29 Mar. 1860.

145. OIOC P.146.42 (BJP [jails] Aug. 1861): Chevers to Gordon, 24 July 1861.

CHAPTER 5
THE ANDAMANS PENAL COLONY

Introduction

This chapter will consider one of the most important penal and spatial legacies of the mutiny-rebellion, Britain's permanent settlement of the Andaman Islands as a colony for the reception of convicts. Before the outbreak of the revolt the British had vague plans to populate the Islands, setting up the Andamans Committee to consider the issue in April 1857. At this time the government saw convicts as a means to an end, as labourers who might secure its long-term aim of productive colonial expansion, notably the protection of shipping and trade routes. In the aftermath of the uprising the British required urgently a place for the exile and imprisonment of mutineer-rebels. The trajectory of proposed settlement therefore changed between the constitution of the committee a month before the revolt began and its departure for the Islands in November 1857. The committee's original plan was to consider the suitability of the Andamans for colonization, but by the time it left India its brief had changed. Government then assumed that the Islands would be settled as a penal colony and the committee was asked to report on where best such a settlement should be located. Clearly, both during pre-settlement surveys and in the months after transportation began the government recognized convicts' economic and social potential as permanent settlers. In part, this was related to the government's desire to promote the colony's self-sufficiency. The suitability of the Islands for colonization was, therefore, central to their selection as a penal site. As we will see, the committee examined carefully the water supply, the quality of the soil, and the extent of cultivable land.

No book addressing the history of incarceration in South Asia would be complete without mentioning the impact of the settlement of the Andamans as a place for the transportation of mutineer-rebels on the Islands' indigenous inhabitants.[1] It is clear that initially their notorious hostility was a major spur to British colonization. Early relations between the Andamanese and overseas visitors were characterized by violence and there were skirmishes even before the first British colony was established.[2] After his survey party visited the Islands during 1789-90, for instance, Lieutenant Colebrooke filed what was to become a typical report, positioning the Islands' indigenous communities outside the scale of 'civilization':

> The men are cunning, crafty and revengeful; and frequently express their aversion to strangers in a loud and threatening tone of voice, exhibiting various signs of defiance, and expressing their contempt by the most indecent gestures ... They will affect to enter into a friendly conference, when, after receiving with a show of humility whatever articles may be presented to them, they set up a shout, and discharge their arrows at the donors. On the appearance of a vessel or boat, they frequently lie in ambush among the trees, and send one of their gang, who is generally the oldest among them, to the water's edge, to endeavour by friendly signs to allure the strangers on shore. Should the crew venture to land without arms, they instantly rush out from their lurking places, and attack them ... Their mode of life is degrading to human nature.

However, he noted his scepticism regarding broader European claims that the Andamanese were cannibals. It was possible that their attacks on strangers were provoked by hunger, he wrote, for their 'mangled and torn' bodies had been found later. There was, however, no positive evidence of it.[3]

After the British established the penal colony, visiting ethnographers and officials stationed at its headquarters in Port Blair studied Andamanese communities, of which there were several distinct groups. Commonly referring to them as aborigines, most officials saw them as direct descendents of the earliest human ancestors. Escalating mortality rates during early contact with British settlers and Indian convicts, from communicable diseases like smallpox and syphilis, led to contemporary comparisons with indigenous communities elsewhere, notably the supposedly dying races of colonial Van Diemen's Land (Tasmania).[4] Violence between British settlers and Indian convicts, on the one hand, and the Andamanese, on the other, continued for some time. As we will see, the Islands' first superintendent, J.P. Walker, turned the hostility of the Andamanese to his advantage with respect to convict management. With only a small penal establishment at his disposal, he transformed the Andamanese into distant 'prison' guards, warning convicts that invariably escape attempts would end in death at the hands of 'savages'.

In a groundbreaking book on the Andaman Islands, Satadru Sen has focused on convict society and its relationship to the incipient colonial state during the second half of the nineteenth century. For our purposes, we would like to draw upon his useful analysis of colonial distinctions between criminal typologies, notably of 'political' and 'ordinary' offenders. As we will see in a discussion of the first plans to organize the penal classes in the new colony, and as Sen elaborates, penal administrators saw the mutineer-rebels of 1857–8 as 'good subjects who had been led astray'. As the secretary to the government of India put it at the beginning of 1858, these were 'men who have been led to the commission of crimes against the State by the example of others, and not men of a desperate or unmanageable character'.[5] Moreover, some Andaman convicts had been sentenced for straightforward military mutiny (desertion, refusal to obey orders and so on), but many more were transported for offences such as dacoity and plunder that were committed during the brief collapse of colonial authority. The government of India categorized the criminality of both, which Sen terms 'intentional' and 'circumstantial' rebellion, as political insubordination.[6]

We will return to the theme of the political offender later, in our discussion of the amnesties offered to convicts after the collapse of the mutiny-rebellion and the resumption of British authority across north India. First, the chapter will examine the factors influencing the decision to resettle the Andamans. Second, we will focus on convict experiences of the journey into transportation. Drawing out some of the complexities of the strong overlaps between military and penal discipline noted by colonial historians in other contexts,[7] we will then see how the notion of the political offender formulated in India played out in practical terms in the Andamans during this period. We will examine in particular how the British authorities organized the early colony, as also the hierarchies and divisions invoked by convicts themselves. Finally, we will discuss conditions during the early years of settlement. The chapter will show that the extraordinary levels of disease, sickness, and death experienced during the first months led, at least in part, to the decision to suspend transportation to the Straits Settlements and Burma altogether and in the future to send all transportation convicts to Port Blair. This assured the long-term future of the Andamans as a penal colony.

The decision to resettle the Andamans

After its abortive attempt at settlement in the late eighteenth century, the East India Company paid little attention to the Andamans, though occasionally its ships sought shelter there, for instance during the Burmese wars of 1826-8. In the 1840s and 1850s, however, indigenous Andamanese communities made a number of attacks on shipwrecked sailors and passengers. After one particularly notorious incident in August 1855, the Company's court of directors asked Governor-General Lord Canning to reconsider the resettlement of the Islands. Canning then called for opinions on the issue. The government of India asked the commissioner of neighbouring Arakan, Henry Hopkinson, to write a report. Arakan was not only similar in landscape and climate to the Andamans, but had also been the site of an Indian penal settlement for some 30 years.[8]

'The relation in which the Andamans shall henceforth stand with reference to our commerce in the Bay of Bengal [and] to our commercial settlements on its coast', Hopkinson wrote, 'form a subject which I certainly do think deserves most earnest attention.' Drawing attention to the 'magnificent situation' of the Islands, near Madras, Calcutta, Akyab, Rangoon, Moulmein, and the Straits, Hopkinson expressed his astonishment that given the problem of attacks on shipping in the region the government wished that they could be 'blotted from the face of the ocean or sunk a thousand fathoms deep below its surface'. Their extent (as much as 2,000 square miles), fine harbours, and fertility made it imperative that they were not 'left in the possession of a handful of degenerate negroes, degraded in habits and intelligence to a level little above the beasts of the forest with which they dwell.' A penal colony might form the nucleus of a colony, or a colony might be allowed to grow up beside it. Moreover, according to Hopkinson, given the likely problems in procuring labour it would be difficult to form a permanent colony without establishing a convict settlement first.[9] Initially, Canning was unconvinced by these arguments. He maintained that there was already ample accommodation for convicts in other penal settlements, the climate was unfavourable, the project would be very expensive, and the Andamanese would remain hostile, at least in the short term. Both the government of India and the court of directors, however, were broadly in favour of Hopkinson's scheme.[10] Their view was only strengthened when shortly afterwards a group of Andamanese killed eight Chinese traders when they landed on the Islands in search of fresh water.[11] The magistrate of Tenasserim reminded the commissioner that in the past year three British vessels had been shipwrecked on or in the vicinity of the Islands: '[I]t appears highly discreditable in a civilised Government to allow such a state of things to exist within a sea, one may say, bounded by its own territories and on the high road to many of its chief emporia.'[12]

The governor-general remained sceptical, though the document detailing his precise objections was never published. While he acknowledged that the occupation of the Andamans by another foreign power would be 'highly inconvenient', and that British settlement would make shipping in the region more secure, before making a decision he first wanted more information on the Islands' harbours, inhabitants, climate, and natural resources.[13] Before making a formal proposal for colonization, therefore, a month before the outbreak of the mutiny-rebellion the court of directors decided to appoint a committee to visit the Islands and prepare a report on their suitability. Taking into account the passage of the southwest monsoon, Canning recommended that the party leave later in the autumn.[14] The committee was, therefore, set up at the height of the mutiny-rebellion by which time it had a noticeably different brief: to select the best site for a penal colony.[15] As an Andamans official put it later, despite the timing the mutiny-rebellion was not the initial reason for British colonization of the Islands, though it later became so. Rather, it was an attempt to control the open hostility of the Andamanese.[16]

With the mass jail-breaking that accompanied the violence of the revolt across north India, the crisis of the prisons gave a new impetus to the decision to settle the Andamans. A further factor was the Straits Settlements' intransigent refusal to accept any more Indian convicts. Indeed, it was in November 1857, the very month the Singapore authorities voiced strong objections to the reception of mutineer-rebels, that the court of directors put together the committee. As we saw in Chapter 4, the government ignored parallel suggestions to relocate mutineers to other colonies in Australia, in the Mascarenes, and in the Caribbean. At the head of the Andamans Committee was F.J. Mouat, inspector-general of jails in Bengal, who was well versed in Indian prison management. Accompanying Mouat were two assistants, Bengal army surgeon G.F. Playfair, and a lieutenant of the Indian navy, J.A. Heathcote. They arrived on the Islands on 11 December. Shortly afterwards, the government of India suspended the transportation of mutineers, deserters, and rebels overseas. Rather, such offenders were to be lodged in Alipur, Bombay or Madras. In a bid to ease the inevitable overcrowding, the government also ordered that some other prisoners could be sent to Singapore or Melaka.[17]

Mouat and his colleagues presented their report to the governor-general a month later. The report noted that almost every trace of the late eighteenth-century British settlement had been destroyed; just a few bricks and tiles and a rough stone jetty remained. Nevertheless, the report maintained that it was by far the best site on the Islands for a penal colony in relation to its abundance of wood and water, its sheltered location, and its landscape, for it would allow the separation and management of convicts of different penal classes. In order to prevent misunderstandings, the committee suggested renaming it Port Blair, in deference to the skills of the original surveyor, Lieutenant Archibald Blair, in selecting the spot.[18] Within two weeks, and as the penal crisis in India deepened, the governor-general decided that a penal colony would be established in the Andamans. At least in the first instance, it would receive mutineers or rebels only. Later on, the government would send all transportation convicts who it was not thought expedient to send to the Straits Settlements or Burma. In failing to connect its decision to the Straits' increasing recalcitrance against maintaining its penal settlements, the government of India was making a very public assertion of authority over its residencies, especially Singapore. Yet the decision to settle the Andamans was inevitably a massive concession to their increasingly important commercial interests.

Given his experience of managing penal settlements, Canning asked the superintendent of convicts in Moulmein, H. Man, to go to Port Blair to make arrangements for the reception, location, employment, and general control of convicts. He was given full executive and judicial authority, and the powers of commissioner under Acts XIV and XVII of 1857. This permitted him to try any person for crimes against the state. The governor-general also ordered Man to take Burmese workers (free or convict) to clear land before the Indian convicts began to arrive, to select and take all the tools and materials he thought necessary, to train a sufficient guard in the use of firearms, and to lay in supplies of rice, wheat, and medicines. Finally, the government of India instructed Man to select and appoint someone to act as convict superintendent. He would remain entirely under Man's authority and control, even after his return to Moulmein.[19] Not long afterwards, Man acted on Mouat's suggestion and appointed J.P. Walker, then superintendent of Agra jail, to the post.[20]

The plan for the management of the Andaman convicts was, from the outset, somewhat different from that in place in the Southeast Asian penal settlements. In contrast to public opinion in the Straits, the government of India argued that mutineer-rebel convicts were not desperate characters (the worst offenders had after all been executed) but men led into crimes against the state by others. They were not 'morally degraded criminals', but 'grievous political offenders'. Therefore, all new arrivals should be placed in a class roughly analogous to the third class in other penal settlements, and the best among them promoted immediately to the position of *tindal* (overseer). A fourth or even fifth class would exist as a punishment class only.

Yet despite the rhetoric, there was a certain nervousness about the political status of these convicts. In the early phase of colonization and until enough land was cleared the government envisaged that the superintendent and his guard would remain on board two ships in the harbour. On no account, it directed, should mutineer or rebel convicts be allowed on board either one.

In contrast, the organization of the convicts into work gangs followed the Southeast Asian system. Each gang would be overseen by a convict *tindal* who would be assisted by a *peon* or two. The *tindal's* duty was to oversee work, and to receive and regulate rations. He was also responsible for the convicts' behaviour and was duty bound to inform the superintendent of any particularly good or bad conduct. In a departure from practice in the Straits Settlements and Burma, and no doubt with one eye on the causes of the mutiny-rebellion, the governor-general directed that men of the same religion should work together in order to avoid objections over common messing. Once this had been done, the superintendent was not to listen to any refusals to obey orders on the grounds of caste.[21]

Finally, in its early planning stage the government of India made it clear that its 'ultimate aim' was to allow the wives and families of the convicts to accompany them. In part, this was related to vague long-term plans to settle the Andamans for broader political, economic, and commercial gain. Mostly, the government saw it as a way to prevent the 'gigantic evil' otherwise likely to occur among a large body of male convicts. It was all too aware of the homosexual scandals that had hit the Australian convict settlement at Norfolk Island after a mutiny there in 1846, especially as the events became integrated into abolitionist discourses around the question of transportation to Australia into the 1850s. An 1859 visitor to the Andamans, Surgeon G.G. Brown, wrote of the benefits of family emigration in the face of the 'frightful revelations' regarding the moral condition of the convicts in Norfolk Island.[22] While attempting to open up the colony to non-political offenders in 1859, Mouat also compared directly Norfolk Island to the exclusively male settlement in the Andamans. Without females, he wrote, the colony would become a 'pandemonium of the worst description'.[23] In 1858, the government of India ordered that although no immediate measures were necessary, a system of family migration should eventually be worked out according to 'judgment and experience'.[24]

The colonization of the Andaman Islands had most inauspicious beginnings. On receiving his instructions, Man could find only seven European soldiers to enlist as convict guards, and so he proposed that the mutineer-rebels be sent to Amherst jail while he made the requisite arrangements in Port Blair. Meantime, he took 50 Burmese convicts and a few European prisoners from the house of correction with him, and they began the process of land clearance. He then travelled back to Amherst from the Andamans to get the necessary stores together. The government of India rejected the prospect of sending convicts to the prison at Amherst, and requested Man's immediate return to the Andamans. Unfortunately, Walker and the first batch of 200 convicts arrived during his absence, leading to a rebuke from the government and a rather defensive explanation from Man.[25]

Because of the decision to transport mutineer-rebels to the Andamans, they were not seen as an appropriate destination for Bahadur Shah, the Mughal Emperor, who was instead sent into exile in Burma. Earlier proposals to send him to South Africa had come to nothing after the local authorities had refused to take him.[26] After the mutiny-rebellion, the British executed 26 members of his family and imprisoned 13 more in Agra jail. Another 15 died. Though the British authorities were unable to connect them with any overt act of rebellion, there was, as they observed at the time, a strong presumption that they shared the feelings of their family. Removal from India was designed to prevent them from becoming 'centres of intrigue and disaffection' in the future.[27] The governor-general proposed that the emperor's brother be sent to Moulmein and that the rest of his family be divided between Moulmein and Karachi. They would not be treated like ordinary prisoners, but would receive ten *rupees* subsistence per month. Initially, government lodged Bahadur Shah, his wife Zinat Mahal, and their two sons in Rangoon. Bahadur Shah apparently passed his days in 'listless apathy', while Zinat Mahal claimed frequently that members of the royal family were helpless victims of the rebels. Both boys, who were aged ten and 15 in 1859, were keen to learn English. Their parents wanted them to be sent to Britain.[28] Bahadur Shah petitioned unsuccessfully for his freedom, and his health continued to fail. He died in November 1862 and was buried in Rangoon.[29]

The convict ship

For most of the convicts sent to the Andaman Islands in the wake of the 1857–8 mutiny-rebellion, the ship was an unfamiliar technological space in which their sense of cultural and geographical displacement began. Indeed, during the first half of the nineteenth century colonial administrators expressed commonly the view that the journey into transportation itself was an important element of the punishment. This was largely due to the caste transgressions that the journey across the black water, or *kala pani*, entailed.

The 1838 Prison Discipline Committee, for instance, described transportation as 'a weapon of tremendous power'.[30] An integral part of life on board ship was the joint chaining and messing of men of all castes, classes, and religions. Water was shared from a common pump, and the washing out of drinking vessels was restricted.[31] If convicts died, none of the usual religious ceremonies took place. Rather their bodies were thrown overboard.[32] Though Fazl-i-Haq did not mention it, Munir Shikohabadi alluded to the impact of *kala pani* in the following verses: 'When they had to leave India and come to this island/The prisoners' evil fate made the water black'.[33] According to the civil surgeon of Allahabad jail, prisoners dreaded being put on board ship. The fact that they were chained together and taken far away from home produced a 'state of depression' conducive to diseases like dysentery and gangrene.[34]

In the immediate aftermath of the outbreak of revolt the government drew up a new set of rules for the regulation of transportation ships. The rules ordered European sergeants, assisted by Indian officers, to keep a diary of the quantity and quality of food and water issued to convicts, the state of the convicts and their quarters, and any complaints. They were also to be present at the opening and closing of the jail wards and at the issue of rations. The officers were responsible for checking that convicts cleaned their quarters properly, that convicts themselves were clean, and that the Indian doctor visited the sick daily. Finally, they were to bring any complaints they could not settle to the notice of the ship's commander. The Indian doctor on each ship was to see each new medical case the moment it was reported, and all sick convicts at daybreak and sunset. The rules also stipulated that he should visit each ward daily to see that it was 'clean and wholesome' and that he should keep a journal. Every morning, the cell doors would be opened and convicts would mount the decks in 'safe' numbers. When the weather was hot they would bathe daily before going back down below decks; twice a week they would wash their clothes. Finally, the 'most respectful and well-behaved' convict in each ward was to be appointed *killaburdar*. These convicts were expected to bring to the sergeant's notice any impropriety, and to oversee the disposal of human waste.[35]

Fears about ritual pollution intensified in the wake of the mutiny-rebellion for, as we have seen, during the revolt there were widely circulating fears about British interference in matters of religion and caste. Many high-caste Hindu mutineer-rebels no doubt approached the prospect of their transportation with serious cultural anxieties. Indeed, in February 1858 officials discovered letters written by transportation prisoners hidden in their bedding. They at first assumed that the letters contained details of a plot with sepoys stationed nearby. However, when they were translated it was found that they were, in fact, private correspondence between prisoners and their families in which they asked their relatives to send money and a supply of dry food for their steamer journey to Calcutta.[36] Many Hindu convicts refused to eat cooked food on board ship, instead taking dry rice and *dhal*, which resulted in bowel complaints. As in mainland jails, administrators made a clear association between high caste and high mortality on board transportation ships.[37]

In a glimpse of convict perspective, two rebels released and returned to India under the amnesty of 1859 expressed their feelings about transportation to the superintendent of Allahabad central jail thus: 'When on the ship they could see no road, trees, land and only the sky above, and the black, green and blue waters around. The sahib-log only knew where to go, and they had to sit day and night looking through telescopes.'[38] A few years later, *Wahabi* rebel Maulana Jafer Thanesari revealed the sense of cultural dislocation he had experienced on board ship. The British officers had not understood any of the Indian languages, he wrote, and the Panjabis were given rice rations rather than their customary wheat. Seasickness was a problem in seas that would 'lash on the ship like a mountain'.[39] High seas and bad weather made transportation a miserable experience for many convicts. In July 1859, for instance, the ship *Fire Queen* experienced very severe weather and had to drop anchor for three days. The convicts got drenched by the unrelenting waves, and it was not long before sickness broke out on board. Four convicts died.[40]

In September 1858, Superintendent Walker reported high rates of sickness and mortality in the Andamans, concluding that one of the principal causes was the transportation of sick convicts to the Islands. Most convicts had undergone long periods of confinement on the mainland before their embarkation. Many of the jails in which they were held had been damaged or destroyed during the mutiny-rebellion, which resulted in overcrowding and poor sanitation. The unhealthiest convicts of all were those from Karachi. As Walker reported, death-rates shortly after arrival ranged from 6.3 to 28.7 per cent and averaged 15.0 per cent. Death-rates at sea, however, remained on the whole relatively low. With the exception of the *Dalhousie*, on which 23 (14.12 per cent) of the convicts died, rates were just one or two and occasionally three per cent (Table 5). The high rate on the *Dalhousie* was apparently the result of the embarkation of all the mutineers then in Alipur jail during an outbreak of cholera. There were also 14 convalescents whom the civil assistant surgeon thought could be sent with advantage to themselves and to other prisoners still in hospital. He had anticipated a short journey to the Andamans, but the ship was delayed for some days before it set sail. The convicts were kept below deck and given only parched rice and *dhal*.[41] Most deaths on convict vessels were put down to dysentery. One or two convicts were said to have gone overboard, though it was difficult to ascertain whether these deaths were accidental or suicide.[42] In one more certain case, convict rebel Jait Sing apparently either pretended to be or was actually seasick and somersaulted overboard.[43] As we saw in Chapter 4, another factor in death-rates at sea was the possibility of convicts awaiting shipment hiding or downplaying their symptoms, in order to avoid being detained in jail without their transported friends or kin. After two convicts died on the *Phoenix* in April 1860, for instance, their shipmates told Superintendent Haughton that the medical officer in Alipur did not want to send them, but agreed to do so on the 'earnest entreaty of the convicts themselves.'[44]

As a result of high death-rates on the early Karachi ships, the government formulated new rules to regulate the treatment of convicts from the North-West Provinces on their way to Calcutta for shipment. The rules ordered the medical superintendent and civil surgeon at Allahabad jail to inspect each inmate and the ship's accommodation before they embarked prisoners for Calcutta, and to detain any sick or infirm men. Each gang would be accompanied by an Indian officer who would issue their rations. At every station along the river, the local magistrate was required to enquire into any complaints by the prisoners. Finally, upon arrival at Alipur the medical officer would inspect the convicts and report to the government of Bengal and the superintendent of Allahabad jail.[45] Conditions on board transportation ships, which after the Company lost its monopoly in 1834 were chartered by private merchants and were not specially fitted out for convicts, did not necessarily show an improvement.

The *Boanerges* arrived in the Andamans in September 1859 under the command of Captain W.B. Skeene. Lieutenant Hurlock was the officer in charge of the guard. During the journey, of the 300 convicts embarked ten died, one committed suicide, and the doctor admitted 65 others to the ship's hospital. On landing, the surviving convicts complained bitterly about the voyage to the Indian overseer of the Islands, Lalla Muttra Doss. Immediately, Superintendent Walker set up a judicial enquiry into the convicts' claims. These hinged on the inadequate issue of water and rations, and the lack of toilet or washing facilities. The enquiry concluded that the convicts had not been treated with the humanity and attention to health and comfort stipulated in the ship's charter. Walker took the case seriously enough to forward it to the lieutenant-governor in Calcutta for consideration.[46] During his enquiry, Walker interviewed several convicts, and though mediated and translated by the peculiar demands of judicial process, their evidence constitute a unique convict perspective on the voyage into transportation in the aftermath of revolt.[47]

The first man called to the stand was Ramnarain Singh, who was enumerated as convict number 3,455. Why he was chosen to testify first is unclear, but presumably he had represented the convicts' complaints to the Indian overseer, and was thus a man of some status held in high regard by his shipmates. If this was the case, Walker too would have recognized his standing. It is not altogether clear who translated his evidence which presumably was not in English. After his experiences in Agra jail, no doubt Walker himself could understand Ramnarain Singh. However, given the cultural interventions in parenthesis it seems likely that a convict clerk translated and wrote down his words:

> I arrived here in a Ship whose name I do not know, three days ago, from Calcutta. The voyage lasted twenty days, and there were three hundred Convicts embarked, all the Convicts experienced great inconvenience *(tukleef)* on board the Ship, the inconvenience consisted in the want of an adequate supply of drinking water and the want of opportunities to ease ourselves and to make water. During the twenty days I was on board, I only had opportunities for easing myself four times, a large number of Convicts were on the deck at a time to ease themselves, and the time allowed was insufficient to allow all to ease themselves. When the opportunity was afforded, we were not allowed water *ab-i-dust* to clean ourselves. Owing to the dirty state of our persons, from the want of water *(ab-i-dust)* to clean ourselves after going to the privy, and the treatment we were there subject to from the European Guard, many did not eat, to avoid as much as possible the necessity for going to the privy. We also suffered great inconvenience from the want of vessels to make water in, there was not a single vessel below into which we could make water, there were no vessels for us to make water into either for use by day or by night; there was no description of vessel, either cask, bucket, or earthen vessel *(gurrah)*. In the apartment I occupied there were seventy or seventy-five Convicts, and for their use during the whole voyage, there was not at any time a vessel into which we could ease ourselves, we experienced great inconvenience from the want of drinking water; we only received from one to one and a half *kutorahs* full of water, a *kutorah* will hold about two pounds (one seer) of water ...

Questions by Lieut. Hurlock, to the deponent. Do you make this complaint of your own free will?
Answer. – Of my own free will *up ne khooshee se* [*apne khushi se*].
Question. – Were you ever sick on board?
Answer. – No.
Question. – How could you escape sickness of your bowels were only moved four times in twenty days?
Answer. – God preserved me, I only eat the Sugar allowed, dissolved in water.
Question. – Did you receive your proper rations while on boardship (sic) with the exception of water?
Answer. – I have no complaint to make about not receiving my rations, but I was unable to eat them, they remained by me.

Although the convicts had represented their grievances to the European sergeant, nothing had come of them. Ramnarain Singh claimed that he had never seen a European officer inspect the convict quarters. Convict sweeper Chimmum confirmed that the four night tubs placed initially on deck had been removed either for washing clothes or for use in the sick ward. One of the Indian doctors on board, Shekh Ramzan Alee, also supported the claims: 'I have known Convicts beg of the Sentries to be removed, and allowed to ease themselves, but I never knew a case where permission was granted.'

Walker next called convict Rugooputee Raee to give evidence; he further corroborated Ramnarain Singh's testimony. Expressing a clear understanding of 'the inconveniences which, as Convicts, we could not but expect to experience' he spoke eloquently of additional factors which were not supposed to be part of the punishment of transportation, especially the denial of the flour ration. 'If we had received it', he said, 'we should have suffered less inconvenience, as we should have made hulwa [halwa], with equal parts of flour, ghee and sugar, which is an article which can be eaten by Hindoos on board ship.' Though Ramnarain Singh had spoken of the shortage of water and toilet facilities, his was the first of many allusions to the precise cultural threat that transportation posed. Walker also called convict *killaburdar* Jugdeo Singh, the man responsible for issuing rations, to the stand. He claimed that he did not know convicts were entitled to an allowance of flour. The doctor Shekh Ramzan Alee agreed that the convicts had not received this ration. His colleague Deedar Allee added that the Hindus told him that they would like a flour allowance in order to make *puris* (deep-fried unleavened bread). The Muslim convicts had suffered much less, he said, because despite the shortage of water and inadequate toilet facilities they ate cooked food. He added: 'Hindoos cannot eat without washing the parts and their hands after easing themselves, and as they were not allowed even Sea-water for the purpose, they did not eat till driven by necessity, and from this they became weak.' He claimed that 'two or three' of the convicts had told him that a man who committed suicide had done so because he was so short of water that he had nothing to drink and was unable to perform his ablutions. He added that because there were no night tubs in the wards, convicts either eased themselves where they slept or into their clothing. They then ripped off the cloth and tied it into a bundle that they threw into the sea. If they made a mess, the convict sweepers complained to the guard and the convicts were flogged. According to another convict witness, Shooghoolam, a man named Mistereewa was taken to the deck, held by two Europeans, and thrashed with what appeared to Walker from his description to be a riding whip. This would not have been the first time that transportation convicts were subjected to the arbitrary authority of a ship's command for some supposed disciplinary transgression.[48] Deedar Allee claimed also to have witnessed a convict so desperate that he was forced to urinate into the guards' compartment. This might be read also as an act of resistance or insubordination.

Extraordinarily, Captain Skeene claimed that he did not know that he was supposed to have been in charge of the convicts. As he saw it, his role was only to supply each man with a gallon of water per day, which he claimed to have done. That neither he nor his officers had the linguistic skills to communicate with the convicts perhaps explains his further assertion: that he had not heard a single complaint during the whole journey. His interpretation of transportation ship rules was that it was the responsibility of the European sergeant to oversee the convicts, not him as officer in charge of the guard. His role was only to prevent 'disturbances or excitement' and to punish insubordination. Skeene claimed that the convicts had received their full compliment of rations, except for smoking tobacco and oil because of associated fire risks; firewood which he thought the non-cooking Hindus did not need; flour that the convict *killaburdar* had refused to issue; and black pepper which had been stowed away accidentally. Hurlock also stated that the convicts had ample opportunities for easing themselves. He relied on a familiar set of cultural representations when he asserted: '[I]f the Convicts did make water into their drinking vessels, or ease themselves into their clothes, they did so from sheer laziness, it being well known to the Commanders of Emigrant Ships and Convict Transports, that Indian Emigrants and Convicts do so from that cause.' Furthermore, he claimed, the convicts had only bathed when compelled.

Walker sent the judicial enquiry to India where the government of Bengal asked the superintendent of marine, J. Rennie, whether the remaining passage money should be forfeited by way of damages. Rennie thought that it should.[49] In a professional closing of the ranks another senior officer in the Indian navy did not agree. He wrote of his experiences of transported convicts and the 'filthy and reckless abandonment in their habits'. Their distress, he went on, was nothing more than the natural consequence of seasickness and the motion of the vessel. The 'horrid alternatives' the convicts described were he said well known to be common and voluntary on transportation ships as well as among native troops. If anybody was to blame, he said, it was the Indian doctors.[50]

A further focus of the Indian investigation was whether prison officials had embarked any sick convicts. The superintendent and the doctor of Alipur were adamant that they had not. The latter presented a somewhat surprising perspective on convict attitudes to the Andamans:

> I had purposely refrained from returning [sick convicts] to Jail, lest they should relapse, and compel me to keep them back, as has sometimes happened much to the chagrin of the Convicts, many of whom are eager and anxious to proceed to the Andamans, where not only are their fetters removed, but their friends and relatives have preceded them. As the change offers a chance, sometimes the only one, of their recovery, I consider it my duty to comply in every practicable instance with their wish for removal.[51]

In the opinion of both the superintendent and the medical officer the convicts who died must have been subject to 'fearful treatment'.[52] To some extent, the Indian doctor Ramzan Alee agreed. On embarkation, he said, he had put 40 convicts under treatment, 33 with chronic and acute dysentery. However, ill health had been aggravated by the overcrowded state of the cabins, poor ventilation, hot weather, and inferior rations. Of the 65 convicts he admitted to the ship's hospital, 30 were suffering from diarrhoea and 21 had symptoms of dysentery.[53]

A further complicating factor in the case was Skeene's claim that the situation had arisen because of bad feeling between Walker and Hurlock during an earlier voyage. This we cannot know, but Skeene claimed that after the *Boanerges* arrived Hurlock refused to acknowledge Walker's authority. Walker subsequently found fault with all the ship's papers and used the convicts to get Hurlock into trouble.[54] For Skeene, convict testimony was worthless. He called for the depositions of 'honest and respectable deponents' instead, writing to Walker on the eve of his departure that 'the whole of this trouble has arisen from your own vindictiveness.[55] The lieutenant-governor disagreed, expressing the opinion that Skeene had failed to execute the full conditions of the charter party. Even making allowances for 'the filthy habits of the Natives when on board Ship', they had no choice but the 'disgusting alternatives' detailed during the enquiry. He and the advocate-general, therefore, suggested withholding the rest of the passage money.[56] They also heaped some of the blame on Hurlock, and the government of India ordered that the commander-in-chief of the Indian navy and the Bombay government take steps to mark his inhumanity and un-officer like conduct.[57]

While the conditions on board the *Boanerges* were shocking, they were not unprecedented.[58] Occasionally, convicts had suffered similarly appalling treatment during the period to 1857–8. Nine of the 97 convicts shipped to the penal settlement in Pinang on the *Imam of Muscat* in 1850 died on the way or shortly after arrival, for instance, mostly of dysentery. Given the low death-rates usually in evidence, this was extraordinary, and later it emerged that at least four of the convicts had refused to take any food while on board.[59] In 1853, six convicts *en route* for Singapore on the *Margaret Skelly* died of dysentery. Many others had disembarked in what the resident councillor of Singapore, F. Church, described as 'a very weak state'. The ship had been at sea for 42 days, but with only 30 days' rations. The convicts complained about their limited allowances.[60] *Subahdar* Shaik Hyder, commander of the Indian guard, claimed that because water ran short the convicts did not have enough to drink or to cook their rice.[61] There was clearly a cultural dimension to the convicts' complaints as well. The ship's commander, Alfred Pearce, claimed that rations could not have been short because the convicts had thrown cooked food overboard.[62] Chief Mate George Holland maintained that the convicts would not take their rations because they were 'too lazy to cook'. On closer analysis it appears that the convicts only refused their rations at the end of the voyage, when the non-cooking Hindu convicts' grain had run out and been substituted with rice.[63] The Bengal authorities were sympathetic to the convicts' claims, and ruled that as the provisions put on board were insufficient the remaining payment for the journey (one-third of the total) should be withheld.[64]

In a similar case in April 1857, 19 of the 131 convicts embarked for Singapore on the *Atlanta* died on board, one on landing, and two others on their way to the convict lines. Two more died within a few days and 40 were still in hospital two months later.[65] The surgeon of the settlement reported that he had 'never witnessed so much misery, disease and wretchedness as existed amongst these men'.[66] The government asked Mouat to conduct an enquiry. He found that because they did not want to be given purgatives some of the convicts had hidden their sickness before embarkation. Also, the vessel's commander told Mouat that although once he had forced the convicts to bathe and wash their clothes and bedding, it had caused so much discontent that he had decided not to do so again. He did not mention the fact that convicts were issued with only one set of clothes and so had nothing to wear on such occasions. Further, the enquiry reported that although the convicts had been allowed the stipulated space (six by half a foot), they were not able to lie down properly. Mouat reported the 'terrible distress' that this must have caused and recommended that in future transportation ships should allow convicts the same space as indentured labourers (six feet by three).[67]

There are suggestive hints in the archives too that there was a significant degree of convict unrest on board the early Andaman ships, though we know almost nothing about it. During the period to 1857–8, planned or actual violent disorder was either discovered or broke out on a dozen ships transporting convicts inland for embarkation or to overseas penal settlements in Mauritius and the Straits. Because convict transportation was organized by the East India Company rather than by private merchants, public enquiries always followed and left an impressive paper trail in the colonial archives.[68] Perhaps due to the political sensitivity associated with the transportation of mutineer-rebels, or more substantively because of the general disorganization that characterized colonial administration and record-keeping during this period, the archive produces only hints of the violent disorder on early mutineer-rebel ships. In the first discernable case, in February 1858 40 prisoners convicted of treason, mutiny, rebellion, and riot embarked on the *Julia* for Singapore. There was an outbreak on board, but we know only that one man was killed. As mutineer-rebels, the convicts became caught up in the Singapore panics and so the government transferred them to Port Blair before they could stand trial. Much to the chagrin of the *Singapore Free Press* they did not face charges in the Andamans either.[69] Later that year, the owners of the ship *Edward* sought compensation for firearms dispensed during the voyage to the Andamans, though there are no details of the circumstances.[70] Curiously, Walker had reported earlier that the convicts had been generally satisfied with their treatment on board.[71]

In a third case that year, 37 mutineers embarked on the *Frere* in Karachi. Though they had attempted previously to escape from jail, officials had not issued the commander with special instructions. Once out at sea the convicts mutinied. They tried to take the ship but failed, with the loss of nine men.[72] The inquiry into the attempted rising noted the poor fit of the convicts' handcuffs. The commissioner of Multan wrote: '[I]t is not advisable to trust to [sic] the security of handcuffs and fetters alone. Unless a prisoner is secured in a manner which humanity must forbid, he cannot be kept in safe custody unless he is constantly watched.'[73] The surgeon in charge of the jail added that fetters and handcuffs could not be made perfectly secure without hurting prisoners. Moreover, those with supple joints or those who lost weight in prison found it quite easy to remove even once well-fitting irons.[74] Fetters were, therefore, a far from perfect penal technology.[75]

'Hindustan in miniature'

Superintendent Walker arrived in the Andamans with the first batch of 200 convicts in March 1858. Three thousand more followed shortly afterwards (Table 4). In total, during the 18 month period from March 1858 to October 1859, the government shipped 3,697 convicts to the Islands, including dozens of men convicted of jail-breaking.[76] In April 1858, the government decided that all persons convicted under Acts XI and XIV of 1857 would be classed as rebels, and it would send accordingly those sentenced to more than three years' imprisonment to the Andamans. This was the case even where they had been sentenced to a term of imprisonment rather than transportation *per se*.[77] By this time, the 83 deserters and mutineers who had already been sent from Bombay to Pinang had also been transferred to Port Blair. Nine of the original batch had died while in the Straits Settlements.[78]

Table 4. Convict ships to the Andamans, 1858–60

Ship	Sailed from	Nos embarked (arrived)	Departed/arrived
Semiramis	Calcutta	200 (n.a.)	d. 4 Mar. 1858 a. 10 Mar. 1858
Roman Emperor	Karachi	175 (171)	d. 27 Feb. 1858 a. 6 Apr. 1858
Edward	Karachi	133 (130)	d. n.a. a. 13 Apr. 1858
Dalhousie	Calcutta	163 (140)	d. 8 Apr. 1858 a. 16 Apr. 1858
Sesostris	Bombay (via Singapore/Pinang)	49/ 83 (n.a.)	d. n.a. a. 12 June 1858
Italian	Bombay	80 (79)	d. n.a. a. 1 July 1858

Ship	Sailed from	Nos embarked (arrived)	Departed/arrived
Coromandel	Calcutta	n.a. (148)	d. n.a. a. 20 July 1858
Fire Queen	Calcutta	47 (47)	d. 4 Aug. 1858 a. 12 Aug. 1858
Australian	Calcutta	282 (n.a.)	d. 26 Aug. 1858 a. n.a.
Louis Henry	Bombay	138 (n.a.)	d. 23 Sept. 858 a. n.a.
Sydney	Calcutta	318 (n.a.)	d. 14 Oct. 1858 a. n.a.
Tubal Cain	Calcutta	65 (n.a.)	d. 28 Oct. 1858 a. n.a.
Royal Bride	Madras	n.a. (24)	d. n.a. a. 20 Oct. 1858
Fire Queen	n.a.	n.a. (77)	d. n.a. a. 8 Nov. 1858
Fire Queen	n.a.	130 (129)	d. n.a. a. 15 Feb. 1859
Countess of Elgin	Karachi/Bombay	223 (220)/ 13 (13)	d. n.a. a. 7 Mar. 1859
Flying Venus	Karachi/Bombay	112 (111)/ 14 (12)	d. n.a. a. 7 Mar. 1859
Melanie	Madras	26 (26)	d. n.a. a. 18 Mar. 1859
Fire Queen	Bengal	5 (5)	d. n.a. a. 23 Mar. 1859
Fire Queen	Bengal	n.a. (150)	d. n.a. a. 25 Apr. 1859
Tubal Cain	n.a.	214 (214)	d. n.a. a. 23 June 1859
Perikop	Karachi/Bombay	n.a. (50/18)	d. n.a. a. 16 July 1859
Fire Queen	Bengal	150 (146)	d. n.a. a. 29 July 1859
Fire Queen	Bengal	n.a. (58)	d. n.a. a. 28 Aug. 1859
Boanerges	Bengal	300 (289)	d. n.a. a. 1 Sept. 1859
Fire Queen	n.a.	n.a. (97)	d. n.a. a. 8 Nov. 1859
Phoenix	n.a.	94 (90)	d. n.a. a. 17 Apr. 1860
Emma Colvin	Karachi	n.a. (94, inc. 7 women)	d. n.a. a. 22 Apr. 1860
Fire Queen	Bengal	n.a. (29)	d. n.a. a. Apr. 1860

Sources: OIOC P.188.53 (IJC 7 May 1858): Walker to Beadon, 6, 13, 17 Apr. 1858; OIOC P.188.53 (IJC 14 May 1858): statement of mutineer and rebel convicts sent to Port Blair from the Alipore Jail, quarter ending 30 Apr. 1858; OIOC P.188.56 (IJC 13 Aug. 1858): Walker to Beadon, 3 July 1858; NAI Home (Judicial 16 July 1858): Walker to Beadon, 12 June 1858; OIOC P.206.60 (IJP 12 Nov. 1858): Walker to Beadon, 4 Sept. 1858, enc. report on the causes of the severe sickness and great mortality which has prevailed amongst the convicts at Port Blair penal settlement in the Andaman Islands, since the formation of the settlement on the 10th March, up to the 25th August 1858 (henceforth 'report on sickness and mortality Port Blair'); OIOC P.206.60 (IJP 12 Nov. 1858): number of rebel convicts sent to Port Blair from Bombay, 1 Aug. – 31 Oct. 1858; OIOC P.206.60 (IJP 12 Nov. 1858): number of rebel convicts sent to Port Blair from Alipur, 1 Aug. – 31 Oct. 1858; OIOC P.206.61 (IJP 29 July 1859): Walker to Beadon, 21 Oct. 1858; OIOC P.260.61 (IJP 29 July 1859): Walker to Beadon, 10 Dec. 1858, 16 Feb 1859, 25 Mar. 1859, 23 June 1859; OIOC P.260.61 (IJP 12 Aug. 1859): Walker to Grey, 18 July 1859, 19 Aug. 1859; OIOC P.260.61 (IJP 19 Aug. 1859): Walker to Grey, 2 Aug. 1859, 10 Sept. 1859; OIOC P.206.62 (IJP 6 Jan. 1860): Haughton to Grey, 13 Nov. 1859; OIOC P.206.62 (IJP 11 May 1860), Haughton to Grey, 21 Apr. 1860, 24 Apr. 1860; OIOC P.206.62 (19 May 1860): Haughton to Grey, 10 Apr. 1860.

In April 1858, a month after his arrival in the Andamans with the first shipload of convicts, Superintendent Walker submitted his first progress report on the colony.[79] The government of India approved most of his suggestions, relieved Man of his responsibilities, and placed Walker in sole charge.[80] Though Man's earlier working contingent had already prepared some ground, as soon as he arrived Walker put the convicts to clearing Chatham Island in the mouth of the harbour. Their organization was decidedly military in orientation, though of course military discipline had considerable overlaps with the disciplinary systems developed for penal labour, both in road gangs in India and in overseas penal settlements. Walker divided the convicts into section gangs of 25, each under a convict section gangsman. Four sections made a subdivision, under the charge of a convict subdivision gangsman. Four subdivisions constituted a division, under the charge of a convict division gangsman, a free overseer, and a native doctor. Where Walker's system departed from the system of prison or convict gang labour used in India and its penal settlements was in the arming of the gangsmen. By the end of April, a couple of hundred convicts were put to work in the relatively remote north side of Phoenix Bay. Fearing attacks from the Andamanese, Walker issued them with muskets and ammunition.[81] Not long afterwards, when 92 convicts escaped and took three of the muskets, he decided to withdrawn them.[82]

Shortly after putting the convicts to work on Chatham, Walker found the water supply inadequate and so he sent three other section gangs to nearby Ross Island. He proposed that it should be made the colony's headquarters. The vegetation was extremely dense and Walker anticipated that unless large numbers of convicts were sent land clearance would take some time. Therefore, he proposed that at least 10,000 convicts be sent annually over the next five years. To his superior officer Man, at this time still in ultimate charge of the penal colony, Walker's plans appeared too ambitious. 'I do not consider we possess as yet sufficient knowledge of the temper of the prisoners, or the feeling with which they regard their deportation', he wrote, 'to warrant my recommending the immediate enormous increased applied for'. With just one Indian overseer to assist him, Man urged Walker to proceed cautiously: '[I]t will be too late to discover that we have made an error when 10 or 20,000 men are congregated'.[83]

Walker, of course, had considerable experience in the management of convicts from his previous post as superintendent of Agra jail. However, in the Andamans he had few assistants. Considering the plan to send all convicted mutineer-rebels to the islands, the establishment of the colony was remarkably small. It consisted of an officer in charge based in Moulmein (Man); Walker as superintendent; Assistant Surgeon Alexander Gamach in medical charge; Assistant Apothecary J. Ringrow; two Indian doctors, Nawab Khan and Kurreem Buksh; two overseers, Mr Richardson and Lalla Muthoora [Muttra] Doss, who had been previously been deputy jailer under Walker in Agra; and a naval guard of 50 commanded by Lieutenant Templer. The only other personnel were two hospital assistants and a hospital sweeper. Walker was keen to recruit his previous assistant jailer Kesree Doss to assist him. The government of India agreed to call for his services,[84] but in the meantime Walker relied intensely on the Islands themselves to provide a sort of 'natural' prison. He saw the jungle, the sea, and the Islands' inhabitants as the most effective guards.[85] Though the first month of settlement passed without any major challenge to Walker's authority, the government of India counselled him against 'being lulled into a false sense of security', and asked him to consider carefully whether any additional force was necessary. In the meantime, it warned, guards should always carry loaded weapons.[86]

In the colony's early days, as Walker himself had anticipated, a substantial proportion of the convicts tried to escape. It seems that many held the belief that beyond the jungle there was a strip of land connecting the Andamans to Burma or India. As during 1857–8, such rumours were central to the transmission of resistance.[87] Just four days after the first batch of convicts arrived, the first man made an unsuccessful bid to flee Chatham by swimming to the mainland. Four days later, 21 convicts built a raft and escaped from Ross Island. A few days afterwards, 11 more Ross convicts absconded. It was not long before one man made his way back to Chatham, half-starved, infested with vermin, and telling tales of great hardship. He said that the convicts had attempted to get on 'the road to Burma', but that they had been unable to find food or fresh water. About a hundred Andamanese attacked them, and killed their leader. Walker noted that the account of this unnamed man had a good effect on the other convicts, and none tried to escape for a while after his return. Convict dreams of freedom from the British yoke had not died with transportation, however. Many thought that they could find service with the 'King of Burma' and return to the Andamans to destroy the penal establishment.[88] Convict Dudhnath Tewari was a mutinous sepoy from the fourteenth regiment, and had been transported from Karachi in the *Roman Emperor* in April 1858. He escaped soon after his arrival and lived with the Andamanese for over a year, learning their language and taking a wife. He returned to the penal settlement voluntarily, after hearing that the Andamanese were planning an attack. In a remarkable display of convict and military solidarity, he said that his object was to save the lives of his 'fellow convicts' and 'fellow soldiers'. He also said that he had escaped initially with the hope of enlisting with the 'Burma *rajah*', whom he and others believed could be found after ten days' march.[89] In the aftermath of Tewari's experiences, rumours about the assistance of an Andamanese '*rajah*' circulated freely. In reality, however, escaped convicts usually returned to the settlement starving, sick or injured. Those who did not come back were assumed to have drowned, starved or been killed.

Though he issued convicts with rations, Walker anticipated the introduction of money gratuities with which convicts could purchase food and clothing from convict managed shops. These shops would be supplied by government stores, which were themselves supplied from Calcutta, and the convict shopkeepers (*banias*) would be allowed to make a small profit (about three per cent). Walker felt that this would encourage thrift among the convicts and would form an important part of convict discipline. He wrote: '[I]ndustry shall bring its own rewards, and idleness its own punishments'. Crucially, each section would be issued with the daily allowance which could rise if it worked more hours than usual. It would be up to a convict *panchayat* (council of arbitrators) to decide what percentage of the usual earnings of the division beyond the three-quarters specified by the rules the sick would be entitled to and what reduction on the share of wages any idlers would receive. Section, subdivision, and division gangsmen would receive additional allowances and commissions on the earnings of their sections, subdivisions, and divisions. When the under secretary to the government of India, R.B. Chapman, visited the colony in November, he reported that this system was working well. The *bania* shops were, he said, keystones of the system. Spectacles, scissors, knives, and razors were all for sale, and in October alone the principal *bania* earned 51 *rupees*, a considerable augmentation to his standard daily allowance of two and a half *rupees*.[90]

By the middle of April 1858, the government had transported over 600 convicts to the colony. By the end of the month, 94 more convicts had absconded, reducing convict strength to such a degree that Walker was forced to withdraw the detachment stationed at Phoenix Bay. Once again, Walker reported a widespread belief among convicts that a *rajah* based on the south west coast of Great (now South) Andaman governed the island. According to him they escaped with the intention of offering him their services as soldiers against the British government. He lamented that escapes would continue until experience proved the hopelessness of success in surviving away from the settlement or reaching the Indian mainland. The government of India agreed, hoping that some of the convicts would return in a poor state.[91] In the meantime, it asked Walker's opinion on the branding of convicts on the breast or arms, a means to prevent them from merging into the general population were they to make it back to India.[92] There was some precedent for this, for the East India Company had practised penal tattooing in India until 1849. Walker responded to the proposal with enthusiasm, suggesting that officers brand the letters P.B./L or P.B./T followed by each convict's number to denote 'Port Blair life' or 'Port Blair term' respectively. However, ultimately the government decided firmly against a measure that it had only recently abolished as a 'barbarous' practice.[93]

Though direct convict testimonies are absent from Walker's account of the early months of colonization, his correspondence includes mediated representations of their experiences of transportation and escape. During the first half of May, over 80 escaped convicts returned to Chatham Island. Some had faced starvation while at large; others had been attacked by indigenous Andamanese. Walker later wrote of the 'unusually strong temptation to escape' by men who would be 'delighted' to have the chance to serve against the British. Indeed, more than a third of all convicts tried to escape within 50 days of arrival. Moreover, with 190 convicts having absconded from three places in the space of just one day, the escapes were pre-planned. According to Walker, convicts took oaths and threatened religious excommunication or even death to those who refused to escape. Walker met this resistance with a degree of force unprecedented in convict management, and used his powers as special commissioner to sentence escapees to death for rebellion against the British government, unless they gave information against their fellow men. As Sen has noted, in this way effectively Walker criminalized the refusal to give information.[94] Despite Walker's draconian threat, convicts refused to testify against each other and on 18 May Walker carried out the mass hanging of 81 returned men. When he reported this to the government of India, he noted that the remaining convicts were working hard and behaving well.[95]

When it learnt of the hangings, the government acted immediately to prevent Walker from the future execution of absconders. Rather, it ordered, they should be flogged and put in irons where they would serve as a visible reminder of the futility of escape.[96] The president in council, J.P. Grant, much lamented Walker's actions, with handwritten notes on the printed proceedings expressing his opinion that the existence of a system which permitted the escape of so many convicts was a dismal failure.[97] In a printed minute he said that he did not wish to charge Walker with inhumanity, but that he believed the early settlement's history was 'melancholy'. The convicts were unlike the ordinary mass of offenders that usually made up the populations of India's prisons and penal settlements. Out of humanity, mutineer-rebels had been transported rather than executed. They were, he said, simply responding to a 'natural impulse' to escape and should not have been punished so severely.[98] When the issue of the power of the Port Blair superintendent to execute convicts emerged later in 1870, it was revealed that Walker's mass hangings were of 'so doubtful nature' that the government of India had destroyed detailed records shortly afterwards.[99]

The problem was of course Walker's reliance on the Islands' difficult terrain and hostile inhabitants rather than a large armed guard as deterrents to escape. As he put it, he told the convicts repeatedly that escape was hopeless: 'I was among the convicts all day – and told them both in groups and individually.'[100] Indeed, one council member went as far as to say that it was technically incorrect to speak of the 'escape' of convicts who were not guarded.[101] Before he received the government's orders prohibiting hanging as a punishment for escape, Walker had executed five more men. Before they were led to the gallows, they had assured him that the Andamanese had killed about half of the 140 men still at large.[102] Walker appears to have shown little remorse in the face of stern criticism. When the government's orders arrived, he responded simply that convict management in the Andamans was quite different from that in India.[103] As M.V. Portman, officer in charge of the Andamanese after 1879 put it, British officers who had served during the revolt could not be expected to treat mutineer-rebels with 'undue leniency'.[104] Indeed, with no place of secure confinement his scope for the punishment of secondary offences was circumscribed. As Surgeon Brown put it a few months later, 'the laws of Draco' were necessary until circumstances permitted a milder code.[105]

After criticism from the government of India, Walker implemented new measures to try to prevent escapes. In particular convicts were mustered four times a day, and counted every second hour during the night by the subdivision and section gangsmen. Walker also told the convicts that if any more escaped he would fetter all of them.[106] Once again he met with government hostility. Putting all convicts in irons would, it said, simply drive them to desperation, increase sickness (through ulceration), and reduce their working power.[107] Indeed, in his March 1859 medical report on the penal colony, Brown reported that he had seen cases where ulceration was so bad that the muscle had been destroyed, exposing the bones and tendons.[108] Although Walker adopted a policy of flogging the often debilitated convicts who returned from escape bids with the not insubstantial punishment of 30 stripes, absconding continued. More tales of hardship emerged, in particular of sanguinary encounters with local communities that left convicts dead or injured.[109] According to Portman's later account, convicts then in the colony told him later that as punishment they had been handcuffed in pairs. The 'worst characters' were taken to the beach and attached to the ground by an iron bar passed through their fetters. They were then made to do whatever work they could manage in the position.[110]

When Chapman visited the Andamans in November 1858, he reported that there was no physical barrier to convict escape. Many convicts still believed that there was a road between the Andamans and India, and that those absconders who had failed to return had found it.[111] According to Walker, by the beginning of 1859 the belief in the Indian road, and also the existence of towns and villages in the interior of Great Andaman, was held extensively by rebel convicts. Mutineer convicts (i.e. sepoys) apparently no longer believed it and so no longer attempted to escape.[112] Rebel convicts, however, were 'a more ignorant and suspicious class'.[113] His successor, J.C. Haughton, formerly a magistrate in Moulmein, shared his opinion, adding that escapes occurred mostly among old offenders tried for escaping from jail or harbouring escaped prisoners under Act V of 1858.[114]

Walker's perceptions of the differing response of mutineers and rebels to their transportation hints at the complexity of the social relationships that characterized the penal colony in the Andamans during these early months, particularly between Walker and his convict charge. Chapman's 1858 memorandum presents a rare glimpse into de facto life in the colony. Unsurprisingly given the mammoth and dangerous task with which they were faced, the European officers were deeply discontented, even Walker who was dissatisfied about his long hours and relatively modest pay. He had difficulty preventing his European guard, who were unhappy at their posting, from mistreating their convict charge. Chapman continued that Walker was in contrast 'exceedingly kind in his manner towards the convicts'. Convicts went to him freely with their wants and grievances, and had complete confidence in him. He compared Walker to 'a zemindar among his villagers'. Yet even Chapman found it difficult to judge the convicts' real feelings. In Walker's presence they were apparently respectful and cheerful. Some of the other officers told him that behind his back they were 'desponding and reckless of their lives'. Chapman also noted also that all convicts were treated alike, that is to say previous rank did not assure their special treatment. Though Walker would not tolerate non-compliance of orders on caste grounds, according to Chapman the convicts 'keep up caste among themselves'. In this respect, Port Blair was 'Hindustan in miniature', with convict *banias* cheating convict customers, and convict *amlahs* (readers, clerks) and *chaprasis* (a generic term for office bearers) charging fees to convict petitioners. Chapman believed that the convicts in the Andamans were accepting their fate, albeit slowly. For him, the only question was whether the regime was penal enough.[115]

The notion that all convicts were treated alike was not quite true, for it is clear that while the government of India maintained that all defendants convicted during the revolt were political offenders, and despite what Chapman reported, Walker himself maintained clear distinctions between 'rebels' and 'mutineers'. We have already seen Walker's claim that they held quite different belief about their chances of escaping from the settlement. The point is further illustrated through details that emerged from an attempt to kill Walker in early 1859, when between 150 and 200 mostly Panjabi convicts plotted his and Overseer Lalla Muttra Doss's assassination. According to Walker they hoped that all the convicts would then join in with a riot and massacre of the European naval guard, seize the ships anchored in the harbour, and escape to India. Fortunately for Walker, another convict named Motee Ram informed him of the plot. Walker assumed that the convict was trying to obtain a reward or a remission of sentence. Nevertheless, he took the precaution of sending the ships away and tightening his personal guard. Motee Ram's account was not, however, exaggerated and on the afternoon of 1 April a group of convicts attacked Walker's office. The convicts stabbed Lalla Muttra Doss while the superintendent fled, chased by a convict armed with an Enfield rifle. Walker reported that when other convicts realized the danger that he was in, they rushed to his assistance, and arrested and disarmed his assailant who died later from his wounds. The reason for the incident, according to Walker, was convicts' feelings of hopelessness and despondency, 'caused by the remembrance of what they have been, and what they are now'. Rumours that the British had been altogether driven from India were at the time rife through the colony. Walker's response was swift. He tried the surviving four convicts, and they were hanged at the end of the month.[116]

According to Walker, mutineer convicts were not involved in the assassination attempt. Moreover, it is clear from his account that those convicts who came to his aid were mostly former sepoys who he had employed as orderlies, section or subdivision gangsmen, and boatmen. These were all posts through which convicts could escape the drudgery and toil of hard labour. As such they were much sought-after positions of authority. Another official wrote that most gangsmen were from the Indian officer class. They were better paid and so could afford the luxuries kept in the stores – tobacco, opium, and even tea and coffee. Also, the *banias* who ran the stores were mostly old sepoys.[117] Though the government did not issue convict uniforms at this time, by early 1859 the divisions between convicts were expressed through dress. According to Brown, working convicts looked 'just like coolies'. Gangsmen on the other hand wore 'smart and respectable looking' clothing, with brass badges obtained from India at their own expense. The only sign of their convict status was a single iron ring around the ankle.[118] In somewhat murky circumstances in 1866, 50 such mutineer convicts were even sent from the Andamans to Sarawak to serve under 'white *rajah*' James Brooke, who took over government on payment of a small annual charge. As they gradually secured their release, in 1871 Brooke requested more convicts. However, only one of the surviving mutineers still in the settlement agreed to go. The rest preferred to stay in Port Blair.[119]

There is no doubt that given the multiple connections between military and penal discipline, Walker relied heavily on mutinous sepoys in his management of the colony during its first twelve months, and that those convicts felt little sense of allegiance with non-military offenders, especially those of low social standing. At the end of 1859, the new superintendent of the Andamans, J.C. Haughton, put it like this: 'Many of the classes cordially hate each other; the transported mutineers look on the men of impure habits with contempt.' Moreover, the breach between convicts and their free soldier overseers was not as wide as Haughton would have liked. He added that Madras Hindus from the *sebundy* guard (irregular troops) paid 'undue respect' to *Brahmins*, and Muslims 'a like partiality for men with religious pretensions of their own creed.'[120] Social status was more important to Indians than the convict/military divide established by the British. Of course, non-military convicts were not all the men who visiting official

Chapman had earlier described as 'common budmashes'. Nuzzur Mahomed Khan, who had pursued the fleeing Walker, had been transported to the Andamans for rebellion in serving under the rebel chief Khan Bahadur Khan in Bareilly. Yet there remains a paradox between mainland notions of the political offender, and early *de facto* Andaman categorisations which drew a much sharper distinction between military and civilian convicts. This classificatory breach emerged in the government of India's response to the plot to assassinate Walker. While the latter recommended the pardoning of large numbers of convicts who had come to his assistance, the government withheld the reward from those of 'bad regiments'.[121]

A further complication in the social hierarchies of the colony was the nature of convict relationships with the Andamanese. Evidently, convicts and European officials were subject to a number of attacks. In one particularly serious incident in April 1859, about 200 Andamanese armed with bows and arrows attacked a similar number of convicts working at Haddo. They killed four convicts. About a week later, around 1,500 Andamanese returned to attack and plunder the settlement once more, mainly for cooking utensils and iron, this time armed with knives and axes from their earlier raid. Walker decided to withdraw the convicts from Haddo and to transfer them to Aberdeen and Viper Island. In May, two escaped convicts returned to the convict camp to inform Walker that the Andamanese were planning a further attack on Aberdeen and Atalanta Point. This gave him the opportunity to organize a successful defence. There is some evidence that the Andamanese singled out convict gangsmen (who wore red turbans, badges, and coloured belts) and the naval guard. Portman claimed that the Andamanese told him later that they objected to the convicts destroying their jungle, but saw that the labouring men were forced to work by their overseers.[122] There are few other contemporary clues regarding Andamanese perceptions of these early years, though Portman also suggested that a turning point in relationships between the Andamanese and the penal settlement came after the British captured three men and took them to Moulmein. When they returned, the Andamanese related that they realized that the British did not wish to harm them. Any seemingly friendly overtures before then were, they claimed, 'mere cunning and treachery' adopted to throw the British off guard while they achieved their goal of plundering the British camp.[123]

It is equally difficult to get a sense of convict feelings about the Andamanese. According to the superintendent of Allahabad central jail, three rebel convicts pardoned and returned to India spoke subsequently of 'strong black cannibals with horse-shaped faces'. They were dismissive of their prospects, stating that because of their fear of guns they would be 'cleared off' with the jungle.[124] In Chapter 4, we discussed convict Munir Shikohabadi's experiences of mainland incarceration in the aftermath of the mutiny-rebellion. Munir wrote further poetry describing his experiences of the penal colony in the Andaman Islands in which he captured the essence of the relationship between its spatial and social dynamics. Clearly scathing of the Islands' indigenous communities, he acknowledged the ambivalent role of the convicts in the process of empire building, squeezed as they were between the British and the Andamanese:

> After being made to leave their homeland, thousands were stuffed into the jungle
> Now even the ghouls native to the wilderness cannot find a place to live
> …
>
> … The downs and ups of the world are gathered in this island
> Here we have seen a superfluity of heights and lows.
>
> If one climbs up a hill it is as if one has wrongly strung up on the gallows
> If one descends it is as if one has fallen into a well …
>
> … Blackness belongs to the jungle people, whiteness to the Europeans
> The prisoners on this island are caught day and night in two-colouredness.[125]

Walker grasped the potential benefits of a scheme of family emigration early on. In his very first report on colony, he wrote that he was encouraging convicts to write to their wives and families requesting that they join them.[126] By then the governor-general was apparently overwhelmed with petitions from convicts' families.[127] Walker's attempts to encourage family migration failed miserably though. He had difficulty in appointing the planned convict family emigration agents in Bengal and the North-West Provinces. The candidates he had in mind were, he said, afraid that they might be deputed to the Islands, and would not run the risk of doing so with respect to caste.[128] Walker's initial enthusiasm met with government approval.[129] However, soon afterwards the government became nervous about how the scheme might be perceived in India. In a veiled allusion to the potential cultural transgressions involved in sea crossings, it feared that the measure might be misconstrued by a suspicious population as well as by transported sepoys and rebels. The secretary to the government of the North-West Provinces wrote of the 'likelihood of indignities in a matter regarding which the native mind is peculiarly sensitive'. He continued: '[A]ny circumstance on which rumours, disadvantageous to the Government, can be founded is turned by the disaffected to their own account, and that when once propagated, such rumours, however wild and imaginary, spread like wild-fire over the country.' As a result, at the end of 1858 the government of India called a halt to the scheme.[130] At the time, in the belief that they could make a comfortable life for their families in the Islands, almost two-thirds of the convicts then in the Andamans (868 out of 1358) had applied for their families to join them.[131]

After the issue of amnesties to mutineer-rebels at the beginning of 1859 (see below), the scheme was revived.[132] Pardoned convicts certainly expressed the view that their suffering was in large part caused by expatriation and separation from their families. Two who were released at the beginning of 1859 wrote that many convicts felt the prospects of a comfortable life for their families were good.[133] The government's motives were rather different. It believed that family emigration was a means of checking widespread homosexual activity, encouraging good behaviour, and promoting productive labour. Brown looked to the examples of convict transportation to America and Australia where, he argued, convict status had not been transmitted from parent to child. He predicted that within a generation in the Andamans the stigma would be entirely lost. Moreover, the presence of families would be an inducement to convicts' industry and steady conduct.[134]

'Perhaps the angels are weeping for the fate of the prisoners'

At the end of the eighteenth century the first abortive Andamans settlement had been decimated by disease. Disease also broke out after colonization in 1858-9, when there were further complicating factors. Some of these related to the general debilitation of much of the Indian population during the socio-economic upheavals of the mutiny-rebellion and after the cholera epidemic that swept across north India at about the same time. This meant that many convicts were in poor health before they were imprisoned, let alone embarked for the Islands. At the same time, medical officials compared the sickness that afflicted convicts in Arakan to that which occurred in the Andamans. Though there is less evidence of the mass hunger strike seen in Arakan, there is no doubt that some Andamans convicts refused to eat. Indeed, the British saw 'depression of spirits' as a contributing factor to death-rates in the Andaman Islands.

In September 1858, Walker presented a report to government on the causes of sickness and mortality in Port Blair. Illness and death were caused primarily by diarrhoea and dysentery, with malarial fevers and ulcers secondary factors. Walker believed that the main cause of sickness was the unhealthy state of the majority of convicts. This was due to their long confinement in Indian jails, many of which, as we have seen, suffered from overcrowding and poor sanitation in the aftermath of the revolt. Indeed, according to Walker, although in many ways the first batch of 200 convicts had been subject to the most hardships, they had suffered the least. This was because they had been in jail for only a short time before their transportation. Echoing the superintendent of Alipur jail in his reports on transportation prisoners received from the North-West Provinces, Walker reported that the unhealthiest convicts of all were the two batches of convicts received from Karachi in April 1858. They looked sickly and feeble, and they were much emaciated with dysentery and scurvy. The prisoners told Walker that they had been in prison for a year, during which time they had undergone multiple jail transfers. Their sea passage had also been relatively long at 40 days. The commander of the *Roman Emperor* reported that half of the men were put on board with dysentery, and that he was surprised that so many had survived the voyage. Of the 175 men embarked, four had died on the passage, 15 had died shortly after arrival, and by August 70 more had succumbed to disease.[135]

The convict ships that followed revealed similarly sorry tales of convicts embarking after suffering sickness in overcrowded jails, and of insufficient rations and supplies. It is clear from Table 5, which shows death-rates by ship, that Walker was not exaggerating the state of the Karachi (Panjabi) convicts.[136] The convicts were mostly mutineers who had fled over the frontier before they surrendered or were captured. According to the surgeon in charge at Multan, they endured 'the greatest imaginable hardships'. If anything, he claimed, transportation had improved their health, for had they remained in India a third of them would have died.[137] Bengal convicts fared slightly better, though cholera broke out among the *Dalhousie* men before their ship had left the Hughli river. Those shipped on the *Coromandel* and *Fire Queen* had awaited their transportation in Alipur jail during an outbreak of diarrhoea and dysentery.[138]

Table 5. Death-rates by ship

Ship	Sailed from	Nos embarked (arrived)	Arrived	Deaths amongst those landed sick	Other deaths amongst those brought by each ship	Per centage of deaths post-arrival per ship
Semiramis	Calcutta	200 (200)	10 Mar.	4	23	13.5
Roman Emperor	Karachi	175 (171)	6 Apr.	11	38	28.7
Edward	Karachi	133 (130)	13 Apr.	4	32	27.7
Dalhousie	Calcutta	163 (140)	16 Apr.	4	11	10.7*
Sesostris	Bombay (via Singapore/P inang)	n.a. (49/83)	12 June	0	10	7.6
Italian	Bombay	80 (79)	1 July	0	5	6.3
Coromandel	Calcutta	n.a. (148)	20 July	3	7	6.8
Fire Queen	Calcutta	47 (47)	12 Aug.	3	3	12.8
Totals		n.a. (1047)		29	129	15.0

* 23.3 per cent including the high number of deaths at sea.
Source: report on sickness and mortality Port Blair, Aug. 1858.

A month or so after the first convicts had landed at Port Blair, the monsoon set in. The tents supplied were totally inadequate for the unrelentingly wet conditions, and the fabric soon tore or rotted. The convicts, therefore, worked and slept in damp clothing and bedding. Even by September, there were not enough huts for all the convicts, and many were still sleeping on damp ground. Many of the convicts were military men, and were therefore not used to hard labour. The work, mainly digging and clearing ground or felling trees, took its toll. Within less than six months, 158 of the 1047 convicts (15 per cent) had died. To those familiar with death-rates in Indian prisons, the only surprise is that mortality was as low as this. Indeed, Walker himself wrote that they were no greater than should have been expected. Of course this figure did not include those convicts who died on board ship (at least 31), those escaped convicts presumed dead or drowned, two suicides, one accidental death or the 87 men executed by Walker.[139] By the end of September, 169 of the 1,330 convicts received (13 per cent) had died in hospital. Including those who had died at work, had committed suicide, had been executed or were presumed dead, the number rose to 429 of the 1,330 convicts received (32 per cent).[140] This figure shocked the government of India, which subsequently reported its 'painful interest' in Andamans affairs.[141]

As in Arakan, Walker partly blamed rates of sickness on convicts' state of mind. He wrote that they were 'quite reckless and desponding', fatalists who cared little what happened to them. He compared the fate of the convicts with that of the Burmese prisoner volunteers who had cleared the ground in anticipation of their arrival. Lured by the promise of remission of sentence, they had not suffered in the same way. Part of Walker's solution was the promotion of family emigration that would, he believed, together with habituation to their massive change in circumstances, lead to a healthier attitude.[142] The senior surgeon of the jails and jail hospitals in the Straits made similar points in his annual report of 1857–8. He reported that almost two-thirds of deaths had occurred among newly arrived convicts. Though this was possibly due to a change in diet (the staple in the Straits was rice not grain), for Surgeon Rose the most important factor was the condition of convicts upon embarkation. As the jails were emptied under a penal policy that endorsed the transportation overseas of prisoners, the Indian authorities took the opportunity to get rid of old and sickly men who were no use in prison manufacture or outdoor work gangs. Two hundred and seven were sent from Bengal to the Straits. As Rose reported, some of them were so ill on arrival that nothing could be done for them. Moreover, though he did not allude to the disappointment of the failed mutiny-rebellion in many ways his other opinions echoed contemporary beliefs about convict sickness in the Andaman Islands and Arakan. His comments about convicts' refusal to eat in particular are worth quoting at length:

> Another cause is the high caste men we received from Bengal; the love of their native country is very great with them, and the idea of never again seeing their homes, their old and sacred places, the monotony of their prison life, and loss of caste, act powerfully both on mind and body; they become careless and indifferent about themselves, their food in particular, and some obstinately refuse to eat at all, emaciation sets in, and death by inanition closes the scene.[143]

Brown's sanitary report early the following year compared similarly the fate of convicts with that of aspiring migrants. He reported that Andaman convicts faced the prospect of never seeing their families again, many of whom had been reduced to extreme poverty. Their exile did not hold out the prospect of a better life for themselves and their families, but was an eternal separation 'which must materially affect the sanitary condition of such a Settlement as Port Blair.'[144]

The perceived relationship between state of mind and body brings us to the issue of suicide. Often, however, the deliberation or accidental nature of potentially suicidal acts was unclear. In the Andamans, by October 1859 a verdict of suicide had been recorded against just one convict death (Table 6). Several convicts and the assistant apothecary, J. Ringrow, had witnessed the suicide of convict Mundraj Gir who walked into the sea. The convicts shouted to him and threw him wood, but he ignored their efforts and drowned himself.[145] Convict Fazl-i-Haq wrote eloquently of the psychological effects of transportation, speaking of his distress, isolation, oppression, melancholy, and depression. The mental effects of loss of honour also emerge forcefully from his writing. One of his principal concerns was the failure to respect religious rites after death. 'When any one from among the people breaths his last,' he wrote, 'an unclean person from the impure ones, who is a sweeper and is like a devil or a monster, drags the dead body by catching the leg and after removing the clothes buries it in a sand hill without a coffin or funeral bath.' According to Haq, were it not for this 'abject treatment', and Islamic injunctions against suicide, no prisoners would have remained alive: '[D]eliverance from the afflictions which one has to suffer here would have been easy.'[146]

Table 6. Fate of convicts shipped to the Andamans, 10 March 1858 – 20 October 1859

Fate of convicts	Nos	Nos as percentage of total
Escaped	336	9.09
Hanged or shot	91	2.46
Suicide	1	0.03
Accidental deaths	11	0.30
Killed by Andamanese	6	0.16
Died of disease	1365	36.92
Released or returned to mainland jails	50	1.35
Remaining in settlement	1837	49.69
Totals	3697	

Source: compiled from OIOC P.206.62 (IJP 6 Jan. 1860): Haughton to Grey, 13 Nov. 1859.

The practice of suicide was invariably more widespread than the figures suggest, though to what extent is difficult to say. First is the impossibility of judging whether escape to almost certain death can be categorized as a 'suicidal act'. More substantively, convicts and officials did not always agree on the causes of deaths. In August 1858, for instance, a dozen Bombay convicts absconded. Three hundred others were sent in pursuit of them, but no trace of them could be found. Most of the convicts, and their Indian overseer, believed that they had drowned themselves. Walker however thought the mass suicide 'improbable'.[147]

Medical officers also noted the high rate of tobacco, alcohol, marijuana, and opium use that convicts had been used to prior to transportation (Table 7), though it is unclear how (if at all) this affected death-rates. Of hospital patients consulted in August 1858, just four per cent said that they were not in the habit of using stimulants. Fourteen per cent said that they had smoked tobacco, four per cent that they had drunk liquor, and 14 per cent said that they had used both both. Ten per cent were accustomed to the use of opium and/or marijuana; 43 per cent to opium and/or marijuana and tobacco; and nine per cent to either or both with tobacco and liquor.[148] Walker believed that these figures might be generalized to the entire convict population.

Table 7. Percentage of men in hospital who made use of narcotics and stimulants, August 1858

Articles the convicts were in the habit of using	Percentage taken from 69 patients then in hospital
Opium or marijuana, or both	10.15
Ditto, with tobacco	43.48
Ditto, with tobacco and liquor	8.69
Tobacco	14.49
Liquor	4.35
Tobacco and liquor	14.49
No stimulants	4.35
	100.00

Source: report on sickness and mortality Port Blair, Aug. 1858.

In the Andamans, it was discovered that denied their usual tobacco rations convicts were smoking roots and leaves. Fearing that this would have a negative impact on their health, Walker recommended the issue of an allowance. There is no question that, as Walker reported, convicts suffered enormously from the effects of the withdrawal of various stimulants, especially opium. Though at the time the subject of the sudden withdrawal of narcotics from prisoners was controversial (Mouat for instance refused to believe that it had any ill effects whatsoever), there was no doubt in Walker's mind that convicts used to stimulants became 'enervated and peculiarly liable to disease'.[149] Indeed, as we have seen Munir Shikohabadi alluded to the harsh effects of opium withdrawal in his verses on Banda jail. Later on in the nineteenth century sepoys stationed in the colony became involved in supplying convicts with the drug.[150]

Almost 70 per cent of men admitted to hospital ended their lives there (Table 8). That the highest proportion of hospital deaths occurred among rather younger men simply reflected the age demographics of the colony.

Table 8. Convict death-rates by age, March 1859

Age	-25 yrs	25-35 yrs	35-45 yrs	45-55 yrs	55+ yrs	Total
Admitted to hospital	98	532	387	125	112	1254
Died	16	124	107	36	43	326
Per centage of deaths on admissions	16.33	23.34	27.65	28.8	38.39	
Per centage of deaths on total deaths	4.9	38.04	32.82	11.05	13.19	

Source: Brown's report.

By the middle of 1859, with the arrival of more convicts from Karachi and Bombay, Surgeon Brown's relatively optimistic picture worsened. In June, Walker wrote that 399 of the 1626 convicts (almost a quarter) were in hospital, and most of the remainder were sick. As a result, work was more or less suspended. Although they had arrived in good health, again a disproportionate number of deaths was recorded against new arrivals from the Panjab.[151] The situation deteriorated even further. In July, the convicts in Aberdeen were so unhealthy that they were taken to Viper Island.[152] At the start of August, almost a third of all convicts (530 of 1780) were hospitalized.[153] The complete change in climate and diet were obvious factors in these high rates. Walker's successor, J.C. Haughton, who assumed office in October 1859, wrote that many of the convicts felt keenly the complete absence of meat.[154] Walker had revealed only rates of sickness and not deaths in most of his 1859 reports. The reason for his omission becomes clear when we consider figures presented by Haughton a month after his arrival. They show just how bad the situation had been, for 36.92 per cent of convicts had died of disease during the period March 1858 to October 1859 (Table 6). Given the surprisingly low death-rates during the earliest months (up to September 1858 just 13 per cent), it is evident that death-rates during the months that followed were devastatingly high. When one also takes into account those convicts who had escaped (and were presumed dead), had committed suicide, had died accidentally, had been executed or had been killed by the Andamanese, it is found that almost half of all convicts transported to Port Blair during the first 19 months died.

Convict Munir Shikohabadi offered an interesting poetic perspective on conditions in the Andamans.[155] His descriptions of the physical hardships inflicted on convicts in relation to rations and labour confirmed the picture painted by official reports at the time. Munir presented an acute sense of the physical isolation and suffering of convicts, and his poetry hinted at the mental anguish suffered by men far removed from – and if their worst fears were realized forgotten by – the mainland:

Even if things are available, the prisoners are in need
They are lucky indeed if they easily get bread and *dhal.*

Starvation thinks the boiled *dhal* is dog's vomit
It considers the wretched rice to be buffalo's straw-cake

As flesh to eat there is the bird of the heart, but meat is as rare as the phoenix
So why should the prisoners on this island not chew the backs of their hands? ...

... Although this island has ground up those whose skin is fair as wheat[156]
Not for even a single day is wheat-flour freely available.

You may saw wood, or dig the earth, or grind mills
Until you are at the point of death,[157] but this will not produce a drop of water in your mouth ...

... The ocean-raining cloud continually pours down day and night
Drowning everyone's field of hope.

Perhaps the angels are weeping for the fate of the prisoners
For every drop contains the lashing of the ocean.

A dark night, terrifying waves and so fearful a whirlpool[158]
Crowds of physical suffering, abundance of mental distress.

How do those lightly laden ones upon the shore know of the state we are in?
Or in what ocean of torment the ship of our existence is tossed?

The fierce wind uproots the palm trees that brush the skies
The foundations of human existence are swept away by the rain ...

... This is the homeland of iguanas, the estate of snakes and scorpions
The hospitality here offers a diet of deadly poison.

Wherever you look there is an abundance of carrion and pork
Which is greatly to the taste of the Chinese, the Burmese, and the
Christians ...

... From dawn to dusk there is the loud noise of crabs and frogs
It is utterly impossible for sleep to come to people's eyes.

The summer here is like the winter in India
The temperature of the sun is hell for the human frame.

Once the summer is over, the rainy season is here for nine months
The rainy season itself embraces the winter.

Even the Londoners turn dark here
Becoming chestnuts if they exercise their greys (horses) ...

... If you were to put cranes' eggs to hatch on this island
It would not be surprising if they produced wild crows.

Munir's final references were to the appalling rates of convict mortality on
the Islands:

You may see more diseases here than in all the rest of the world
It is as if the human body had become a sack of illnesses.

His whole life's reserves of strength are destroyed
If anyone should innocently give hospitality to fever.

There is a complete shortage of medicine, while diseases are available
without being asked for
There is a dearth of being in one's senses and an abundance of
delirium.

On this island there is not even a report of medicine
Perhaps the Christians who follow Jesus[159] have imprisoned it!

On the day that death dived into the sea and reached this island
It does not emerge, being so frightened when it sees the water.[160]

This last verse, a perfect metaphor for convict fears of the Andamans, marks
the end of the Andamans section of his poem.

Convict Fazl-i-Haq presented another memoir of the acute sufferings of a
formerly affluent man:

This book of mine is no doubt the work of a heart-broken and suffering prisoner who is sighing for what has been lost to him, who is afflicted with every kind of injury, who has no power of bearing hardship even for a short time ... [He] is now in fetters and in p[er]plexity and trapped in a snare ... He is in the grip of great misfortunes and bad luck and is in the custody of a fro[wn]ing tyrant who has deprived him of all that he had of beauty and style in fashion and dress, and has put him to test by forcing him to live in the valleys of sorrows and in the narrow prisons which are places where dark sufferings assemble ... He is needy and disappointed as is put to so severe a trial through adversities ... He is in the detention of a white-faced, black-hearted, blue-eyed, stern-looking, red-haired, inconstant and dissimulating person. This fellow has deprived him (author) of what he had from clothes and has clad him in the coarsest garments and the roughest possible dress ... He has been separated completely from his family by imprisonment and is yearning for them ... His arms have been weakened by the severest blows. He is dejected, lonely and forlorn and subjected to drudgery; he has been exiled from his country and town. He is distressed, afflicted, and in banishment; he has been made to suffer, and separated from his family and children ...[161]

Fazl-i-Haq also wrote of the geography of confinement, of the inclement weather and the 'hilly roads full of troubles'. The Andamans wind was 'hotter than *simum*' (the desert wind of Arabia and north Africa), the food as disagreeable as *colocynthis* (bitter cucumber), and the water 'more harmful than snake poison.' He continued:

Its sky is a cloud which rains sorrows and its raining clouds shower afflictions and miseries. The ground is spread over with stones like measles and small pox (on the diseased body). Its air, because of calamities, is full of disasters. Every house in this place, built with grass and weeds, is infested with lasting illness and misery; from its roof always drizzle drops like the tears of my eyes which never stop. Its air is contaminated and therefore a source of diseases. Illness is cheap, but medicines are dear. Epidemics are frequent ... For the wounded there is no cure, for the healthy no security, and for the sick no treatment ... No anxiety in the world could be guessed upon the pains that one has to bear in this place.

Fazl-i-Haq was in a privileged position. Like Munir, he was not put to hard labour but worked as a clerk. He thanked God that he was not weighed down with heavy chains and fetters like other convicts. The convict overseer, he wrote, was 'a harsh, stern, hard-hearted man', who showed 'very kind of malice and enmity against them.'[162] In the Islands he became friends with Munir, who even wrote a short poem about their conversations on the art of poetry itself.[163] By the time he completed his writing, Fazl-i-Haq had given up all hope of release. His only regret was that his sufferings had precluded him from completing his manuscript.[164] Munir recorded his death in poetic form, writing that he 'joined the company of the grave and winding sheet' in 1861. Despite his fears about funeral rites, Fazl-i-Haq was buried in a *mazar* (tomb) just outside Port Blair at South Point.[165]

Political amnesty and the opening up of the islands to 'ordinary' offenders

On the day that India was placed under the control of the British crown, 1 November 1858, the governor-general issued an amnesty to mutineers, deserters, rebels, and prisoners awaiting trial for mutiny offences. In the Panjab alone, almost a thousand men turned themselves in. The figure for the North-West Provinces was even higher: 2,300. The majority (806) were from Kanpur.[166] Continuing disturbances in the districts made the pardon of those mutineer-rebels already convicted politically inexpedient.[167] Two years later, however, with the return of stability to the districts, the government of India decided that all prisoners undergoing sentence in mainland prisons or at Port Blair for mutiny offences would be made subject to the amnesty. In effect this extended the earlier provisions to those who would have been entitled to pardon had they been at large or unconvicted at the time the government proclaimed amnesty. The government called for returns from prison officers detailing who might be excluded on the grounds of their previous history or subsequent conduct in prison, or whose return home they considered dangerous. Some offenders were made subject to a blanket disqualification: those who had willingly and knowingly harboured murderers, those who had led or instigated revolt, and those who had belonged to and been present with a regiment or detachment that had killed its officers. All others were to be released with immediate effect.[168]

There were difficulties in the enforcement of the amnesty, as revealed in the fine line between the categorization of ordinary and political offenders. When three cases were referred to Patna from Port Blair, for instance, the commissioner reported that the men in question had taken advantage of the state of anarchy that had existed in Hazaribagh district to plunder 'for their own benefit'. They each belonged to the 'predatory tribes' (*chuars*) operating in the district; one of them had even been undergoing sentence for dacoity in Hazaribagh jail when it was liberated. The commissioner regarded the prospect of their release from the Andamans with alarm: 'To let such ruffians loose on society would only be to encourage them and their fraternity to commit more crimes of the same nature'.[169] As the Bengal secretary to government put it, the difference between those plunderers who qualified for release under the amnesty and those who did not was whether they were convicted of plunder arising out of and immediately connected with the political disturbances, rather than of plunder 'by individuals of the criminal classes for the mere sake of plunder'.[170] Some district magistrates and administrators agreed with him. The magistrate of Shahabad wrote that it would be 'most dangerous' to release all convicted robbers and dacoits merely because their offences took place at a particular time.[171] The lieutenant-governor of Bengal had a rather different opinion. According to him, there was a great difference between offences committed 'at a time of anarchy when there is no Law and those committed against the Law when it is really in force'. Therefore *all* serious crimes such as gang robbery or plundering committed during the mutiny-rebellion were treasonable, and with the few stated exceptions (harbouring murderers, leading or instigating revolt, belonging to and being present when a British officer was killed), *all* offenders convicted at the time were entitled to clemency.[172] Under this definition by mid-1862 the government had released more than two hundred prisoners from Bengal jails alone.[173]

The failure to draw a clear distinction between mutineer-rebels and convicts sentenced for crimes during the mutiny-rebellion was not without consequence in the Andamans either. In November 1858, of the 1301 convicts from Bengal, less than half (524 or 40 per cent) were sentenced for mutiny, desertion or rebellion. Two hundred and fifty were sentenced for dacoity and highway robbery (19 per cent), 215 for plunder (17 per cent), 102 for murder and wounding (eight per cent), 79 for burglary, theft or cattle stealing (six per cent), 54 for affray and riot (four per cent), seven for arson, three for rape, and two for poisoning (one per cent). Sixty-five more (five per cent) had been convicted of escaping from jail. Because they had been convicted at the time of the mutiny-rebellion, the government considered all as political offenders. However, according to government of India official Chapman, who visited the Islands in 1858, 'a goodly portion are [sic] certainly common budmashes'. We have seen how sepoy convicts separated themselves from those viewed as ordinary offenders. In turn, if Chapman is to be believed, ordinary convicts were unwilling to claim responsibility for specific rebel acts. The most that they would ever confess was having been caught up in a storm of events *('is tufaan mein').*[174]

In 1862, the government of India passed a further resolution, remitting additional sentences passed on prisoners who had escaped from jail during the mutiny-rebellion. This was particularly significant in the case of the Andamans because by the provisions of Act V of 1858, all prisoners who had escaped from jail but did not surrender themselves within a month of the passing of the act were liable to transportation for life. Though the act was repealed by more discretionary legislation in 1860, in the meantime all escaped prisoners were transported to the Andamans. The Bengal authorities thus asked the superintendent at Port Blair to prepare a list of all such convicts.[175] This was not completed until the end of 1864, when there were 38 still in the Islands. Most had been tried during 1858-9; a handful in 1860 or 1861. The largest number (seven) had escaped from Gaya jail, six from Bareilly, and four from Jaunpur.[176] The government did not release all of them. One of them had escaped once before, another had acted as a leader in the rebellion. The government did not see either man as a fit subject for pardon.[177]

Convict poet Munir Shikohabadi secured his release in a rather more unusual way. After the revolt, the *Nawab* of Rampur, Yusuf Ali Khan, who had remained loyal to the British, attended an assembly held by the British in Allahabad. He apparently heard a rendition one of Munir's *ghazals* (lyrical poems). The *nawab* was so taken with the performance that he petitioned the British on Munir Shikohabadi's behalf, so helping to secure his release in 1864.[178] Munir himself wrote of it as follows:[189]

Today, Munir, I have been granted release from captivity
By the grace of God I have been blessed with this happy noon.

I am on my way from this island to Calcutta
O God, grant me a happy journey to India!

Thanks be that I have come aboard this swift vessel
Let the anchor be raised and the time of victory be blessed.

My prayers have been granted
And happy fate smiles upon me ...[180]

Conclusion

Many convict mutineer-rebels felt an extreme sense of desperation upon their transportation to the Andamans. Conditions were appalling, and death-rates were unparalleled in any contemporary mainland jail. It is little wonder that so many men tried to escape. Convict rumours about the landscape and spatial dynamics of the Islands abounded, as did beliefs about the progress of the revolt in India. We should be cautious about ascribing any clear sense of 'convict' identity to these first Andamans transportees, however, for it is clear that there were substantial hierarchies between military and 'ordinary' rebels. Convicts were central to the organization of the penal colony in the Islands and their sense of social difference shaped the early regime in important ways. Although no doubt perpetuated by the exigencies of establishing a new colony, the mutineer-rebels perceived and expressed divisions among themselves.

The number of mutineer-rebels subject to penal transportation was always finite. By the start of 1859, the revolt had more or less come to an end and the supply of political convicts had all but dried up.[181] This presented the government with the prospect of ending transportation to the Andamans altogether. By this time, however, the government felt acutely that to abandon it would be a massive waste of the effort and resources it had already committed, and so it began to formulate long-term plans. It recognized the importance of convict labour to permanent settlement schemes, especially in land clearance. As we have seen, two related arguments emerged: the supply of labour ought to be increased and only fit and healthy convicts should be transported. By March 1859 one visitor to the Andamans (Surgeon Brown) was writing that the Andaman Islands might become a source of riches, 'a new outlet for the knowledge, civilization, commerce, and' ironically, perhaps, given the circumstances of their colonization 'Christianity of our country.' He went on: 'The punishment of a section of Bengal convicts is but a small object compared with the attainment of a great end.'[182]

It was ultimately the need for labour in clearing and settling more of the Islands which led to the opening up of the colony to all transportation offenders, not just those convicted of mutiny-rebellion offences. There were two provisos. In an acknowledgement of the labour demands of the islands, it was agreed that only able-bodied healthy convicts would be sent. Second, ordinary convicts would not be allowed to mix with mutineer-rebels.[183] The average annual number of transportation convicts in the five years up to 1857 had been 466; Mouat saw no reason why the Andamans should expect to receive more convicts than this. Walker in the meantime asked to continue his system of selecting gangsmen from 'political' convicts, by which he meant sepoys. They were, he said, far superior to the free overseers he had seen in mainland jails.[184] In practice, due to the insufficiency of cleared land it was difficult to follow the government of India's direction that mutineer-rebels be kept separate from ordinary offenders. Once again, the government's decision about who constituted a 'rebel' seemed illogical to officers on the ground. In his first report as superintendent of Port Blair, Haughton wrote that almost half the convicts sent during the first half of 1859 were 'ordinary' offenders. In fact, as Walker clarified in his memorandum on the report, the special commissioners had convicted them of crimes 'incidentally to the unsettled state of the country' making them rebels in the eyes of government.[185] Finally, the government of India decided that, as far as possible, *badmash* should be separated from those of station and respectability.[186] As J.S. Campbell and H.W. Norman noted in their major 1874 report on the Andamans, the problem with mixing political and other offenders was the 'danger of intrigue and the promotion of disaffection'.[187] By May 1860, the mutineer-rebels still in the colony had been sent to Ross Island, and ordinary offenders to Viper Island and Atalanta Point.[188]

Notes

1. By far the most comprehensive account of the relationship between the penal settlement and the Andamanese is Satadru Sen, 'Policing the Savage: Segregation, Labor and State Medicine in the Andamans', *Journal of Asian Studies*, 58, 3 (1997), 753-73. See also Sita Venkateswar, *Development and Ethnocide: colonial practices in the Andaman Islands*, Copenhagen, International Work Group for Indigenous Affairs, 2004, 92-111.

2. Portman, *A History of our Relations, vol. I*, 57-70.

3. *Ibid.*, 69.

4. G.E. Dobson, 'On the Andamans and Andamanese', *Journal of the Anthropological Institute*, 4 (1875), 457-67; W.H. Flower, 'On the Osteology and Affinities of the Andaman Islands', *Journal of the Anthropological Institute*, 9 (1880), 108-33; A. Lane Fox, 'Observations on Mr Man's Collection of Andaman and Nicobarese Objects', *Journal of the Anthropological Institute*, 7 (1878), 434-70; E.H. Man, 'On the Andamanese and Nicobarese Objects presented to Major-General Pitt Rivers', *Journal of the Anthropological Institute*, 9 (1882), 268-94; E.H. Man, *On the Aboriginal Inhabitants of the Andaman Islands*, London, Trübner and Co., 1885; Portman, *A History of our Relations;* C.H. Read, 'Mr Portman's Photographs of Andamanese', *Journal of the Anthropological Institute*, 12 (1893), 401-3; R.C. Temple, *Andaman and Nicobar Islands*, Calcutta, Superintendent of Government Printing, 1909.

5. OIOC P.188.49 (IJC 15 Jan. 1858): Beadon to Man, 15 Jan. 1858.

6. Sen, *Disciplining Punishment*, 61-6 (quotes 62, 63).

7. Douglas M. Peers, 'Sepoys, Soldiers and the Lash: Race, Caste and Army Discipline in India, 1820-50', *Journal of Imperial and Commonwealth History*, 23, 2 (1995), 211-47.

8. Dalrymple to Grey, 28 Nov. 1855; Grey to Dalrymple, 29 Feb. 1856, cited in Portman, *A History of our Relations, vol. I*, 188-90.

9. Hopkinson to Grey, 8 Feb. 1856, cited in *ibid.*, 190-7 (quote 191).

10. Grey to Dalrymple, 29 Feb. 1856, cited in *ibid.*, 189.

11. Governor-General Canning to the Court of Directors, 22 Apr. 1856, enc. A. Bogle, Commissioner Tenasserim and Martaban Provinces, to Edmonstone, cited in *ibid.*, 197-204.

12. J.C. Haughton, Magistrate Tenasserim and Martaban Provinces, to Bogle, 3 Mar.

1856, cited in *ibid.*, 198.

13. Canning's Minute, cited in *ibid.*, 203-4.
14. Canning to the Court of Directors, 8 Apr. 1857, cited in *ibid.*, 206-7.
15. OIOC P.188.49 (IJC 15 Jan. 1858): Beadon to Mouat, G.F. Playfair, and J.A. Heathcote, 20 Nov. 1857.
16. Portman, *A History of our Relations, vol. I*, 186.
17. OIOC P.188.48 (IJC 14 Dec. 1857): Beadon to Young, H. Forbes, Acting Secretary to Government Madras, and W. Hart, Secretary to Government Bombay, 1 Dec. 1857.
18. OIOC P.188.49 (IJC 15 Jan. 1858): Mouat, Playfair, and Heathcote to Beadon, 1 Jan. 1858; Beadon to H. Man, Executive Engineer and Superintendent of Convicts Moulmein, 15 Jan. 1858. See also Portman, *A History of our Relations, vol. I*, 208-9, 213-4, 217-41.
19. *Ibid.*: Beadon to Man, 15 Jan. 1858. See also Portman, *A History of our Relations, vol. I*, 242-7.
20. OIOC P.188.50 (IJC 12 Feb. 1858): Message despatched with the Governor-General to Edmonstone, n.d.; OIOC P.188.54 (IJC 18 June 1858): Man to Beadon, 11 May 1858.
21. OIOC P.188.49 (IJC 15 Jan. 1858): Beadon to Man, 15 Jan. 1858.
22. OIOC P.206.61 (IJP 29 July 1859): G.G. Brown's Report on the Sanitary State of the Andamans, n.d. Mar. 1859 (henceforth 'Brown's report').
23. OIOC P.146.15 (BJC 10 Mar. 1858): Mouat to Buckland, 22 Feb. 1859 (also at OIOC P.206.61 [IJP 29 July 1859]).
24. OIOC P.188.49 (IJC 15 Jan. 1858): Beadon to Man, 15 Jan. 1858.
25. OIOC P.188.54 (IJC 18 June 1858): Man to Beadon, 11 May 1858.
26. Martin, *The Indian Empire, vol. III*, 186-8.
27. OIOC P.146.21 (BJP 8 Sept. 1859): Davies to Beadon, 26 Apr. 1859.
28. *Ibid.*: Simson to Davies, 27 May 1859; OIOC L.PS.6.466: Report by Captain H.N. Davies in charge of Ex-King of Delhi and other State prisoners at Rangoon, 10 July 1859. There are extensive extracts from this report in Dalrymple, *The Last Mughal*, 465-73.
29. Dalrymple, *The Last Mughal*, 474.
30. *Report of the Committee on Prison Discipline*, 86.
31. Chapman's memo.
32. OIOC P.188.50 (IJC 9 Apr. 1858): S. Hellard, Commander *Dalhousie*, to Beadon, 4 Apr. 1858.
33. The literal translation of 'evil fate' is 'black-fatedness' (unpublished English translation in the possession of Christopher Shackle).
34. OIOC P.206.61 (IJP 3 June. 1859): J. Irving, Civil Surgeon Allahabad Central Prison, to Thornhill, 2 Aug. 1859. Marina Carter has documented similar psycho-cultural explanations for heavy fatalities on board Indian indentured labourers' ships during the same period. See *Servants, Sirdars and Settlers*, 127-8.
35. OIOC P.146.4 (BJC 26 Nov 1857): Regulations for convict ships, 6 Nov. 1857.
36. Memorandum of Lieutenant-Colonel S.F. Hannay, Debrooghur, 15 Feb. 1858, cited in PP 1857-58 (2449): Papers relative to mutinies in East Indies.
37. NAI Home (Judicial 3 June 1859): C. Hathaway, Inspector-General of Prisons Panjab, to Thornton, 21 Mar. 1859. (Also in OIOC P.206.61 [IJP 3 June 1859]).
38. OIOC P.206.61 (IJP 29 July 1859): T. Farquhar, Superintendent Allahabad Central Prison, to Muir, 14 Jan. 1859. 'Sahib-log' = European gentleman, i.e. captain.
39. Maulana Jaferr Thanesari, *In Exile (A Strange Story)*, Delhi, Urdu Makaz, 1964, 96

(unpublished English translation in the private possession of Satadru Sen).

40. OIOC P.206.61 (IJP, 19 Aug. 1859): Walker to Grey, 2 Aug. 1859.

41. OIOC P.188.53 (IJP 11 June 1858): Civil Assistant Surgeon 24 Parganas to Officiating Superintendent Surgeon of Bengal, 8 Apr. 1858.

42. OIOC P.407.11 (BomJC 6 July 1858): Walker to Beadon, 14 April 1858; OIOC P.407.13 (BomJC 21 Sept. 1858): Walker to Beadon, 13 April 1858, 1 July 1858.

43. OIOC P.206.60 (IJP 12 Nov. 1858): W.J. Shum, Acting Master Indian Navy, to C.D. Campbell, Senior Naval Officer, 31 Oct. 1858.

44. OIOC P.146.27 (BJP [jails] May 1860): Haughton to Grey, 21 Apr. 1860.

45. OIOC P.146.17 (BJP 19 May 1859): Couper to Young, 5 May 1859. (See also NAI Home [Judicial, 3 June 1859] nos 7-13).

46. OIOC P.146.21 (BJP 27 Oct. 1859): Walker to Rivers Thompson, 10 Sept. 1859, enc. Judicial Enquiry Regarding the Treatment of the Convicts on Board the Ship *Boanerges*, 5-8 Sept. 1859. The following discussion is based on this document.

47. There are a number of parallels with the period to 1857–8. See Clare Anderson, '"The Ferringees are Flying - the ship is ours!": the convict middle passage in colonial South and Southeast Asia, 1790-1860', *Indian Economic and Social History Review*, 41, 3 (2005), 143-86.

48. Anderson, '"The Ferringees are Flying!"', 167-71.

49. OIOC P.146.26 (BJP [jails] Apr. 1860): J. Rennie, Superintendent of Marine, to J.P. Grant, Lieutenant-Governor of Bengal, 9 Nov. 1859.

50. *Ibid.*: Campbell to Thompson, 18 Nov. 1859.

51. *Ibid.*: Montresor to Thompson, 24 Nov. 1859.

52. *Ibid.*

53. *Ibid.*: Report of the management and health of the native convicts under my charge, Ramjan Alli (Ramzan Alee), n.d.

54. *Ibid.*: W.B. Skeene, Commander *Boanerges*, to Messrs Gillanders, Arbuthnot and Co., Agents *Boanerges*, 21 Nov. 1859.

55. *Ibid.*: Skeene to Walker, 14 Sept. 1859.

56. *Ibid.*: Thompson to H. Browne, Under Secretary to Government of India Home Department, 24 Apr. 1860; OIOC P.146.28 (BJP [jails], June 1860): Opinion of Advocate-General W. Ritchie, 30 May 1860.

57. OIOC P.146.27 (BJP [jails], May 1860): Browne to W.F. Marriott, Acting Secretary to Government Bombay, 11 May 1860.

58. Anderson, '"The Ferringees are Flying"'.

59. OIOC P.405.1 (BomJC 20 Mar. 1850): Blundell to J.G. Lumsden, Secretary to Government Bombay, 17 Jan. 1850; P.405.3 (BomJC 14 Apr. 1850): E. Baynes, Superintendent Convicts Bombay, to Lumsden, 18 Mar. 1850, enc. D. Costello, Civil Surgeon Tannah Jail, to R. Keays, Session Judge Konkan, 13 Mar. 1850.

60. OIOC P.144.55 (BJC 16 Mar. 1854): F. Church, Resident Councillor Singapore, to E.A. Samuells, Superintendent Alipur jail, 30 Sept. 1830.

61. *Ibid.*: Information of Shekh Hyder, 22 Dec. 1853.

62. *Ibid.*: Alfred Pearce, Commander *Margaret Skelly*, to Church, 31 Oct. 1853.

63. *Ibid.*: Information of Chief Mate George Holland, 22 Dec. 1853.

64. OIOC P.144.55 (BJC 16 Mar. 1854): Beadon to F.E. Rogers, Superintendent Marine, 6 Mar. 1854.

65. OIOC P.146.4 (BJC 26 Nov. 1857): R. Macpherson, Executive Engineer and Superintendent Convicts and Roads Singapore, to Mackenzie, n.d. (June 1857).

66. *Ibid.*: J. Rose, Senior Surgeon Straits Settlements, to Secretary Medical Board Calcutta, 25 Apr. 1857.

67. *Ibid.*: Mouat to Buckland, 15 June 1857.
68. Anderson, "'The Ferringees are Flying'".
69. OIOC P.407.10 (BomJC 6 July 1858): Beadon to Buckland, 24 Apr. 1858; OIOC P.407.13 (BomJC 21 Sept. 1858): Blundell to H.L. Anderson, Secretary to Government Bombay, 15 June 1858; *Singapore Free Press*, 22 July 1858.
70. OIOC P.188.56 (IJC 13 Aug. 1858): Walker to Beadon, 8 July 1858.
71. OIOC P.407.11 (BomJC 6 July 1858): Walker to Beadon, 14 Apr. 1858.
72. OIOC P.407.30 (BomJC 4 July 1859): H.B.E. Frere, Commissioner Sindh, to Anderson, 4 June 1859.
73. *Ibid.*: G.W. Hamilton, Commissioner Multan, to Thornton, 8 Nov. 1858.
74. *Ibid.*: J. McIntire, Surgeon in Civil Medical Charge, to Major F.E. Voyle, Deputy Commissioner Multan, 26 Oct. 1858.
75. Anderson, "'The Ferringees are Flying'", 159-61.
76. OIOC P.234.46 (NWPJC Oct. 1858): List of Prisoners Despatched from Mirzapur Jail to Alipur Jail, 3 Sept. 1858; OIOC P.206.62 (IJP 6 Jan. 1860): J.C. Haughton, Superintendent Port Blair, to Grey, 13 Nov. 1859.
77. OIOC P.188.56 (IJC 20 Aug. 1858): Chapman to Buckland, 16 Aug. 1858.
78. *Ibid.*: Blundell to Beadon, 2 July 1858, enc. Nominal Roll of the Convicts Shipped at Penang *per Sesostris*, 6 June 1858, Nominal Roll of Nine Convicts of the Mutineers Received from Bombay, who have died since their arrival.
79. Unless noted otherwise, the following descriptions are taken from OIOC P.188.53 (IJC 7 May 1858): Walker to Beadon, 6 Apr. 1858. The report is also located at NAI Home (Judicial 7 May 1858), nos 24-46. For extensive extracts from original correspondence, readers might refer to Portman, *A History of our Relations, vol. I*, ch. 8.
80. OIOC P.188.53 (IJC 7 May 1858): Beadon to Walker, 7 May 1858; Beadon to Man, 7 May 1858.
81. *Ibid.*: Walker to Beadon, 17 Apr. 1858.
82. *Ibid.*: Walker to Beadon, 23 Apr. 1858.
83. *Ibid.*: Man to Beadon, n.d. (Apr. 1858).
84. *Ibid.*: Beadon to Muir, 7 May 1858.
85. Anderson, 'The Politics of Convict Space', 44.
86. OIOC P.188.53 (IJC 7 May 1858): Beadon to Walker, 7 May 1858.
87. Guha, *Elementary Aspects*, 251-68.
88. Brown's report.
89. OIOC P.206.61 (IJP 29 July 1859): Statement of convict no. 276 Doodnath Tewarry, 26 May 1859; Portman, *A History of our Relations, vol. I*, 279-86.
90. *Ibid.*: Memorandum of R.B. Chapman, Under Secretary to Government of India, n.d. (Nov. 1858) (henceforth 'Chapman's memo').
91. OIOC P.188.53 (IJC 7 May 1858): Walker to Beadon, 23 Apr. 1858; Beadon to Walker, 7 May 1858; NAI Home (Judicial 28 May 1858): Walker to Beadon, 1 May 1858.
92. OIOC P.188.53 (IJC 7 May 1858): Chapman to Walker, 26 May 1858. Earlier, Man had suggested the measure. On penal tattooing and branding in colonial India and its penal settlements, see Anderson, *Legible Bodies*, ch. 2.
93. NAI Home (Judicial 3 Sept. 1858): Walker to Beadon, 8 July 1858.
94. Sen, *Disciplining Punishment*, 191.
95. NAI Home (Judicial 28 May 1858): Walker to Beadon, 1 May 1858; NAI Home (Judicial 30 July 1858): Walker to Beadon, 7 May 1858; NAI Home (Judicial 16 July 1858): Walker to Beadon, 12 June 1858.
96. NAI Home (Judicial 11 June 1858): Beadon to Walker, 11 June 1858.

97. NAI Home (Judicial 28 May 1858): Note of J.P. Grant, President in Council, n.d.

98. NAI Home (Judicial 16 July 1858): Minute of Grant, 25 June 1858.

99. NAI Home (Judicial 24 Sept. 1870): H. Man, Superintendent Port Blair, to E.C. Bayley, Secretary to Government of India, 12 Aug. 1870.

100. NAI Home (Judicial 16 July 1858): Walker to Beadon, 12 June 1858.

101. *Ibid.*: Minute of H. Ricketts, n.d.

102. *Ibid.*: Walker to Beadon, 12 June 1858.

103. OIOC P.206.60 (IJP 17 Sept. 1858): Walker to Beadon, 7 Aug. 1858.

104. Portman, *A History of our Relations, vol. I*, 257.

105. Brown's report.

106. OIOC P.206.60 (IJP 22 Oct. 1858): Walker to Beadon, 14 Aug. 1858.

107. *Ibid.*: Beadon to Walker, 20 Oct. 1858.

108. Brown's report.

109. OIOC P.206.60 (IJP 12 Nov. 1858): Walker to Beadon, 4 Sept. 1858.

110. Portman, *A History of our Relations, vol. I*, 257.

111. Chapman's memo.

112. OIOC P.206.61 (IJP 29 July 1859): Walker to Beadon, 4 Feb. 1859.

113. *Ibid.*: Walker to Beadon, 25 Mar. 1859.

114. OIOC P.206.62 (IJP 19 May 1860): Haughton to Grey, 10 Apr. 1860.

115. Chapman's memo.

116. OIOC P.206.61 (IJP 29 July 1859): Walker to Grey, 29 Apr. 1859.

117. Brown's report.

118. Brown's report. On the expression of penal hierarchies through dress, see Anderson, *Legible Bodies*, ch. 4.

119. OIOC P.699 (IJP 25 Feb. 1871): Application from *Rajah* Brooke for another batch of convicts for service at Sarawak, Port Blair, 30 Jan. 1871.

120. OIOC P.206.62 (IJP 6 Jan. 1860): Haughton to Grey, 29 Nov. 1859.

121. OIOC P.206.61 (IJP 29 July 1859): Grey to Walker, 20 July 1859.

122. Portman, *A History of our Relations, vol. I*, 277-9.

123. Portman, *A History of our Relations, vol. I*, 306. The men's visit to Moulmein is recounted by Commissioner of the Tenasserim and Martaban Provinces Albert Fytche, 'On certain Aborigines of the Andaman Islands', *Transactions of the Ethnological Society of London*, 5 (1867), 239-42.

124. OIOC P.206.61 (IJP 29 July 1859): T. Farquhar, Superintendent Allahabad Jail, to Muir, 14 Jan. 1859.

125. This also invokes a sense of 'double-dealing' (unpublished English translation in the possession of Christopher Shackle).

126. OIOC P.188.53 (IJP 7 May 1858): Walker to Beadon, 6 Apr. 1858.

127. *Bombay Gazette*, 22 Nov. 1858.

128. OIOC P.206.60 (IJP 12 Nov. 1858): Walker to Beadon, 4 Sept. 1858.

129. OIOC P.188.53 (IJP 7 May 1858): Beadon to Walker, 7 May 1858.

130. OIOC P.206.61 (IJP 29 July 1859): Muir to Grey, 9 Oct. 1858.

131. OIOC P.206.61 (IJP 29 July 1859): Farquhar to Muir, 14 Jan. 1859; Walker to Grey, 6 Nov. 1859.

132. *Ibid.*: Grey to Walker, 20 Feb. 1859. For a detailed account of family migration to the Andamans during the second half of the nineteenth century, see Satadru Sen, 'Rationing Sex: female convicts in the Andamans', *South Asia*, 30, 1 (1999), 29-59.

133. OIOC P.206.61 (IJP 29 July 1859): Farquhar to Muir, 14 Jan. 1859.

134. Brown's report. In a biblical allusion, he referred to the 'convict stain' as the 'mark of Cain' (in the Old Testament, Cain was marked and then sent into exile).

135. Report on sickness and mortality Port Blair, Aug. 1858.
136. *Ibid.*
137. OIOC P.206.60 (IJP 10 Dec. 1858): J. Macintyre, Surgeon in Civil Medical Charge, to Voyle, 10 Oct. 1858.
138. Report on sickness and mortality Port Blair, Aug. 1858.
139. *Ibid.*
140. OIOC P.206.60 (IJP 12 Nov. 1858): Walker to Beadon, 28 Sept. 1858.
141. *Ibid.*: Beadon to Walker, 6 Nov. 1858.
142. *Ibid.*: Walker to Beadon, 4 Sept. 1858. Once again, we might compare the mental state of transported mutineer-rebels with that of transported French communards. See Bullard, *Exile to Paradise*, ch. 7.
143. OIOC P.206.60 (IJP 12 Nov. 1858): Report on the jails and jail hospitals of the Straits Settlements for the official year 1857-58, by Senior Surgeon Rose, n.d.
144. Brown's report.
145. OIOC P.206.60 (IJP 1 Oct. 1858): Walker to Beadon, 5 Aug. 1858.
146. Haq, 'The Story', 27, 53-5 (quote 54).
147. NAI Home (Judicial 22 Oct. 1858): Walker to Beadon, 14 Aug. 1858.
148. James H. Mills argues that marijuana was a site of knowledge formation about inmates in colonial asylums, though there is no evidence of such discussions in the Andamans. James H. Mills, *Madness, Cannabis and Colonialism: The 'Native-Only' Lunatic Asylums of British India, 1857-1900*, Basingstoke, Macmillan, 2000, ch. 2.
149. Report on sickness and mortality Port Blair, Aug. 1858.
150. NAI Home (Port Blair Oct. 1877) no. 10: Sepoys found with opium in their possession. The authorities later set up licensed opium shops in an attempt to regulate the supply of the drug. It banned sales to convicts, but recognized that nevertheless probationary self-supporting convicts were able to obtain the drug, usually from Madras sepoys stationed at Ross Island. See NAI Home (Port Blair June 1893) nos 7-14: Licensed opium shops.
151. OIOC P.206.61 (IJP 29 July 1859): Walker to Grey, 21 June 1859.
152. *Ibid.*: Walker to Grey, 8 July 1859.
153. *Ibid.*: Walker to Grey, 2 Aug. 1859.
154. *Ibid.*: Haughton to Grey, 11 Oct. 1859.
155. Unpublished English translation in the possession of Christopher Shackle.
156. Wheaten complexions were at this time seen as an indication of high birth (like Shikohabadi himself).
157. Literally translated as 'with life on the lips'.
158. The poem incorporates neatly these two italicized half verses from a famous Persian poem by the great fourteenth-century Persian poet Hafiz, which was written in the same metre as Shikohabadi's.
159. Jesus was famous for his healing powers.
160. Unpublished English translation in the possession of Christopher Shackle.
161. Haq, 'The Story', 26-7.
162. Haq, 'The Story', 52-3, 54.
163. Unpublished English translation in the possession of Christopher Shackle.
164. Haq, 'The Story', 54-7.
165. Husain, *Bahadur Shah II*, 298.
166. OIOC P.206.62 (IJP 26 Oct. 1860): Davies to Simson, 2 Feb. 1859; Statement of mutineers and deserters pardoned from Nov. 1858 to May 1860 (North-West Provinces).

167. *Ibid.*: Extract from the proceedings of the Government of India Foreign Department, 15 Nov. 1860, enc. Governor-General's Minute, 4 Dec. 1858.
168. OIOC P.146.34 (BJP [jails] Dec. 1860): Grey to W.S. Seton-Karr, Officiating Secretary to Government Bengal, 19 Nov. 1860.
169. OIOC P.146.44 (BJP [jails] Oct. 1861): Dalton to H. Bell, Under Secretary to Government Bengal, 19 Aug. 1861.
170. OIOC P.146.41 (BJP [jails] June 1861): Grey to Lushington, 1 June 1861.
171. OIOC P.146.52 (BJP [jails] Sept. 1862): Mouat to Gordon, 23 June 1862.
172. *Ibid.*: Gordon to Mouat, 18 July 1862.
173. OIOC P.146.49 (BJP [jails] Apr. 1862): List of prisoners confined in the several jails of the lower provinces for offences connected with the mutiny of 1857, ordered to be released.
174. Chapman's memo.
175. OIOC P.146.51 (BJP [jails] June – Aug. 1862): Grey to Couper, 8 Mar. 1862; Bayley's memo, 11 June 1862.
176. OIOC P.206.71 (IJP Jan. – June 1865): Roll of prisoners undergoing sentence of transportation at Port Blair under Act V of 1858, 14 Dec. 1864.
177. OIOC P.207.72 (IJP July – Dec. 1865): H. Beverley, Officiating Under Secretary to Government Bengal, to A.P. Howell, Under Secretary to Government of India, 4 July 1865.
178. Qureshi, *Munshi Sayyid Ismail Husain Munir Shikohabadi*, 36-7.
179. Riaz ud Din, *Intikhab-e kalam-e*, 93.
180. Unpublished English translation in the possession of Christopher Shackle.
181. OIOC P.206.60 (IJP 10 Dec. 1858): Walker to Beadon, 4 Sept. 1858; Beadon to Walker, 3 Dec. 1858.
182. Brown's report.
183. OIOC P.206.61 (IJP 29 July 1859): Mouat to Buckland, 22 Feb. 1859; Grey to Young, 21 July 1859; Grey to Haughton, 8 Nov. 1859.
184. *Ibid.*: Mouat to Rivers Thompson, 3 Sept. 1859; Walker to Grey, 10 Sept. 1859.
185. OIOC P.206.62 (IJP 6 Jan. 1860): Haughton to Grey, 13 Nov. 1859.
186. *Ibid.*: Grey to Haughton, 29 Dec. 1859.
187. NAI Home (Port Blair Aug. 1874): J.S. Campbell and H.W. Norman, Report on the Penal Settlement in the Andamans.
188. OIOC P.206.62 (IJP 16 July 1860): Haughton to Grey, 9 May 1860.

CHAPTER 6
CONCLUSION

In the aftermath of the revolt, the government of India followed a policy of non-interference in Indian affairs relating to religion and caste. Nervous of a repeat of the widespread military and civil unrest experienced during 1857–8, the government was keen to dispel the apparently popular belief that its aim was the cultural defilement or even wholesale conversion of the entire population to Christianity. British administrators were also eager to untangle the seemingly tight knot that bound together the question of native 'loyalty' and 'treachery', and increasingly came to understand individual posturing with or against the state in relation to broader collective groups and relationships. In its drive for cultural understanding, if not empathy, the government created what is now commonly described as an 'ethnographic state', through which it differentiated, distinguished, and sharpened categories of religion and caste. These fed into colonial forms of governance generally, particularly new modes of recruitment into the Bengal army, as also the specifics of colonial alignment with particular sections of the Indian population. Indian communities were themselves central to the formation of such social discourses and practices. As during the pre-colonial period they continued their attempts to reposition themselves socially, economically, and culturally according to their own needs and desires.[1]

Yet, as we have seen, colonial concerns about the relationships between the individual, society, religion, caste, and tribe were not solely a post-1858 development. Such concerns were central to colonial efforts to develop and to enforce the codes and practices of penal confinement during the first half of the nineteenth century. Moreover, during this period jails became established spaces in which prisoners and free communities contested, defended, and forged new kinds of religious or caste based identities. The many controversies that the clashes between the colonial state and its subject peoples caused during the first half of the nineteenth century were characterized by the deep conviction on the part of the British that they may have been interfering in *tradition*, but they were not intervening in *religion*. Indeed, the vigorous defence of disciplinary measures mounted by penal administrators in this respect was often predicated on a deep ignorance of the effect that colonial policies had with regard to social privilege and marginalization. Prisoners and their kin engaged not in an inappropriate defence of religious or caste practices, as the British often claimed, but in bids for enhanced status and social mobility. The use of colonial institutions for this purpose was part of a much longer process through which Indians of all communities negotiated cultural change.

Given the history of north Indian jails during the first half of the nineteenth century, it is not surprising that they assumed an important role in north Indian experiences of the 1857–8 uprising. The breaking open of prisons was one of the most populist moments of the mutiny-rebellion, and a key element of urban revolt. Sepoys, *sowars,* and rebels damaged or destroyed dozens of jails and set thousands of prisoners free. However, just as prison unrest during the first half of the nineteenth century inspired only limited solidarity between jails and free communities, so too was there a somewhat ambivalent relationship between mutineers, rebels, and escaped prisoners. The prison was a target of, and indeed assumed significance within, the revolt because it had become an innovatory space of unprecedented colonial intervention into Indian affairs. Nonetheless, mutineer-rebel sympathies lay with their high-caste or high status brethren and not with the general prison population. Thus they did not liberate some inmates as such, but pressed them into portage or other duties.

In the aftermath of revolt, with thousands of prisoners at large and a dearth of secure prison accommodation, the colonial state faced an unprecedented penal crisis. The revolt catalysed the beginning of the process of the closure of the Southeast Asian penal settlements in the Straits Settlements and Burma, and secured the establishment of a new penal colony in the Andaman Islands for the reception of mutineer-rebels. However, on the Indian mainland, other than repairing and securing jails the government made few radical changes in the architecture of confinement or in forms of jail discipline. Innovations such as the move to cellular accommodation and the withdrawal of prisoners from outdoor labour developed further changes in progress since the 1840s. More important were post-revolt changes in how prisoners and prisons were represented and imagined, particularly as metaphors for the broader cultural intrusions of colonial rule. We can trace also the development of colonial notions of the 'political' as distinct from the 'criminal' prisoner to 1857–8, though the meaning of that category continued to shift over time.[2] Moreover, the unintended effect of the ethnographic state's solidification of ideas about collective social categories was prisoners' increasing use of jails as vehicles of social mobility.

During the late nineteenth and early twentieth centuries, jails became clearly defined political arenas in which anti-colonial agitators and nationalists played out the struggle for independence. The British transported about five hundred nationalists to the Andaman Islands, where they were incarcerated in an architecturally imposing radiating cellular jail that opened in 1906. Jail going and hunger-striking were central to the fight for freedom and many political prisoners wrote memoirs of their experiences of incarceration. As the notion that India itself was one vast prison became embedded in anti-colonial discourses, imprisonment took on a new metaphorical meaning that gave it enhanced significance.[3] Nationalists viewed jail chains in particular as material symbols of colonial subjection. V.D. Savarkar wrote, for instance, that supporters of the Meerut sepoys in 1857 sought not only the removal of their fetters, 'but also the chains of slavery lying for one hundred years around the neck of our dear Motherland!' He went on to draw parallels with the twentieth-century freedom struggle: 'the chains of these patriots must be smashed, the chains of the Motherland must be smashed, and the banner of Independence must wave forth!'[4] And yet the roots of these practices and discourses can be found during the first half of the nineteenth century. As we have seen, from its first decades hunger-striking was one prisoner response to colonial jails and penal settlements. Moreover, in his narrative account of revolt and transportation Fazl-i-Haq used the terms 'jailer', 'tyrant', and 'custody' to represent the role of the East India Company in revolt, imprisonment, and transportation.[5]

It is interesting to dwell for a moment on the question of why Fazl-i-Haq's narrative, as also the poetry of Munir Shikohabadi, has been largely forgotten by Indian nationalists, including Savarkar who claimed that there were no mutineer-rebel accounts of the Andamans, and historians. In the case of Munir, it is probably because the Lakhnao school of Urdu poetry fell subsequently from literary favour.[6] Fazl-i-Haq's narrative is more complex. He drew attention to British retributive brutality, but at the same time was highly critical of both the rebel army and the rebel government. He accused mutinous sepoys of disgraceful and dishonourable conduct that produced laxity, chaos, and a breakdown in law and order. He claimed that the rebel army consisted of cowardly 'men from the gutter' who were ignorant, untrustworthy, and debauched. The rebel government's officers were 'illiterate, ease-loving, impertinent, noise-making, lazy and feeble fellows and flatters, hangers on, and sycophants'. Though scathing of a number of Muslim leaders (including Bahadar Shah), Fazl-i-Haq was most sympathetic to *jihadis* and believed generally that Muslims both rebelled and suffered in greater numbers than Hindus.[7] Historically, the violent British response to mutiny has been downplayed by historians, and this perhaps explains the absence of Fazl-i-Haq's narrative in some accounts. Moreover, his critique of the social (and to a large degree the sexual) disorder that underlay the revolt and of Hindu alliances with the British, together with his sympathy for Muslims, has been equally unpalatable to interpretations seeking to stress the social cohesiveness and national basis of the uprising.[8]

Despite the amnesties under which the government released some imprisoned or transported mutineer-rebels, many such convicts remained in the Andaman Islands to serve out their time. Some died before the amnesties came into force, and others were precluded from their provisions. *Wahabi* rebel Thanesari, who was shipped to the Islands in 1866, wrote of seeing 'many kings, nawabs, landlords, judges, scholars, deputy collectors, writers, administrators, commanders, governors etc.' transported to the Islands in connection with the 1857 revolt. He lamented that these 'honorable Indian gentlemen' were treated in the same way as low-caste convicts.[9] A report published in *The Times* in 1873 also wrote of the 'hundred romances' that could be written about the convicts, including Thanesari who by then was a clerk in convict headquarters. There remained several other mutineer-rebels in the colony.[10] In 1890, 67 convicts convicted during 1857–8 were still alive. Savarkar claimed that when he was transported to the Andamans in 1911, a surviving mutineer sent a message of congratulation for his incarceration 'for an attempt to overthrow the Raj similar to the one they had planned in their day'.[11]

Since the coming of Indian independence in 1947, the Andaman archipelago has undergone a profound transformation in cultural memory. Its association with the punishment of political offenders has transformed it into a symbolic space of anti-colonial struggle and martyrdom.[12] And yet the prison as an institution of punishment has proved remarkably enduring in independent India, as in post-colonial nations elsewhere. Indeed, colonial forms of penal discipline have fed into the governance of successor states in significant ways. Even the architecturally imposing cellular jail at Port Blair, which opened in 1906 and incarcerated all subsequent freedom fighters, was used as a local prison until it was designated a national memorial in 1969. Indian ambivalence about prisons and prisoners, of course, can be traced to the early decades of the nineteenth century and into the 1857–8 rebellion. Moreover, the revolt reveals the long history of prisons as both places of rebellion and as symbolic sites in and through which Indian communities negotiated broader social, economic, and political contests.

Notes

1 Bayly, *Caste, Society and Politics*; Cohn, *Colonialism and Its Forms of Knowledge*; Dirks, *Castes of Mind*; Metcalf, *The Aftermath of Revolt*; Omissi, *The Sepoy and the Raj*.

2. Singh, *Political Prisoners in India*, 2-3.

3. Arnold, 'The Self and the Cell'; Singh, *Political Prisoners in India*.

4. Savarkar, *The Indian War of Independence*, 93.

5. Haq, 'The Story', 26-7, 28 (n. 1).

6. Shackle, 'Munir Shikohabadi'.

7. Haq, 'The Story', 30-1, 42 (quotes 31, 42).

8. Indeed, it is interesting that the extract of Fazl-i-Haq's work chosen for inclusion in *FSUP I* (appendix A) focuses on (religious) causes rather than the trajectory of revolt.

9. Thanesari, *In Exile*, 69.

10. *The Times*, 26 Dec. 1873.

11. Savarkar, *The Story*, 73.

12. Clare Anderson, 'The politics of convict space: Indian penal settlements and the Andamans', in Carolyn Strange and Alison Bashford (eds), *Isolation: Places and Practices of Exclusion*, London, Routledge, 2003, 46-51; Sen, *Disciplining Punishment*, 274-72.

BIBLIOGRAPHY

Primary Sources

(i)   Unpublished material

JNU Library, New Delhi, P.C. Joshi Collection
'The Story of the War of Independence, 1857–8, by 'Allamah Fadl-i-Haqq of Khayrabad'.

National Archives of India, Delhi (NAI)
Home (Judicial), 1858-9, 1870.
Home (Port Blair), 1874, 1877, 1893.

National Archives of Mauritius, Coromandel (NAM)
Miscellaneous departmental correspondence (RA), 1820, 1860.

Oriental and India Office Collections, British Library, London (OIOC)
Bengal Judicial Criminal Consultations, (BJC) 1796-1858.
Bengal Judicial Proceedings (BJP), 1859-62.
Bengal Public Proceedings (BPP), 1858.
Bombay Judicial Criminal Consultations (BomJC), 1858.
F98/31 (Temple Papers): F.J. Mouat, *The Prison System of India*, London, National Association for the Promotion of Social Science, 1872.
India Judicial Criminal Consultations (IJC), 1857–8.
India Judicial Proceedings (IJP), 1859-65, 1871-2.
North West Provinces Criminal Judicial Consultations (NWPJC), 1858-9.
Political and Secret Department Proceedings (L.PS), 1859.
Bengal Judicial Letters (L.PJ), 1858.
W5824: Narrative of events attending the outbreak of disturbances and the restoration of authority in the district of Meerut, in 1857–8.

Parliamentary Papers
PP 1857-58 (2294): Papers relative to mutinies in East Indies: Appendix.
PP 1857-58 (2295): Papers relative to mutinies in East Indies: Appendix.
PP 1857-58 (2302): Papers relative to mutinies in East Indies: Appendix A.
PP 1857-58 (2316): Papers relative to mutinies in East Indies: Appendix B.
PP 1857-58 (2330): Papers relative to mutinies East Indies: Appendix B.
PP 1857-58 (2363): Papers relative to mutinies in East Indies: Appendix B.
PP 1857-58 (2448): Papers relative to mutinies in East Indies.
PP 1857-58 (2449): Papers relative to mutinies in East Indies.
PP 1859 Session I (238): Papers relating to mutiny in Punjab, 1857.

PP 1875 (24): Mauritius (Treatment of Immigrants), Report of the Royal Commissioners appointed to inquire into the Treatment of Immigrants in Mauritius, 1875.

Tamil Nadu State Archives, Chennai (TNSA)
Judicial Proceedings, 1858.

(ii)   Published material

Anon, 'Prison Discipline in India', *Calcutta Review*, 12, 6 (1846), 449-99.

Charles Ball, *A History of the Indian Mutiny: giving a detailed account of the Sepoy insurrection in India; and a concise history of the great military events which have tended to consolidate British empire in Hindostan, vol. I*, London, London Printing and Publishing Co., 1858.

William Crooke, 'Songs of the Mutiny', *The Indian Antiquary*, 40 (1911), 123-24, 165-69.

K.K. Datta, *Selections from Unpublished Correspondence of the Judge-Magistrate and the Judge of Patna, 1790-1857*, Patna, Superintendent Government Printing Bihar, 1954.

G.E. Dobson, 'On the Andamans and Andamanese', *Journal of the Anthropological Institute*, 4 (1875), 457-67.

Alexander Duff, *The Indian Rebellion: Its Causes and Results*, London, James Nisbet and Co., 1858.

William Edwards, *Personal Adventures During the Indian Rebellion in Rohilcund, Futtehghur, and Oude*, London, Smith, Elder, and Co., 1858.

A. Lane Fox, 'Observations on Mr Man's Collection of Andaman and Nicobarese Objects', *Journal of the Anthropological Institute*, 7 (1878), 434-70.

W.H. Flower, 'On the Osteology and Affinities of the Andaman Islands', *Journal of the Anthropological Institute*, 9 (1880), 108-33.

Albert Fytche, 'On certain Aborigines of the Andaman Islands', *Transactions of the Ethnological Society of London*, 5 (1867), 239-42.

Ghalib, 1797-1869, Life and Letters, translated and edited by Ralph Russell and Khurshidul Islam, New Delhi, Oxford University Press, 1994.

Barendra Kumar Ghose, *The Tale of My Exile*, Pondicherry, Arya Office, 1922.

John James Halls, *Two Months in Arrah in 1857*, London, Longman, Green, Longman, and Roberts, 1860.

Kaye's and Malleson's History of the Indian Mutiny of 1857–8 (6 vols), London, W.H. Allen, 1888-9.

Fazl-i-Haq Khairabadi, *Saurat-ul-Hindya*, Lahore, Maktabah-yi Q☐driyah, 1974.

S. Moinul Haq, 'The Story of the War of Independence, 1857–8 (being an English translation of Allamah Fadl-i-Haqq's Risalah on the War)', *Journal of the Pakistan Historical Society*, 5, 1 (1957), 23-57.

Sayyid Ahmed Khan, *The Causes of the Indian Revolt, written by Syed Ahmed Khan Bahadur in Urdu in the Year 1858, and translated into English by his two European friends*, Benares, Medical Hall Press, 1873.

T.C. Loch, *Report on the jails of Bengal, Behar and Orissa for the year 1854-5*, Calcutta, Thomas Jones *Calcutta Gazette* Office, 1856.

James Lunt (ed.), *From Sepoy to Subadar being the life and adventures of Subedar Sita Ram, a Native Officer of the Bengal Army written and related by himself, translated and first published by Lieutenant-colonel Norgate, Bengal Staff Corps at Lahore, 1873*, London, Routledge and Kegan Paul, 1970.

J.F.A. McNair, *Prisoners Their Own Warders: A Record of the Convict Prison at Singapore in the Stratis Settlements established 1825, Discontinued 1873, together with a Cursory History of the Convict Establishments at Bencoolen, Penang and Malacca from the Year 1797*, Westminster, Archibald Constable and Co.: 1899.

E.H. Man, 'On the Andamanese and Nicobarese Objects presented to Major-General Pitt Rivers', *Journal of the Anthropological Institute*, 9 (1882), 268-94.

-, *On the Aboriginal Inhabitants of the Andaman Islands*. London, Trübner and Co., 1885.

Robert Montgomery Martin, *The Indian Empire: history, topography, geology, … government, finance, and commerce. With a full account of the Mutiny of the Bengal Army, vol. III*, London, London Printing and Publishing Co., 1858-61.

Charles Theophilus Metcalfe, *Two Native Narratives of the Mutiny in Delhi, translated from the originals*, Westminster, Archibald Constable and Co., 1898.

F.J. Mouat, *Report on the Jails of the Lower Provinces of the Bengal Presidency for 1855-6*, Calcutta, John Gray, 1856.

-, *Report on the Jails of the Lower Provinces of the Bengal Presidency for 1856-7*, Calcutta, John Gray *Calcutta Gazette* Office/P.M. Cranenburgh, Military Orphan Press, 1857.

-, 'On Prison Statistics and Discipline in Lower Bengal', *Journal of the Statistical Society of London*, 25, 2 (1862), 175-218.

-, 'On Prison Discipline and Statistics in Lower Bengal', *Journal of the Statistical Society of London*, 30, 1 (1867), 21-57.

B. Parmanand, *The Story of My Life*, New Delhi, S. Chand and Co., 1982.

M.V. Portman, *A History of our Relations with the Andamanese*, Calcutta, Superintendent Government Printing, 1899.

Prison Returns of the North West Provinces, 1860, Allahabad, Government Press, 1861.

Prison Returns of the North Western Provinces, 1861, Allahabad, Government Press, 1862.

Charles Raikes, *Notes on the Revolt in the North-Western Provinces of India*, London, Longman, Brown, Green, Longmans and Roberts, 1858.

C.H. Read, 'Mr Portman's Photographs of Andamanese', *Journal of the Anthropological Institute*, 12 (1893), 401-3.

Report of the Committee on Prison Discipline, 8 Jan. 1838, Calcutta, Baptist Mission Press, 1838.

Report of the Inspector of Prisons on the Management of the Jails, from 1845 to 1851, and on the present state of prison discipline in the North West Provinces, Agra, Secundra Orphan Press, 1852.

Report of the Inspector General of Prisons, North Western Provinces, for the year 1852, Agra, Secundra Orphan Press, 1853.

Report of the Inspector General of Prisons, North Western Provinces, for the year 1853, Agra, Secundra Orphan Press, 1854.

Report of the Inspector General of Prisons, North Western Provinces, for the year 1854, Roorkee, Thomason C.E. College Press, 1855.

Report of the Inspector-General of Prisons in the Punjab for the year 1858, Lahore, Punjabee Press, 1859.

Report of the Inspector-General of Prisons in the Punjab, for the year 1853, Agra, Secundra Orphan Press, 1854.

Report of the Inspector-General of Prisons in the Punjab for the year 1859, Lahore, Chronicle Press, 1860.

T.R.E. Rice, *A History of the Indian Mutiny*, London, W.H. Allen, 1885.

S.A.A. Rizvi and B. Bhargarva (eds), *Freedom Struggle in Uttar Pradesh* (5 vols), Lucknow, Publications Bureau, Information Department Uttar Pradesh, 1957-60.

Frederick Roberts, *An Eye Witness Account of the Indian Mutiny*, New Delhi, Mittal Publications, 1983 (first published 1896).

V.D. Savarkar, *The Indian War of Independence, 1857*, Bombay, Phoenix Publications, 1947.

-, *The Story of My Transportation for Life*, Sadbhakti Publications, Bombay, 1950.

Bejoy Kumar Sinha, *In Andamans, the Indian Bastille*, Kanpur, Profulla, C. Mitra, 1939.

R.C. Temple, *Andaman and Nicobar Islands*, Calcutta, Superintendent of Government Printing, 1909.

Mark Thornhill, *The Personal Adventures and Experiences of a Magistrate during the Rise, Progress and Suppression of the Indian Mutiny*, London, John Murray, 1884.

C.G. Wiehe, *Journal of a Tour of Inspection of the Principal Jails in India made by the Inspector General of Prisons, Bombay Presidency, in December 1862 and January and February* 1863, Byculla, Education Society Press, 1865.

(iii)   Newspapers

Bengal Hurkaru, 1834, 1842, 1846, 1857.
Bombay Gazette, 1834, 1858.
Friend of India, 1842.
Singapore Free Press, 1858.
The Times, 1857, 1873.

Secondary Sources

(i)   Published Material

Qeyamuddin Ahmad, *The Wahabi Movement in India*, Calcutta, Firma K.L. Mukhopadhyay, 1966.

S.N. Aggarwal, *The Heroes of Cellular Jail*, Patiala, Publication Bureau, Punjabi University, 1995.

George K. Alapatt, 'The Sepoy Mutiny of 1857: Indian Indentured Labour and Plantation Politics in British Guiana', *Journal of Indian History*, 59, 1-3 (1981), 295-314.

Clare Anderson, *Convicts in the Indian Ocean: transportation from South Asia to Mauritius, 1815-53*, Basingstoke, Macmillan, 2000.

-, 'The politics of convict space: Indian penal settlements and the Andamans', in Strange and Bashford (eds), *Isolation*, 40-55.

-, *Legible Bodies: race, criminality and colonialism in South Asia*, Oxford, Berg, 2004.

-, '"The Ferringees are Flying - the ship is ours!": the convict middle passage in colonial South and Southeast Asia, 1790-1860', *Indian Economic and Social History Review*, 41, 3 (2005), 143-86.

-, 'Sepoys, Servants and Settlers: convict transportation in the Indian Ocean, 1787-1945', in Dikotter and Brown (eds), *Cultures of Confinement*, 185-220.

A. Piatt Andrew, 'Indian Currency Problems of the Last Decade', *Quarterly Journal of Economics* (1901), 483-516.

David Arnold and David Hardiman (eds), *Subaltern Studies VIII, Essays in Honour of Ranajit Guha*, New Delhi, Oxford University Press, 1994.

David Arnold and Stuart Blackburn (eds), *Telling Lives in India: Biography, Autobiography, and Life History*, Bloomington, Indiana University Press, 2004.

David Arnold, 'The Colonial Prison: Power, Knowledge, and Penology in 19th-Century India', in Arnold and Hardiman (eds), *Subaltern Studies VIII*, 148-87.

-, *Colonizing the Body: State Medicine and Epidemic Disease in Nineteenth-Century India*, Berkeley, University of California Press, 1993.

-, 'The Self and the Cell: Indian Prison Narratives as Life Histories', in Arnold and Blackburn (eds), *Telling Lives in India*, 29-53.

-, 'The Contested Prison: India 1790-1945', in Dikotter and Brown (eds), *Cultures of Confinement*, 147-84.

David Baker, 'Colonial Beginnings and the Indian Response: The Revolt of 1857-58 in

Madhya Pradesh', *Modern Asian Studies*, 25, 3 (1991), 511-43.

C.A. Bayly, *The New Cambridge History of India II.i: Indian society and the making of the British Empire*, Cambridge, Cambridge University Press, 1988.

-, *Empire and Information: intelligence gathering and social communication in India, 1780-1870*, Cambridge, Cambridge University Press, 1999.

Susan Bayly, *Caste, Society and Politics in India from the Eighteenth Century to the Modern Age*, Cambridge, Cambridge University Press, 1999.

Barbara Bender and Margo Winer (eds), *Contested Landscapes; Landscapes of Movement and Exile*, Oxford, Berg, 2001.

Gautam Bhadra, 'Four Rebels of Eighteen-Fifty-Seven', in Ranajit Guha (ed.), *Subaltern Studies IV: Writings on South Asian History and Society*, New Delhi, Oxford University Press, 1985, 229-75.

Alison Blunt, 'Embodying war: British women and defilement in the Indian 'Mutiny', 1857-8', *Journal of Historical Geography*, 26, 3 (2000), 403-28.

E.I. Brodkin, 'The Struggle for Succession: rebels and loyalists in the Indian Rebellion of 1857', *Modern Asian Studies*, 6, 3 (1972), 277-90.

Alice Bullard, *Exile to Paradise: Savagery and Civilization in Paris and the South Pacific, 1790-1900*, Stanford, Stanford University Press, 2000.

Marina Carter, *Servants, Sirdars and Settlers: Indians in Mauritius, 1834-1874*, Oxford, Oxford University Press, 1995.

Gautam Chakravarty, *The Indian Mutiny and the British Imagination*, Cambridge, Cambridge University Press, 2005.

Haraprasad Chattopadhyaya, *The Sepoy Mutiny, 1857: a social study and analysis*, Calcutta, Bookland Private Ltd, 1957.

S.B. Chaudhuri, *Civil Disturbances during the British Rule in India, 1765-1857*, Calcutta, World Press, 1955.

-, *Civil Rebellion in the Indian Mutinies*, Calcutta, World Press, 1957.

P.C. Roy Choudhury, *1857 in Bihar (Chotanagpur and Santhal Parganas)*, Patna, Gazetteers' Revision Office, Revenue Department, 1957.

Bernard S. Cohn, *Colonialism and Its Forms of Knowledge: The British in India*, Oxford, Oxford University Press, 1997.

Eleanor Conlin Cassella, '"Doing Trade": a Sexual Economy of 19th Century Australian Female Convict Prisons', *World Archaeology*, 32, 2 (2000), 209-21.

-, 'Landscapes of Punishment and Resistance: a Female Convict Settlement in Tasmania', in Bender and Winer (eds), *Contested Landscapes*, 143-59.

-, 'To Watch or Restrain: Female Convict Prisons in 19th Century Tasmania, Australia', *International Journal of Historical Archaeology*, 5, 1 (2001), 45-72.

Ian Copland, 'Christianity as an arm of Empire: the ambiguous case of India under the Company, c. 1813-1858', *The Historical Journal*, 49, 4 (2006), 1025-54.

William Dalrymple, *The Last Mughal: the fall of a dynasty, Delhi, 1857*, London, Bloomsbury, 2006.

K.K. Datta, *Biography of Kunwar Singh and Amar Singh*, Patna, K.P. Jayaswal Research Institute, 1957.

Frank Dikotter and Ian Brown (eds), *Cultures of Confinement: a history of the prison in global perspective*, London, Christopher Hurst, 2007.

Riaz ud Din (ed.), *Intikhab-e kalam-e Munir Shikohabad*, Lucknow, Uttar Pradesh Urdu Academy, 1982.

Nicholas B. Dirks, *Castes of Mind: colonialism and the making of modern India*, Princeton, University of Princeton Press, 2001.

Ian Duffield, '"Stated this Offence": high-density convict micro-narratives', in Frost and

Maxwell-Stewart (eds), *Chain Letters*, 119-35.

David Finkelstein and Douglas M. Peers (eds), *Negotiating India in the Nineteenth-Century Media*, Basingstoke, Macmillan, 2000.

Sandria Freitag, 'Crime in the Social Order of Colonial North India', *Modern Asian Studies*, 25, 2 (1991), 227-61.

Lucy Frost and Hamish Maxwell-Stewart (eds), *Chain Letters: narrating convict lives*, Melbourne, Melbourne University Press, 2001.

Lucy Frost and Hamish Maxwell-Stewart, 'Introduction', in Frost and Maxwell-Stewart (eds), *Chain Letters*, 1-5.

John Furnivall, 'The Fashioning of Leviathan', *Journal of the Burma Research Society*, 29, 1 (1939), 36-43.

Indira Ghose, *Women Travellers in Colonial India: the power of the female gaze*, New Delhi, Oxford University Press, 1998.

Durba Ghosh, 'Decoding the Nameless: gender, subjectivity, and historical methodologies in reading the archives of colonial India', in Kathleen Wilson (ed.), *A New Imperial History: Culture, Identity, and Modernity in Britain and the Empire, 1660-1840*, Cambridge, Cambridge University Press, 2004, 297-316.

Ranajit Guha (ed.), *Subaltern Studies II: Writings on South Asian History and Society*, New Delhi, Oxford University Press, 1983.

Ranajit Guha, *Elementary Aspects of Peasant Insurgency in Colonial India*, New Delhi, Oxford University Press, 1983.

-, 'The Prose of Counter-Insurgency', in Guha (ed.), *Subaltern Studies II*, 1-42.

Sumit Guha, 'An Indian Penal Regime: Maharashtra in the Eighteenth Century', *Past and Present*, 147 (1995), 100-26.

Irfan Habib, 'The Coming of 1857', *Social Scientist*, 296-9 (1998), 6-15.

P. Hardy, *The Muslims of British India*, Cambridge, Cambridge University Press, 1972.

Mushirul Hasan and Narayani Gupta, *India's Colonial Encounter: essays in memory of Eric Stokes*, New Delhi, Manohar, 1993.

Iqbal Husain, 'Fazle Haq of Khairabad – A Scholarly Rebel of 1857', *Proceedings of the Indian History Congress* (1987), 355-65.

Mahdi Husain, *Bahadur Shah II and the war of 1857 in Delhi with its unforgettable scenes*, New Delhi, M.N. Publishers, 1987.

N. Iqbal Singh, *The Andaman Story*, New Delhi, Vikas, 1978.

Kenneth W. Jones, *The New Cambridge History of India III.i: Socio-religious reform movements in British India*, Cambridge, Cambridge University Press, 1989.

P.C. Joshi (ed.), *Rebellion 1857: A Symposium*, New Delhi, People's Publishing House, 1957.

P.C. Joshi, '1857 in Our History', in Joshi (ed.), *Rebellion 1857*, 119-222.

-, '1857 in Folk Songs', in Joshi (ed.), *Rebellion 1857*, 271-87.

Ratanlal Joshi, *The Martyrs*, Bombay, Udbodhak Granthmala, 1994.

Ujjwal Kumar Singh, *Political Prisoners in India*, New Delhi, Oxford University Press, 1998.

Joyce Lebra-Chapman, *The Rani of Jhansi: a study in female heroism*, Honolulu, University of Hawaii Press, 1986.

Philippa Levine, *Gender and Empire (Oxford History of the British Empire Companion Series)*, Oxford, Oxford University Press, 2004.

R.C. Majumdar, *The Sepoy Mutiny and the Revolt of 1857*, Calcutta, S.S. Chaudhuri, 1957.

-, *Penal Settlement in Andamans*, New Delhi, Gazetteers Unit, Department of Culture, Ministry of Education and Social Welfare, 1975.

Jamal Malik, 'Letters, prison sketches and autobiographical literature: The case of Fadl-e Haqq Khairabadi in the Andaman Penal Colony', *Indian Economic and Social History Review*, 43, 1 (2006), 77-100.

L.P. Mathur, *Kala Pani: History of Andaman and Nicobar Islands with a study of India's Freedom Struggle*, New Delhi, Eastern Book Company, 1992.

Thomas R. Metcalf, *The Aftermath of Revolt: India, 1857-1870*, Princeton, University of Princeton Press, 1964.

Delia Millar, *The Victorian Watercolours and Drawings in the Collection of Her Majesty the Queen, vol. II*, London, Philip Wilson, 1995.

James H. Mills, *Madness, Cannabis and Colonialism: The 'Native-Only' Lunatic Asylums of British India, 1857-1900*, Basingstoke, Macmillan, 2000.

James H. Mills and Satadru Sen (eds), *Confronting the Body: the politics of physicality in colonial and post-colonial India*, London, Anthem, 2004.

Rudrangshu Mukherjee, *Awadh in Revolt 1857-1858: a study of popular resistance*, New Delhi, Oxford University Press, 1984 (second edition with revised introduction, New Delhi, Permanent Black, 2002).

Stephen Nicholas (ed.), *Convict Workers; Reinterpreting Australia's Past*, Cambridge, Cambridge University Press, 1988.

Stephen Nicholas and Peter R. Shergold, 'Transportation as Global Migration', in Nicholas (ed.), *Convict Workers*, 28-42.

Sten Nilsson and Narayani Gupta, *The Painter's Eye: Egron Lundgren and India*, Stockholm, National Museum, 1991.

David Omissi, *The Sepoy and the Raj: The Indian Army, 1860-1940*, Basingstoke, Macmillan, 1994.

Alex Padamsee, *Representations of Indian Muslims in British Colonial Discourse*, Basingstoke, Palgrave Macmillan, 2005.

Gyanendra Pandey, *The Construction of Communalism in Colonial North India*, New Delhi, Oxford University Press, 1990.

Hyungji Park, '"The Story of Our Lives": *The Moonstone* and the Indian Mutiny in *All the Year Round*', in Finkelstein and Peers (eds), *Negotiating India*, 84-109.

Nancy L. Paxton, 'Mobilizing Chivalry: rape in British novels about the Indian Uprising of 1857', *Victorian Studies*, 36, 1 (1992), 5-30.

-, *Writing under the Raj: Gender, Race, and Rape in the British Colonial Imagination, 1830-1947*, New Brunswick, Rutgers University Press, 1999.

Douglas M. Peers, 'Sepoys, Soldiers and the Lash: Race, Caste and Army Discipline in India, 1820-50', *Journal of Imperial and Commonwealth History*, 23, 2 (1995), 211-47.

Laura Peters, '"Double-dyed Traitors and Infernal Villains": *Illustrated London News, Household Words*, Charles Dickens and the Indian Rebellion', in Finkelstein and Peers (eds), *Negotiating India*, 110-34.

Anoma Pieris, 'On Dropping Bricks and Other Disconcerting Subjects: unearthing convict histories in Singapore', *Fabrications*, 15, 2 (2005), 77-94.

E. Daniel Potts, *British Baptist Missionaries in India 1793-1837: the history of Serampore and its missions*, Cambridge, Cambridge University Press, 1967.

Avril A. Powell, *Muslims and Missionaries in Pre-Mutiny India*, London, Curzon, 1993.

Siraj ul Haq Qureshi, *Munshi Sayyid Ismail Husain Munir Shikohabadi aur unki sha'iri*, Karachi, Academic Publishers, 1989.

Rajesh Rai, 'Sepoys, convicts and the "bazaar" contingent: the emergence and exclusion of "Hindustani" pioneers at the Singapore frontier', *Journal of Southeast Asian Studies*, 35, 1 (2004), 1-19.

Pankaj Rag, '1857: Need for Alternative Sources', *Social Scientist*, 296-9 (1998), 113-47.

Rajat Kanta Ray, 'Race, Religion and Realm: The Political Theory of "The Reigning Indian Crusade", 1857', in Hasan and Gupta, *India's Colonial Encounter*, 133-82.

Peter Robb, 'The impact of British rule on religious community: reflections on the trial of Maulvi Ahmadullah of Patna in 1865', in Robb (ed.), *Society and Ideology*, 142-76.

Peter Robb (ed.), *Society and Ideology: Essays in South Asian History, presented to Professor K.A. Ballhatchet*, New Delhi, Oxford University Press, 1993.

Tapti Roy, 'Visions of the Rebels: A Study of 1857 in Bundelkhand', *Modern Asian Studies*, 27, 1 (1993), 205-28.

-, *The Politics of a Popular Uprising: Bundelkhand in 1857*, New Delhi, Oxford University Press, 1994.

R B Sakasena, *A History of Urdu Literature*, Allahabad, Ram Narain Lal, 1927.

Henry Scholberg, *The Indian Literature of the Great Rebellion*, New Delhi, Promilla, 1993.

James C. Scott, *Domination and the Arts of Resistance: hidden transcripts*, New Haven, Yale University Press, 1992.

S.N. Sen, *Eighteen Fifty-Seven*, New Delhi, Publications Division, Ministry of Education and Broadcasting, Government of India, 1957.

Satadru Sen, 'Policing the Savage: Segregation, Labor and State Medicine in the Andamans', *Journal of Asian Studies*, 58, 3 (1997), 753-73.

-, 'Rationing Sex: female convicts in the Andamans', *South Asia*, 30, 1 (1999), 29-59.

-, *Disciplining Punishment: Colonialism and Convict Society in the Andaman Islands*, New Delhi, Oxford University Press, 2000.

-, 'The female jails of colonial India', *Indian Economic and Social History Review*, 39, 4 (2002), 417-38.

-, 'Contexts, Representation and the Colonized Convict: Maulana Thanesari in the Andaman Islands', *Crime, History and Societies*, 8, 2 (2004), 117-39.

Christopher Shackle, 'Munir Shikohabadi on his imprisonment', forthcoming in Shobna Nijhawan (ed.), *Writings in Hindu and Urdu on Indian Nationalism*, New Delhi, Permanent Black, 2007.

K.S. Singh, 'The "Tribals" and the 1857 Uprising', *Social Scientist*, 296-9 (1998), 76-85.

Radhika Singha, '"Providential" Circumstances: The Thuggee Campaign of the 1830s and Legal Innovation', *Modern Asian Studies*, 27, 1 (1993), 83-146.

-, Radhika Singha, *A Despotism of Law: Crime and Justice in Early Colonial India*, New Delhi, Oxford University Press, 1998.

S.K. Sinha, *Veer Kuer Singh: The Great Warrior of 1857*, New Delhi, Konark Pubishers, 1997.

Stefan Sperl and Christopher Shackle (eds), *Qasida poetry in Islamic Africa and Asia*, Leiden, Brill, 1996.

Harindra Srivastava, *Five Stormy Years: Savarkar in London, June 1906 - June 1911*, New Delhi, Allied Publishers, 1983.

E.T. Stokes, *The Peasant and the Raj: Studies in Agrarian Society and Peasant Rebellion in Colonial India*, Cambridge, Cambridge University Press, 1978.

E.T. Stokes (ed. C.A. Bayly), *The Peasant Armed: the Indian Revolt of 1857*, Oxford, Clarendon, 1986.

Carolyn Strange and Alison Bashford (eds), *Isolation: Places and Practices of Exclusion*, London, Routledge, 2003.

Faruqui Anjum Taban, 'The Coming of the Revolt in Awadh: The Evidence of Urdu Newspapers', *Social Scientist*, 296-9 (1998), 16-24.

P.J.O. Taylor, *A Companion to the 'Indian Mutiny' of 1857*, New Delhi, Oxford University Press, 1996.

C.M. Turnbull, 'Convicts in the Straits Settlements, 1826-67', *Journal of the Malay Branch of the Royal Asiatic Society*, 43, 1 (1970), 87-103.

-, *A History of Singapore, 1819-1988*, Oxford, Oxford University Press, 1989.

Megan Vaughan, *Creating the Creole Island: Slavery in Eighteenth-Century Mauritius*, Durham, Duke University Press, 2005.

Sita Venkateswar, *Development and Ethnocide: colonial practices in the Andaman Islands*, Copenhagen, International Work Group for Indigenous Affairs, 2004.

Anand A. Yang (ed.), *Crime and Criminality in British India*, Tucson, University of Arizona Press, 1985.

Anand A. Yang, 'Disciplining "Natives": prisons and prisoners in early nineteenth century India', *South Asia*, 10, 2 (1987), 29-45.

-, *Bazaar India: Markets, Society, and the Colonial State in Bihar*, Berkeley, University of California Press, 1998.

-, 'Indian convict workers in Southeast Asia in the late eighteenth and early nineteenth centuries', *Journal of World History*, 14, 2 (2003), 179-208.

-, 'The Lotah Emeutes of 1855: Caste, Religion and prisons in North India in the Early Nineteenth Century', in Mills and Sen (eds), *Confronting the Body*, 102-17.

Peter Zinoman, *The Colonial Bastille: a history of imprisonment in Vietnam, 1862-1940*, Berkeley, University of California Press, 2001.

(ii)   Unpublished Material

Sumit Guha, 'Surviving the maelstrom: the north Indian adventures of Vishnubhat Godse, 1857-1858', paper presented at British Association of South Asian Studies annual conference, Birkbeck College, University of London, Apr. 2006.

Anoma Pieris, 'Hidden Hands and Divided Landscapes: Penal Labor and Colonial Citizenship in Singapore and the Straits Settlements, 1825-1873', PhD in Architecture, UC Berkeley, 2003.

Taylor Sherman, 'Political Prisoners and Hunger Strikes in Indian Jails, 1929-1938', paper presented at *Convicts Discussion Workshop III*, University of Leicester, Jan. 2006.

Maulana Jaferr Thanesari, *In Exile (A Strange Story)*, Delhi, Urdu Makaz, 1964 (unpublished English translation in the private possession of Satadru Sen).

INDEX OF PRISONS

INDEX

R

S